THE
MYTHS
OF
INFLATION
AND
INVESTING

THE MYTHS OF INFLATION AND INVESTING

by

Steven C. Leuthold

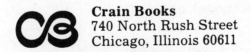

Crain Books
740 North Rush Street
Chicago, Illinois 60611

Contents

Preface

During the last decade the investment community has been besieged with information about inflation. Statistics, projections, sophisticated models, assumptions and correlations have poured out of Wall Street, Washington and academia. Indeed, inflation is of vital interest to investors, corporate planners, economists, politicians and the man on the street.

Unfortunately, much of the information is limited and misleading. Many of the expert opinions appear to be misguided and ill-founded. Many of today's truisms may, in fact, be fallacies. What is almost uniformly believed to be inflation fact often is inflation myth. It also appears that much of today's inflation-based investment theory, theory that plays a vital part in investment decisions involving many billions of dollars annually, does not always stand the test of time.

Ten years ago it was almost uniformly accepted that inflation was good for the stock market and that stocks were a hedge against inflation. Today's investors have serious doubts about this once universal truth. Many would even say it's a damned lie. These beliefs, once so widely accepted, have cost investors of large and small accounts — pension funds, banks and individuals — very dearly during the last decade. Our examination of the historic documentation underlying these beliefs has revealed them to be more myth than reality. Unfortunately, this research project was not started until 1973, after much of the damage had been done. Even at that late date, this research represented one of the first attempts to test the stocks-as-an-inflation-hedge thesis.

In the old "Dragnet" television series, Jack Webb continually admonished witnesses: "Just the facts, ma'am, just the facts." Opinions were of little value to this deadpan cynic. Today we hear many opinions about inflation, its characteristics, its causes and its effects. If we are bombarded with the same opinions or theories coming from a gaggle of respected experts, the opinions too often assume the status of truisms. Regretfully, few of us bother to check the facts. Why bother checking out something everybody knows is true, something everyone else seems to accept?

Long ago, powerful men (and powerful governments) learned that if people hear the same message enough times from enough respected sources and if they see it in print enough times, they accept the message. There are not many Joe Fridays around — skeptics who want only the facts instead of accepting the opinions.

For years almost everyone knew that the world was flat, that the sun revolved around the earth, that tomatoes were poisonous, that nuclear power plants were safe and that the stock market was a hedge against inflation. The experts, the respected people who ought to know, said so. Thus, it must be so. We assumed the evidence must be overwhelmingly supportive. The case must be proven beyond a reasonable doubt.

Today we hear respected inflation and investment experts high on their pedestals declaring with great confidence and authority: "Inflation is a permanent part of our economic system." And: "We can live with 6 per cent to 7 per cent inflation." And: "This is a new era. Inflation has never been above this." And: "Nominal long-term interest rates are, of course, comprised of the perceived inflation rate and a 'real' return of 2 per cent to 3 per cent." And: "We know the Consumer Price Index, if anything, understates inflation."

In this book we critically examine these and other widely held beliefs and supposed truisms relating to inflation. Some are blatantly wrong. Some are highly questionable. Others are only partially supported by the evidence.

As Joe Friday knew in "Dragnet," convictions depend primarily on the facts, not opinions, no matter how "expert" the opinions might be. If there is a reasonable doubt, there should be no conviction. This book, while containing many facts, also presents some opinions. Several of these opinions run counter to current popular beliefs about inflation. Some of these you may choose to accept; some you will not. But even if you accept the ideas and opinions, don't bet the farm on them. Take the blinders off.

The primary purpose of this book is to stimulate continuing critical appraisal. Too often in the worlds of finance and economics, opinions are presented as pseudo facts, universal truisms or even natural laws. Disbelievers are labeled naive or unsophisticated. The opinion givers are typically highly respected authorities in their fields, the experts.

Unfortunately, it does not always follow that the experts have documented their conclusions or have engaged in substantive supportive research on the subject. It seems ego, like love, can be blinding.

The message is clear: Be a skeptic. Be an agnostic. Be a cynic. Remember back in the 1960s everyone *knew* that stocks were an inflation hedge (including this author). Ignorance may have been bliss for a while, but it has become awfully painful and expensive.

— S.C.L.

Acknowledgements

This manuscript has been in the works for 10 years, although over most of that period I was not really aware this was the case. It started with a series of special research studies for the institutional clients of Piper, Jaffray & Hopwood. Piper provided me with a great deal of latitude to carry on the initial research. Since 1977, Charles Miller and Tom Powers of Funds Advisory, Houston, Texas, have supported and encouraged expanding the work. I have been fortunate indeed for associations with these two firms. Without their support and tolerance, this book would never have evolved.

I am indebted to many for collecting and publishing the various series of economic statistical data employed in this book. The Department of Commerce, the National Bureau of Economic Research, the Bureau of Labor Statistics, and Securities Research Company were some of the organizations that provided this foundation data. Sidney Homer's landmark work, *A History of Interest Rates,* was invaluable. And E. H. Phelps Brown and Sheila V. Hopkins of Oxford deserve special acknowledgement for their painstaking work researching historic inflationary trends. The Cowles Commission studies also provided valuable resource materials. Hyperinflation research originally published by Axe Houghton provided valuable historic insight.

I am also indebted to many for intellectual stimulation. Published material by David Warsh of *Forbes,* Norman McCrae of the *Economist* and Richard Ruggles of Yale come immediately to mind. Peter Bernstein and David Dreman provided encouragement and occasionally corrected some of my fuzzy thinking. Terry Ellis and Fred Robertson of Fixed Income Advisory Company took a helpful critical look at the work on interest rates. History Professor Dick Laue helped me keep my historic facts straight. George Sadler of the American Productivity Center did the same with the chapters devoted to productivity.

Valuable research assistance was provided by Richard Bruce, Jon Heimerman, Keith Blaich, and especially Jim Floyd. Cleo Elsner, Rosamaria Magiera, and Maureen DeCamp put up with a

x

lot as the manuscript evolved and also are responsible for many of the charts and tables.

Steve Gilkenson and Michael Clowes of *Pensions and Investments* provided encouragement, suggestions, and constructive editing. And, without Crain Books' Kathryn Sederberg taking this whole project in hand, the manuscript would probably never have seen the light of day.

Finally, I would like to dedicate this manuscript to Trish Leuthold. She lived with me while I lived with this. It was not easy. This must be true love.

— S.C.L.

Chapter 1

U.S. Inflation History: The Causes, Effects and History

Which of the following statements are true?

1. The real key to understanding inflation is money supply.

2. Recent U.S. inflationary levels are unprecedented.

3. Transition from inflation to deflation has rarely been a gradual process.

4. From 1790 to 1979, the long-term inflation rate in the U.S. was approximately 3 per cent.

5. U.S. inflation history reveals that deflation is relatively rare, occurring less than 20 per cent of the time.

6. Significant wars have always been accompanied by inflation.

What is inflation? Webster defines it as swelling, expanding, "an increase in volume of money and credit relative to the available goods resulting in a substantial and continuing rise in the general price level."

In this book inflation simply means a rising level of prices for consumer goods, commodities, raw materials and services. If a market basket of groceries costs $80 today and the same market basket of items costs $100 a year from now, THAT'S INFLATION. If it costs $3,000 to furnish a room today and the same furnishings cost $4,000 a year from now, THAT'S INFLATION. If it costs $3,000 to manufacture a car today and $4,000 to turn out that identical car a year from now, THAT'S INFLATION. If it cost you $20,000 to live a year ago, and now the same existence costs you $25,000 a year, THAT'S INFLATION.

Causes of Inflation

Rising prices and inflation are not simply the product of expanding the money supply or the result of too much money chasing too few goods.

There are many reasons why prices rise and there are many causes of inflation. Rising prices and inflation are not, as many seem to think, simply the product of expanding the money supply or simply the result of too much money chasing too few goods, though both are factors. Inflation, like cancer, has many causes. Here are some of the causes of inflation:

- When the demand for something goes up but the supply stays the same, the price usually goes up. More people are drinking wine these days, but only a fixed amount of the 1972 vintage now exists. It cannot be expanded. The buyers compete for the limited supply and the price rises. Also, if the demand for a new product exceeds the supply, prices will go to a premium until production can catch up with demand. This is demand pull inflation.

- When supply contracts and demand remains constant, prices in a free market environment go up. Thus, when beef supplies or coffee supplies shrink because of weather conditions or producer decisions, the same number of buyers compete for a smaller supply. If the price rises too high, some users shift to an alternative, say chicken or tea. And when supply and demand are closer in balance, prices will stabilize or come down. This is also demand pull inflation.

- If supply can be artificially restricted or tightly controlled, producers can raise prices at will. The Organization of Petroleum Exporting Countries (OPEC) and the international diamond cartel are examples. If the producers are tightly organized in a cartel, they can arbitrarily raise prices. If the item is a necessity, like oil, the user has few short-term alternatives. Demand can be quite inelastic. Labor unions have similar characteristics in being able arbitrarily to raise the prices of labor. In many areas, the labor user has no alternative source of supply, at least in the short run.

- If the cost of labor or the price of oil is arbitrarily raised, the producer affected must pay the price, shut down or otherwise compensate. Typically, the producer pays the price and attempts to raise the price of his product to cover the added costs. But, if the user of his product will not pay the higher price, the producer might be forced to shut down because his business is no longer profitable, unless he can improve productivity or reduce other costs. These alternatives can be very difficult to implement quickly. This is cost-push inflation. Increased costs are added on to the next level.

- If the government issuing the currency in circulation is spending more than it is taking in and the currency in circulation is not fully backed by gold or silver, the government can, in effect, cover its overspending by creating more money. In the days before paper money and credit this was accomplished by reducing the gold or silver content of the coins. Today it is accomplished by issuing Treasury checks to the nation's banks, allowing them to lend more money to people. This is usually accompanied by an increase in the amount of currency in circulation. This dilution or degrading of the currency typically results in more dollars, francs or pounds being needed to buy the same amount of goods. Prices, thus, go up across the board. This is monetary debasement.

- If goverment grows faster than a nation's economy, it must either degrade the currency or extract a growing portion of its citizens' income to cover the increased costs. This increase in taxation typically reduces the disposable income of the citizens. Now, if the citizens can be convinced and satisfied that the increased role of the government is worth this reduction in take home pay, things can balance out. However, if the citizens are not willing to accept this reduction, if they feel they can no longer make ends meet with a smaller check, if they feel they can make better use of the lost dollars than the government, then tremendous pressures develop for pay increases to compensate for these "lost" tax dollars.

- Governments sometimes try to hide taxes by imposing them on corporations, the implication being that the public won't have to pay anything because business will pay it out of its profits. But business treats taxes as it treats all other costs. Unless the costs can be passed on to the consumer through price increases, profits will be reduced, perhaps even eliminated, and the company may go out of business. If the profits are reduced, it will be more difficult for companies to raise capital. Their growth may slow, halt or turn into a fatal decline. When faced with increased taxation, companies must either reduce costs and operate more efficiently or raise prices to offset the increased taxes or costs of regulation, thus passing the costs on to the consumers. The latter is most common. The power to tax is the power to destroy, unless a business is able to raise prices to compensate.

- Government has other ways of artificially upsetting and controlling the normal functions of an economic system. Minimum wage legislation, price supports, over-regulation, excessive bureaucratic burdens, all are factors in increasing prices, adding costs and creating artificially high floor prices for materials and labor, thus contributing to inflation.

In almost all periods of history, inflation has been a combination of several distinct species, four of which are now present in the U.S. economy.

These are obviously not all the causes of today's inflationary pressures. But the point is that inflation is a complex subject, a multifaceted problem with no simple solutions. In fact, in almost all periods of history inflation has been a combination of several distinct species. Here are five distinct species. Four of them are now present in the U.S. economy.

1. **Isolated Factor Inflation.** These are inflationary pressures that come out of left field. They are transitory, and while having a significant temporary impact on price levels, they tend to correct themselves. These pressures include such things as adverse effects of weather on agricultural production, plagues, epidemics, oil cartels, the actions of groups cornering a market such as the wheat market, or temporary exchange rate panics.

2. **War Inflation.** Major wars have almost without exception been a major cause of inflation. The economic systems of nations involved in major conflicts are often forced to run flat out. Industrial production supporting the war effort runs full steam ahead. Labor and material shortages develop. In the past, agricultural production declined in wartime because farmers took up swords and rifles. Shortages of consumer items developed because the means of production were directed toward the war effort. Government borrowing and spending typically increased. Even when the wars were over, inflation continued at an alarming rate as the pent up demands for consumer goods were satisfied. Savings and unused credit were an enormous stimulative force, at least in the victorious nations.

3. **Business Cycle Inflation.** Economies expand and contract. Perhaps the extremes, booms and busts, are a thing of the past, perhaps not. At any rate, periods of excessive optimism and excessive pessimism will exist as long as men and women populate the earth. At one time back in the 1960s, more than a few economists actually believed we

could iron out the contractions by managing the economy. Nevertheless, as an economy expands, consumers and businessmen prosper and gain confidence, typically resulting in too much money chasing too few goods. Production cannot keep pace with demand and prices start rising. This overheating is followed by a cooling as demand contracts and prices taper off or fall. The ebb and flow of these cyclical pressures are often an overlay accentuating the underlying long-term trend.

4. **Monetary Debasement Inflation.** This is goverment printing press inflation. The existing government attempts to keep a troubled economic system functioning by creating a larger supply of money. This is by far the most dangerous kind of inflation because of its snowballing characteristics. It feeds on itself and is very difficult to control, much less stop. Oil cartels eventually break up. Wars end. Business cycles eventually run down. But the printing press often does not stop until the economic system is in ruins. Hyperinflation, or bushel basket inflation, leaves very few economic survivors.

5. **Metamorphic Inflation.** This form of inflation can last for long periods, even 100 years or more. It is the product of pervasive socio-economic change, change the old economic order could not accommodate. Eventually, as the evolutionary change matures and slows, a modified economic system evolves which can cope with the new order of things.

Inflation and the U.S.

Several years ago a noted U.S. economist made the statement that inflation was inevitable in our economy, and, in fact, good for the economy. Today some reputable economists still maintain our economy can adapt to and live a long-term inflation rate of 6 per cent. Pension officers and their consultants are building these high rates into their long-term models, juggling the projected rates of return around, trying to make it all work out.

Is inflation a permanent fixture in the U.S. economy? Can we adapt to a long-term rate of 6 per cent? What is reasonable inflation? What is intolerable?

The following charts trace U.S. inflation and deflation back over most of the country's history. The first chart displays annual changes in the Consumer Price Index, or a reasonable facsimile, from 1790 to date. The bars represent the annual inflation or deflation rates (below the line), while the wriggling line represents the cumulative inflation picture. The second chart portrays the ebbs and flows, the cyclical nature of inflation and deflation, with a five-year centered moving average of annual rates.

Recent high levels of inflation are not a new phenomenon; inflation runs in cycles and has not been a permanent fixture in the U.S. economy.

Here are some of the conclusions and observations arrived at from close scrutiny of these charts:

- The recent high levels of U.S. inflation are not a new phenomenon, having, on a moving average basis, been exceeded in the 1790s, the 1860s and the 1910s. Two other periods also come very close to approximating recent experience, and numerous individual years exceeded 1979's peak.
- Inflation runs in cycles, and, in the past, clearly has not been a permanent fixture in the U.S. economy.
- In all but one case inflationary peaks have been followed by a significant correction period of deflation. Even in that exception (1949 to 1955) there were two years of actual deflation. The advent of the Korean War probably prevented the typical deflationary correction, a correction that would have carried the moving average into negative territory.
- It's obvious that major wars and high inflation go hand in hand. The Revolutionary War, the War of 1812, the Civil War, World War I, World War II, the

**Annual Changes in Consumer Price Index:
1790 Through 1979**

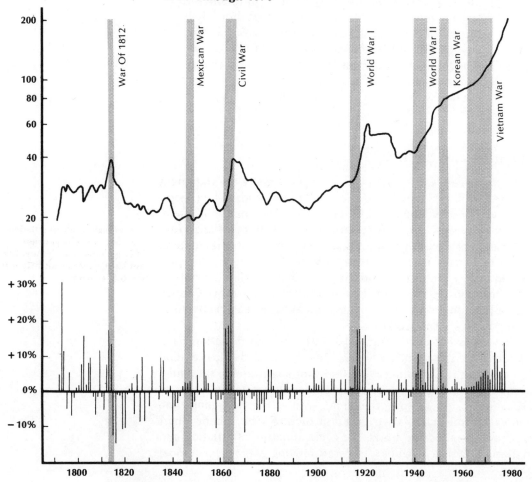

Vietnam War, the Korean War and, to a lesser degree, the Spanish American War (not on chart) were accompanied by some inflation.

- As a superheated war economy cools off, inflation has historically subsided. However, with the exception of the Civil War, relatively high rates of inflation have prevailed for several years after each war's conclusion, probably a function of pent-up consumer demand. As this is satiated, the deflationary correction begins developing.

- The shift from an inflationary environment to that of deflation often has been sudden and dramatic. For instance, in 1813 and 1814, inflation was 17 per cent and 13 per cent, respectively, followed by 13 per cent and 15 per cent deflation in 1815 and 1816. In 1863 and 1864, inflation was 16 per cent and 35 per cent, followed by no inflation in 1865 and 5 per cent deflation in 1866. In 1919 and 1920, inflation was 15 per cent and 16 per cent, but 1921 and 1922 brough deflation of 11 per cent and 6 per cent. Inflation ran at 14 per cent and 8 per cent, respectively, in 1947 and 1948, but 1949 was a deflationary year. The Korean War quickly put the country back into an inflationary mode, 8 per cent in 1951, but by 1954 and 1955, there was minor deflation.

- Some may see the existence of a long-term 50 to 55-year inflationary-deflationary Kondratief-type cycle or wave in this chart (peaks around 1814, 1864, 1919 and 1974). Partly because of limited definitive historical evidence, we remain intellectually skeptical of this purported "natural law."

- Currently the five-year centered moving average of inflation may be about to turn down from a peak. In the past this has indicated that a correction of inflation excess is under way. This supports the current thesis of some economists, who say inflation peaked in 1979 and the U.S. is about to embark on a secular inflationary decline. Considering past movements and barring a new major war, it is certainly possible that inflation may be down to 3 per cent or 2 per cent in the mid-1980s, and the advent of actual deflation is not out of the question.

Analyzing the inflation/deflation data from 1792 through 1979, it is clear that long-term inflation experience in the U.S. is far lower than is generally believed. The annual compound growth rate in consumer prices is 1.2 per cent for 189 years. The arithmetical average of annual data is 1.5 per cent and the median is 1.7 per cent.

Also running counter to the belief that inflation usually has been characteristic of the U.S. economy, the study found that inflation, on an annual basis, exceeded 1 per cent only 51 per cent of the time, while deflation of 1 per cent or more was present 21

U.S. historic inflation is far lower than most believe, with a compound annual growth rate for consumer prices of 1.2 per cent over 189 years.

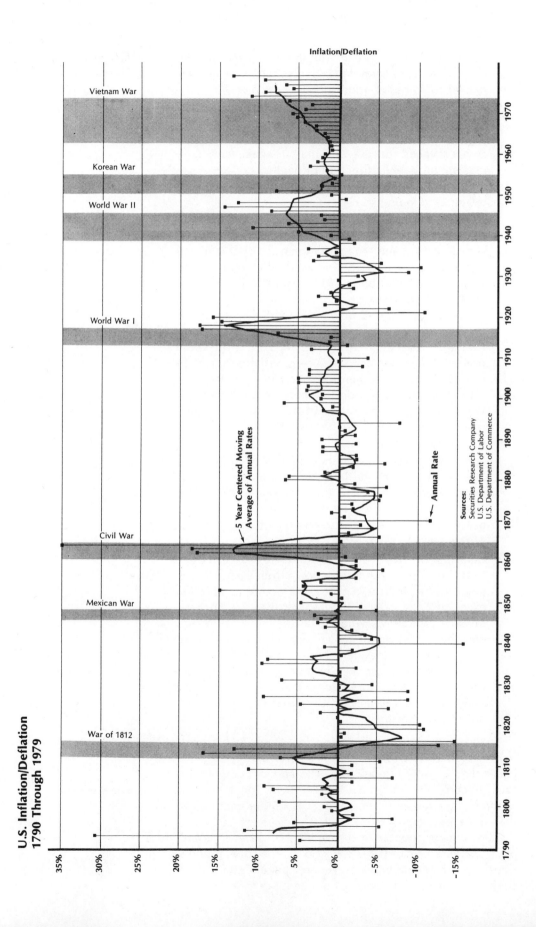

U.S. Inflation/Deflation
1790 Through 1979

Inflation/Deflation

Vietnam War

Korean War

World War II

World War I

Civil War

5 Year Centered Moving Average of Annual Rates

Mexican War

War of 1812

Annual Rate

Sources:
Securities Research Company
U.S. Department of Labor
U.S. Department of Commerce

35%   30%   25%   20%   15%   10%   5%   0%   -5%   -10%   -15%

1790   1800   1810   1820   1830   1840   1850   1860   1870   1880   1890   1900   1910   1920   1930   1940   1950   1960   1970

per cent of the time. Price stability (less than 1 per cent inflation or deflation) existed in 28 per cent of the years.

In total, 56 per cent of the years experienced some upward movement in consumer prices, while 44 per cent of the years consumer prices were unchanged or down.

This ancient U.S. history may not represent future experience because times have changed. But, interestingly, another aspect of the research covering more than 1,000 years of price movements in established economies of the world showed that prices rose about 60 per cent of the time and fell 40 per cent of the time. The 1,000-year annual compound rate of growth for consumer prices worked out to less than 1 per cent per year.

When all the smoke is blown away, it appears that the root cause of today's abnormally high inflation levels in the U.S. is the U.S. government's continuing policy of spending more money than it takes in, covering the difference by degrading the currency. Business and labor, by raising prices, are only trying to keep up. Keep in mind that this can and, in fact, may be changing in the U.S. because the electorate is beginning to rebel.

When today's economists project future long-term inflation at 6 per cent, they ought to take a look at history and at a compound interest table. If 6 per cent inflation is experienced for the next 40 years, today's $7,000 compact car would cost $70,000. A $100,000 house (which is no longer such an exorbitant price) would cost $1 million 40 years from now. And that $9 bottle of scotch would be about $90. Six per cent inflation compounded over 40 years equals a 10-fold gain in the cost of everything. Still, economists say, "Yes, we can live with 6 per cent inflation."

Happily, in the past only metamorphic inflation has persisted for long periods. Inflation from all other causes generally has ended after a relatively brief period. It appears we are at the end of a long period of metamorphic inflation, which is a symptom of massive structural change in any economy and its underlying society. Inflation may well be under control within a few years. The inflation experience of the last two decades is not the die cast for the next 10, 20 or 30 years. Chapters 15-17 explain why.

The root cause of today's abnormally high inflation levels in the U.S. is the government's continuing policy of spending more money than it takes in.

Chapter 2

The Myth of Common Stocks and Inflation

What is normally the best environment for the stock market?

A. Years of extraordinary inflation

B. Years of neutrally high inflation

C. Years of moderate inflation

D. Years of price stability

E. Years of moderate deflation

F. Years of extraordinary deflation

G. Nothing is good for the stock market.

In the halcyon days of the 1960s, when the stock market seemed to be marching forever onward and upward, almost all investors believed the stock market was a hedge against inflation. Indeed, it was commonly believed that inflation was good for the stock market.

Then, as inflation surged ahead in the 1970s and the stock market surged down, investors began to question the prevailing wisdom about the stock market and inflation. Perhaps, they thought, the stock market was not a hedge against inflation. Perhaps inflation was bad for the stock market. Currently there is a growing belief that deflation would be good for the stock market. We also have some frustrated investors who say nothing is good for the stock market.

Strangely, those frustrated investors may be closest to the truth because our research demonstrates that the best stock market performance takes place in years of price stability — years when essentially *nothing* is happening on the inflation/deflation front; years when the cost of goods and services is up or down 1 per cent or less. Thus, at least in terms of inflation and deflation, nothing *is* good for the stock market.

Many investors will say this is not a particularly stunning revelation, but many aspects of our research will be outlined in succeeding chapters and they will provide new insights into the stock market's relationship with and response to various levels of inflation and deflation.

When a similar study was presented by the Leuthold Group in 1975, its conclusions surprised most professional investors because no one had bothered to research the validity of the idea of stocks as an inflation hedge. Wall Street and the investment business in general, even in this age of computerization and informational sophistication, often seemed mired in myths, folklore, cliches, old wives' tales and tradition.

It seems that any advocate with a loud enough voice can gain a substantial following *if* he has a high enough pedestal and is persistent. Facts and history don't have to substantiate the position. Critical analysis is rare. Few bother to check the facts themselves, and those who do investigate usually don't bother to publicly rebut the false concepts. They just don't believe them.

Thus, fallacies like "the dollar can never be devalued" or "stocks are an excellent inflation hedge" can endure as common knowledge and fact for a long time.

Now, however, the experience of the 1970s has turned many investors away from the "stocks as an inflation hedge gospel." A few faithful disciples, though, are doggedly hanging on to it, rationalizing that we must view the hedge over the *very long term*. This long-term argument will be dealt with later.

Now a new thesis seems to be emerging, one that is gaining followers and converts at an amazingly rapid rate. This thesis says: "What would really be good for the stock market is a good dose of deflation!" But is this new thesis any more valid than the previous one?

Inflation is not good for the stock market nor is the stock market an effective hedge against inflation.

It seems facts and history don't have to substantiate the position of any persistent advocate who has a loud enough voice and a high enough pedestal.

History as a Guide

Before accepting either of these contrary positions, take a good look at the past relationship between inflationary years and the stock market movements, and deflationary years and the stock market movements. History, while not always providing definitive answers, can be a most helpful guide.

For this purpose, we dug out the level of annual inflation or deflation in the U.S. economy during the past 108 years, 1872 through 1979, using the Consumer Price Index or a predecessor as proxy. Then the annual percentage changes of the stock market were calculated, excluding dividends. For the 1872 to 1936 period, we used the Cowles All Stocks Index as a source. From that point on, we used the Dow Jones Industrial Average. The DJIA was used for this later period because it was convenient and widely followed, not because it was the best index.

Finally, we divided the 108 years of economic and market history into six environments:

1. **Years of extraordinary inflation.** In these periods inflation ranged from 8 per cent to 18 per cent. We found that 13 per cent of the years studied (14 of the 108) fell into this category.

2. **Years of relatively high inflation.** These ranged from 4 per cent to 7 per cent inflation per year. Some 18.5 per cent of the years studied (20 of 108 years) fell into this category.

3. **Years of moderate inflation.** Inflation ranged from 2 per cent to 3 per cent per year, and 19.4 per cent of the years (21 of 108) fell into this category.

4. **Years of price stability.** The range was from 1 per cent inflation to 1 per cent deflation, and 27.8 per cent of the years (30 of 108) met the qualifications.

5. **Years of moderate deflation.** Annual *deflation* rates ranged from 2 per cent to 4 per cent and 12 per cent of the years studied (13 of 108) fell into this category.

6. **Years of extraordinary deflation.** The annual *deflation* rate ranged from 5 per cent to 11 per cent. Only 9.3 per cent of the years (10 of 108) fell into this category.

Inflation has not been a constant factor with which investors have had to contend.

Thus, there were 55 years of inflation (extraordinary, relatively high or moderate), 23 years of deflation (moderate or extraordinary) and only 30 years of relative price stability. Inflation, thus, has not been a constant factor with which investors have had to contend. But what has been its impact on stock market investments, investments which many people felt provided the best protection against inflation's ravages?

The tables and charts in this chapter provide part of the answer. They assume a theoretical investor owned stocks only in the years that qualified for a particular category of inflation or deflation years. In reality, of course, these qualifying years were not consecutive.

But the calculation is still an effective way to demonstrate the relative investment attractiveness of each environment. Dividends are not included.

How has the market performed during the whole 108-year period? It was up in 61.1 per cent, or 66, of the years with a median gain of 15.1 per cent in the rising years. It was down in 38.9 per cent of the years, with a median loss of 12.3 per cent. The median year performance was a gain of 3.3 per cent, and the compound annual return for the whole period was 2.6 per cent. These figures do not include dividends. Dividends averaged about 4.8 per cent, indicating a compound annual total return rate of about 7.4 per cent from 1872 through the end of 1978. But this is only part of the picture. A clearer picture emerges if we look separately at each category.

A Deeper Look

If an investor put money into the market only during the years of extraordinary inflation (when it ranged between 8 per cent and 18 per cent), he would have been invested for 14 years. Assuming a $1,000 starting value and that those years were consecutive, the terminal value of the initial investment would be only $821 for a compound annual loss of 1.4 per cent. Years of extraordinary inflation, thus, appear to be poor years for stock market investments.

Years of relatively high inflation are even worse. The investor could have been in the market for 20 such years in the period under examination, and his $1,000 investment would have declined to $296 for a compound annual loss of 5.9 per cent.

Moderate inflation years provide better results. There were 21 such years in our survey, and a $1,000 investment would have grown in an environment of 2 per cent to 3 per cent inflation to $4,223 for a compound annual return of 7.1 per cent.

There were 30 years of relative stability in our survey period, and a $1,000 investment in these years would have produced a terminal value of $10,063, or a compound annual growth rate of 8 per cent.

Years of moderate deflation would have produced a compound annual growth rate of 7.8 per cent, giving a terminal value after 13 years of $2,655.

Finally, years of extraordinary deflation, of which there were 10 in the period examined, were as bad for the stock market as years of relatively high inflation, reducing the starting value of $1,000 to only $544 for a compound annual decline of 5.9 per cent.

These results are summarized in the table and the chart on the following page.

The question arises as to why the extraordinary inflation was less damaging to a $1,000 investment than the relatively high inflation? In part this may be the result of a statistical quirk. But it also reflects the fact that in some of the years of extraordinary inflation, the inflation rate was decelerating, and, as will be

Years of extraordinary deflation have been as bad for the stock market as years of relatively high inflation.

Theoretical Investment Results

(Starting Capital: $1,000)

Environment	Years Invested	Starting Value	Terminal Value	Compound Annual Growth
Extraordinary Inflation (8%-18%)................	14	$1,000	$ 821	−1.4%
Relatively High Inflation (4%-7%).................	20	1,000	296	−5.9
Moderate Inflation (2%-3%).................	21	1,000	4,223	+7.1
Stability (1% Inflation-1% Deflation)	30	1,000	10,063	+8.0
Moderate Deflation (2%-4%).................	13	1,000	2,655	+7.8
Extraordinary Deflation (5%-11%)................	10	1,000	544	−5.9

108 Years Of Investing (1872–1979)
In Six Inflationary/Deflationary Environments
Annual Compound Rate

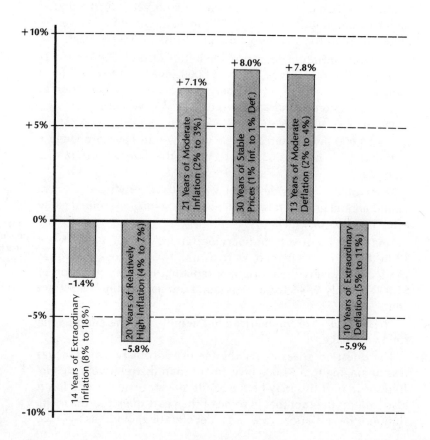

discussed in detail later, a decelerating rate of inflation is good for the stock market.

The investment performance disparity is even more dramatic when viewed in terms of median annual stock market performance found in each environment. In years of extraordinary inflation (8 per cent through 18 per cent), the median annual stock market return was 2.8 per cent. In years of relatively high inflation (4 per cent through 7 per cent), the median return was 2 per cent. In periods of moderate inflation (2 per cent through 3 per cent), the median return was 10.9 per cent, while in periods of relative price stability (minus 1 per cent deflation through 1 per cent inflation), median return was 13.6 per cent. Periods of moderate deflation (2 per cent through 4 per cent) and extraordinary deflation (5 per cent through 11 per cent) produced returns of 8.5 per cent per year and minus 3.5 per cent per year.

The disparity in investment performance in different economic environments is even more dramatic when viewed in terms of median annual stock market performance.

This is summarized below and in the chart on the next page.

Median Annual Stock Market Performance

Environment	Median Annual Change
Extraordinary Inflation (8%-18%)	+ 2.8%
Relatively High Inflation (4%-7%)	+ 2.0
Moderate Inflation (2%-3%)	+10.9
Stability (1% Inflation-1% Deflation) . .	+13.6
Moderate Deflation (2%-4%)	+ 8.5
Extraordinary Deflation (5%-11%)	− 3.5

Thus, it is apparent that years of relative moderation in terms of inflation or deflation have provided the best environment for the stock market. As long as inflation has not been more than 2 per cent to 3 per cent per year and deflation has not been greater than 2 per cent to 4 per cent per year, the stock market has prospered.

Adjusting the Picture

But these figures give only half of the picture because they do not take into consideration the annual loss or gain in buying power caused by the annual rate of inflation or deflation. If we adjust the return picture to constant dollars, the picture changes significantly.

First, the years of extraordinary inflation were the worst investment environment because the purchasing power of $1,000 declined to only $138 during the 14 years, giving a compound annual negative return of 13.2 per cent.

When we adjust the picture to constant dollars, the years of extraordinary inflation were the worst investment environment.

Years of relatively high inflation were little better. Here the purchasing power of $1,000 declined during the 20 years to only $166, for a negative return of 8.6 per cent.

**108 Years of Investing (1872-1979)
In Six Inflationary/Deflationary Environments**

Median Annual Performance

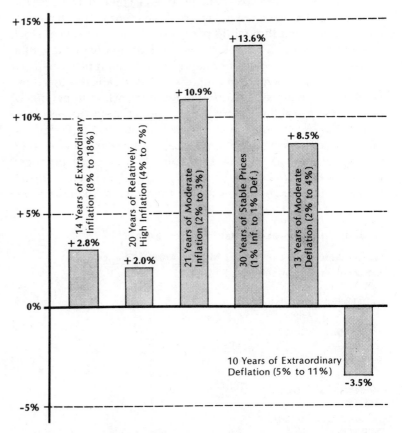

The real return during periods of moderate inflation (2 per cent to 3 per cent) was 4.6 per cent, as the initial $1,000 increased in buying power to $2,571. In the 30 years of stability, the purchasing power of $1,000 increased to $9,257 for a 7.7 per cent real return, while in 13 years of moderate deflation (2 per cent to 4 per cent), the purchasing power increased to $3,577 for a real return of 10.3 per cent.

Even extraordinary deflation provided a better return than extraordinary or relatively high inflation. In periods of extraordinary deflation, though the initial $1,000 declined to $544 in the market, the purchasing power actually increased to $1,207, giving a constant dollar compound annual growth rate of 1.9 per cent. These results are shown in the table and the chart on the following page.

Thus, in terms of real purchasing power, periods of moderate deflation have been the best for the stock market investor. While the market has not increased as much as in periods of relative stability, it has increased sufficiently that with the decline in prices the constant dollar return is greater.

Unfortunately for the stock market investor, years of moderate deflation are not as common as years of moderate inflation or relatively high inflation, and years of extraordinary in-

In terms of real purchasing power, periods of moderate deflation have been best for the stock market investor.

Constant Dollar Compound Annual Growth

Environment	Years Invested	Starting Value	Constant Dollar Terminal Value	Constant Dollar Compound Annual Growth
Extraordinary Inflation (8%-18%).................	14	$1,000	$ 138	−13.2%
Relatively High Inflation (4%-7%)...................	20	1,000	166	− 8.6
Moderate Inflation (2%-3%)...................	21	1,000	2,571	+ 4.6
Stability (1% Inflation-1% Deflation)	30	1,000	9,257	+ 7.7
Moderate Deflation (2%-4%)...................	13	1,000	3,577	+10.3
Extraordinary Deflation (5%-11%).................	10	1,000	1,207	+ 1.9

108 Years Of Investing (1872–1979)
In Six Inflationary/Deflationary Environments
Constant Dollars
(Adjusted For Inflation/Deflation)

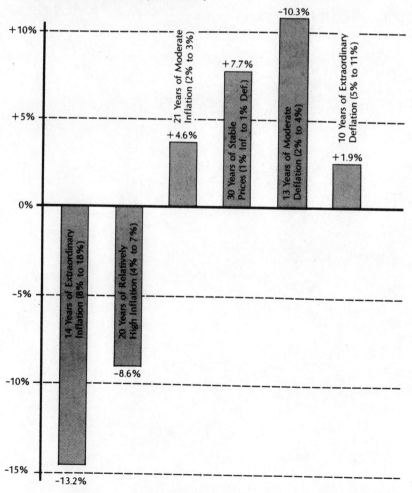

flation, the worst of all possible environments, are just as common.

Happily, the second best environment in terms of constant dollar returns also has been the most common environment, years of relative price stability. In the years when the inflation rate was 1 per cent or less or the deflation rate was 1 per cent or less, the constant dollar compound annual rate of growth was 7.7 per cent. As we noted before, the 30 years of relative price stability provided the best environment purely in terms of market returns.

In the next chapter we will examine these periods in more detail.

Chapter 3
Taking a Closer Look

Which of the following statements are true?

1. The stock market usually serves as an inflation hedge.

2. There is a simple correlation between the current inflation rate and the following year's rate.

3. The stock market, year to year, rises about 60 per cent of the time.

4. Long-term inflation in the U.S. is in excess of 2.5 per cent per year.

5. Shifts from inflation to deflation are typically gradual.

Most people enjoy watching professional football halftime highlights on television, even if they are not gridiron fanatics. The exciting action and spectacular plays are compressed into about 10 minutes. There's no need to sit through the commercials, time outs and three-yards-and-a-cloud-of-dust plays.

Assuming most readers are not hardcore fanatics on this subject, let's summarize and present the highlights of the inflation/deflation market direction research. At the same time, we will focus more closely on each of the periods discussed briefly in the previous chapter.

For those who wish to pore over the detailed statistical data, they are included at the end of this chapter. The tables and statistics presented there might be useful as a reference source or for winning cocktail party wagers or for impressing investment committees.

The Investment Environment

The preceding chapter indicated that high levels of inflation and deflation typically are accompanied by a relatively poor stock market. The best environment for the stock market seems to be stability. As long as inflation or deflation does not exceed 3 per cent there is no adverse effect on stock prices. And the constant dollar table in the previous chapter (page 17) shows that the stock market is a very poor hedge against higher levels of inflation.

Inflation at levels of 4 per cent and above has a negative effect on the stock market.

Taking a closer look, what has been the stock market's comparative record in years when inflation was 4 per cent or more?

Contrary to the almost universally accepted dogma of the 1950s and 1960s, which held that common stocks were the best inflation hedge, history clearly reveals the market provided no protection at all when inflation was at or above 4 per cent. It is interesting to note that when it was generally accepted that stocks were an inflation hedge, inflation only equaled or exceeded 4 per cent in four widely spaced years — 1951, 1957, 1968 and 1969.

During the past 108 years there have been 34 years with annual inflation rates of 4 per cent or higher. In only seven of these years did the stock market manage to keep pace with or rise more than the inflation rate (excluding dividends). In those 108 years, including 1979, there have been eight years when inflation blazed at levels of 10 per cent or higher. The stock market was not able to outperform the inflation rate in even one of those eight years. (See tables below.) In the years of extraordinary inflation, the market was up eight years and down six, but the compound annual growth rate for the period was minus 1.4 per cent, while in constant dollars the compound annual rate eroded to minus 13.2 per cent. In the periods of relatively high inflation — 4 per cent to 7 per cent — the market was up 11 years and down nine, but again finished with a negative compound annual growth rate — minus 5.8 per cent, while in constant dollars the loss mounted to an 8.6 per cent compound annual rate.

In not one of the eight years when inflation blazed at 10 per cent and higher was the stock market above to outperform the inflation rate.

The following tables show the 14 years of extraordinary inflation and the 20 years of relatively high inflation as well as the market returns for these years, including the annual returns in constant dollars.

HOW THE INVESTMENT OF $100 FARED IN SPECIFIC INVESTMENT ENVIRONMENTS

A. Extraordinary Inflation Environment
(8% thru 18%)

14 Years	Beginning Value	Inflation Erosion to	Stock Market % Change	Constant Dollar Year End Value	Constant Dollar % Change
1916 (8%)	$100	$92	+ 3.4%	$ 95.13	− 4.9%
1917 (17%)	100	83	− 30.7	57.51	− 42.5
1918 (18%)	100	82	+ 16.1	95.20	− 4.8
1919 (15%)	100	85	+ 13.1	96.13	− 3.9
1920 (16%)	100	84	− 23.7	64.09	− 35.9
1942 (11%)	100	89	+ 7.6	95.76	− 4.2
1946 (9%)	100	91	− 8.1	83.62	− 16.4
1947 (14%)	100	86	+ 2.2	87.89	− 12.1
1948 (8%)	100	92	− 2.1	90.07	− 9.9
1951 (8%)	100	92	+ 14.4	105.25	+ 5.3
1974 (11%)	100	89	− 27.6	64.44	− 35.6
1975 (9%)	100	91	+ 38.3	125.85	+ 25.9
1978 (9%)	100	91	− 3.2	87.80	− 12.2
1979 (13%)	100	87	+ 4.2	90.03	− 10.0
(12%)	Average		+ 0.3%		− 11.5%
	Compound Annual Growth		− 1.4%		− 13.2%

B. Relatively High Inflation Environment
(4% thru 7%)

20 Years	Beginning Value	Inflation Erosion to	Stock Market % Change	Constant Dollar Year End Value	Constant Dollar % Change
1880 (7%)	$100	$93	+ 19.0%	$110.67	+ 10.7%
1881 (6%)	100	94	+ 2.8	96.63	− 3.4
1899 (7%)	100	93	+ 6.5	99.05	− 1.0
1902 (4%)	100	96	+ 1.3	97.25	− 2.7
1903 (4%)	100	96	− 18.5	78.24	− 21.8
1906 (4%)	100	96	+ 3.2	99.07	− 0.9
1907 (4%)	100	96	− 33.3	64.03	− 36.0
1910 (4%)	100	96	− 12.3	84.19	− 15.8
1912 (4%)	100	96	+ 2.9	98.78	− 1.2
1937 (4%)	100	96	− 32.8	64.51	− 35.5
1941 (5%)	100	95	− 15.4	80.37	+ 19.6
1943 (6%)	100	94	+ 13.8	106.97	+ 7.0
1957 (4%)	100	96	− 12.8	83.71	− 16.3
1968 (4%)	100	96	+ 4.3	100.13	+ 0.1
1969 (5%)	100	95	− 15.2	80.56	− 19.4
1970 (6%)	100	94	+ 4.8	98.51	− 1.5
1971 (4%)	100	96	+ 6.1	101.86	+ 1.9
1973 (6%)	100	94	− 16.6	81.22	− 18.9
1976 (7%)	100	94	+ 17.9	110.83	+ 10.8
1977 (7%)	100	93	− 17.3	76.91	− 23.1
(5%)	Average		− 4.6%		− 7.4%
	Compound Annual Growth		− 5.8%		− 8.6%

What has been the historic stock market behavior in periods of moderate inflation—2 per cent to 3 per cent? Consider the following:

C. Moderate Inflation Environment
(2% thru 3%)

21 Years	Beginning Value	Inflation Erosion to	Stock Market % Change	Constant Dollar Year End Value	Constant Dollar % Change
1882 (2%)	$100	$98	− 2.9%	$ 95.16	− 4.8%
1887 (2%)	100	98	− 6.5	91.63	− 8.4
1888 (2%)	100	98	− 2.4	95.65	− 4.3
1890 (2%)	100	98	−13.6	84.67	−15.3
1897 (2%)	100	98	+12.9	110.64	+10.6
1900 (2%)	100	98	+14.1	111.82	+11.8
1901 (2%)	100	98	+15.8	113.48	+13.5
1923 (2%)	100	98	− 2.4	95.65	− 4.3
1925 (3%)	100	97	+22.8	119.12	+19.1
1934 (3%)	100	97	− 1.1	95.93	− 4.1
1935 (3%)	100	97	+37.0	132.89	+32.9
1944 (2%)	100	98	+12.1	109.86	+ 9.9
1945 (2%)	100	98	+26.7	124.17	+24.2
1952 (2%)	100	98	+ 8.4	106.23	+ 6.2
1956 (2%)	100	98	+ 2.3	100.25	+ 0.3
1958 (3%)	100	97	+34.0	129.98	+30.0
1960 (2%)	100	98	− 9.3	88.89	−11.1
1965 (2%)	100	98	+10.9	108.68	+ 8.7
1966 (3%)	100	97	−19.0	78.57	−21.4
1967 (3%)	100	97	+15.2	111.74	+11.7
1972 (3%)	100	97	+14.6	111.16	+11.2
(2%)	**Average**		+ 8.1%		+ 5.5%
	Compound Annual Growth		+ 7.1%		+ 4.6%

If you had invested only in the 21 years when inflation was in the 2 per cent to 3 per cent range, you would have had 7.1 per cent compound annual rate of return (excluding dividends). Even after factoring out inflation (in constant dollars), the return would have been 4.6 per cent. The market declined more than 15 per cent only one year—1966—in this environment; and there were only eight years out of 21 when the market returns were negative.

In summary, inflation at these lower levels would seem to have no adverse effect on the stock market. However, the investment record, although good, falls significantly short of the market performance found in the environment of price stability *if* viewed in terms of constant dollars.

The stock market appears to react most favorably in periods of relative price stability, when inflation is 1 per cent or less, or when deflation is 1 per cent or less. In only eight of the 30 years in which these conditions existed was there a losing market, and only in 1893 did the decline exceed 15 per cent.

The compound annual growth rate for these years was 8 per cent (about 13 per cent when dividends are included) with a one year high of 44 per cent in 1954. Even in constant dollars, the

(1% or Less Inflation/Deflation)

30 Years	Inflation/ Deflation	Beginning Value	Adjustment Inflation/ Deflation	Stock Market % Change	Constant Dollar Year End Value	Constant Dollar % Change
1872	1% D	$100	$101	+ 6.9%	$107.97	+ 8.0%
1892	1% D	100	101	+ 1.4	102.41	+ 2.4
1893	-0-	100	100	− 19.8	80.20	− 19.8
1895	-0-	100	100	+ 1.0	101.00	+ 1.0
1896	-0-	100	100	− 2.3	97.70	− 2.3
1898	1% I	100	99	+ 18.6	117.41	+ 17.4
1904	-0-	100	100	+ 25.6	125.60	+ 25.6
1905	-0-	100	100	+ 16.0	116.00	+ 16.0
1909	-0-	100	100	+ 14.3	114.30	+ 14.3
1911	-0-	100	100	+ 1.0	101.00	+ 1.0
1913	1% D	100	101	− 14.2	86.66	− 13.3
1914	1% I	100	99	− 9.0	90.09	− 9.9
1915	1% I	100	99	+ 31.6	130.28	+ 30.3
1924	-0-	100	100	+ 18.6	118.60	+ 18.6
1926	1% I	100	99	+ 5.1	104.05	+ 4.1
1928	1% I	100	99	+ 28.8	127.51	+ 27.5
1929	-0-	100	100	− 10.3	89.70	− 10.3
1936	-0-	100	100	+ 28.9	128.90	+ 28.9
1939	1% D	100	101	− 3.0	97.99	− 2.0
1940	1% I	100	99	− 12.7	86.43	− 13.6
1949	1% D	100	101	+ 12.9	114.03	+ 14.0
1950	1% I	100	99	+ 17.6	116.42	+ 16.4
1953	1% I	100	99	− 3.8	95.24	− 4.8
1954	1% I	100	99	+ 44.0	142.56	+ 42.6
1955	-0-	100	100	+ 20.8	120.80	+ 20.8
1959	1% I	100	99	+ 16.4	115.24	+ 15.2
1961	1% I	100	99	+ 18.7	117.51	+ 17.5
1962	1% I	100	99	− 10.8	88.31	− 11.7
1963	1% I	100	99	+ 17.0	115.83	+ 15.8
1964	1% I	100	99	+ 14.6	113.45	+ 13.5
	-0-	**Average**		+ 9.1%		+ 8.8%
		Compound Annual Growth		+ 8.0%		+ 7.7%

growth rate was an impressive 7.7 per cent. Unfortunately, the last years in which these stable conditions existed were 1961, 1962, 1963, and 1964.

As noted in the previous chapter, years of moderate deflation also appear to be favorable for the market. In the 13 years of moderate deflation (prices declining between 2 per cent and 4 per cent), the market advanced in nine years and declined in four. A person who confined investing to only those years would have experienced a 7.8 per cent compound annual growth rate, not much lower than in the years of relative price stability. In constant dollar terms, he would have done even better because on an inflation-adjusted basis the growth rate was 10.3 per cent compounded annually. However, the sample here is relatively small—only 13 years—and also ancient, with only three instances since the turn of the century. Therefore, it is difficult to say with confidence that moderate deflation is the best environment for the market.

Although the market reacts well in years of moderate deflation, the sample is small and ancient, and it is difficult to aver that moderate deflation is best for the market.

E. Moderate Deflation Environment
(2% thru 4%)

13 Years	Beginning Value	Inflation Erosion to	Stock Market % Change	Constant Dollar Year End Value	Constant Dollar % Change
1873 (2%)	$100	$102	− 13.0%	$ 88.74	− 11.3%
1874 (2%)	100	102	+ 3.2	105.26	+ 5.3
1877 (4%)	100	104	− 9.5	94.12	− 5.9
1879 (2%)	100	102	+ 43.0	145.86	+ 45.9
1883 (2%)	100	102	− 8.7	93.13	− 6.9
1885 (2%)	100	102	+ 19.8	122.20	+ 22.2
1886 (2%)	100	102	+ 8.5	110.67	+ 10.7
1889 (2%)	100	102	+ 3.2	105.26	+ 5.3
1891 (2%)	100	102	+ 18.2	120.56	+ 20.6
1908 (3%)	100	103	+ 37.3	141.42	+ 41.4
1927 (2%)	100	102	+ 26.3	128.83	+ 28.8
1930 (3%)	100	103	− 28.9	73.23	− 26.8
1938 (2%)	100	102	+ 28.1	130.66	+ 30.7
(2%) Average			+ 9.8%		+ 12.3%
Compound Annual Growth			+ 7.8%		+ 10.3%

In the 10 years of extraordinary deflation, when prices fell between 5 per cent and 11 per cent, investment experience was generally not good. Only 1922, when the market was up 20.1 per cent, and 1933, when the market was up 49.4 per cent, were good years. An investor who limited his investing to this kind of environment would have experienced a 5.9 per cent compound annual loss, although, because of the high levels of deflation, his result on a constant dollar basis was actually a 1.9 per cent gain.

F. Extraordinary Deflation Environment
(5% thru 11%)

10 Years	Beginning Value	Deflation Adjustment	Stock Market % Change	Constant Dollar Year End Value	Constant Dollar % Change
1875 (5%)	$100	$105	− 4.2%	$100.59	+ 0.6%
1876 (5%)	100	105	− 18.0	86.10	− 13.9
1878 (6%)	100	106	+ 6.3	112.68	+ 12.7
1884 (6%)	100	106	− 18.7	86.18	− 3.8
1894 (8%)	100	108	− 2.8	104.98	+ 5.0
1921 (11%)	100	111	+ 7.3	119.10	+ 19.1
1922 (6%)	100	106	+ 20.1	127.31	+ 27.3
1931 (9%)	100	109	− 46.6	58.21	− 41.8
1932 (10%)	100	110	− 19.4	88.66	− 11.3
1933 (5%)	100	105	+ 49.5	156.98	+ 57.0
(7%) Average			− 2.7%		+ 5.1%
Compound Annual Growth			− 5.9%		+ 1.9%

Thus, the best environment for investing in the stock market seems to be years of relative price stability, with some evidence that this is followed closely by years of moderate deflation. Investing in years of extraordinary inflation, relatively high inflation or extraordinary deflation brought poor results.

But can you make money in the stock market with all this knowledge?

From a practical standpoint, the catch, of course, is knowing at the beginning of a particular year what the inflation or deflation rate for that year will be. One approach would be to assume that next year's inflation or deflation rate will approximate this year's. Unfortunately, this does not work well at all. There is very little year to year inflation or deflation stability. Analyzing the historic data, we find that the odds of a particular year's inflation/deflation environment being repeated in the following year are less than 50-50.

The catch is knowing at the beginning of the year what the inflation or deflation rate will be.

If This Year's Environment Is:	The Odds Next Year's Environment Will Be the Same Are:
Extraordinary Deflation	38%
Moderate Deflation	16
Price Stability	35
Moderate Inflation	23
High Inflation	17
Extraordinary Inflation	45

So, even though the research indicates there is a correlation between annual stock market movements and the annual rate of inflation or deflation, this information, although helpful to the investor, does not qualify as an investment panacea. It is not a magic key to successful investment strategy because it depends on one's ability to *predict* inflation or deflation levels one year in advance. And *predicting* next year's inflation or deflation, especially when inflation is currently high, could be as difficult as predicting next year's stock market. This will be dealt with further in a later chapter.

Predicting next year's inflation or deflation is as difficult as predicting next year's stock market.

Most people will be surprised to learn the inflation rate during the span of this study. Most would probably guess it has been about 3 per cent per year, but in fact it has been but half that. Equally surprising may be that during this 108 year period there were 38 years when there was no inflation, including 31 years of deflation. Unfortunately, that still left us with 70 years of inflation of one degree or another, and, thus, with a problem for the stock market investor.

In 11 of the 108 years, inflation exceeded 8 per cent, and in only one of those years, 1975, did the stock market beat inflation. In three of the 11 years, the market was horrible.

Eleven Years When Inflation Topped 8%

Inflation	Year	Stock Market Change
9%	1978	− 3%
9	1946	− 8
9	1975	+ 38
11	1942	+ 7
11	1974	− 28
13	1979	+ 4
14	1947	+ 2
15	1919	+ 13
16	1920	− 24
17	1917	− 31
18	1918	+ 16

Contrary to what might be expected, the shift from an inflationary environment to a deflationary one need not be gradual. It can be quite abrupt. For example, in 1919 the country suffered through 15 per cent inflation, and in 1920 it had 16 per cent inflation, but in 1921 it had 11 per cent *deflation*. Similarly, in 1947 the country had 14 per cent inflation followed by 8 per cent inflation in 1948, and then 1 per cent deflation in 1949. The table at the end of this chapter shows consecutive years of inflation and stock market data.

What then of those who say the stock market is a long-term hedge against inflation. The evidence cited by the believers usually consists of presenting long-term stock market investment results of say, 25 years, 50 years or more, and comparing this with the long-term inflation rate.

Because the stock market gained more than was lost to inflation during this period, the conclusion is that stocks are a hedge against inflation.

This is, at best, a questionable conclusion, as will be examined elsewhere in this book. In all of the time periods cited, stock market growth rates most closely correlate with book value growth, earnings growth and dividends growth. The stock market gains during these periods are recognition of these fundamental growth factors. These are the prime movers, not inflation. If the long-term growth of these fundamental factors ceases or slows down, the stock market will follow suit, no matter that inflation continues to surge ahead.

"Aha," the diehard stock market/inflation advocate might say "won't inflation itself cause earnings, book value and dividends to grow at a similar rate?"

It's the old chicken and egg argument. Sometimes, it will, but certainly not all the time, especially when inflation is running 5 per cent or more per year. A look at recent experience might be of interest. From Dec. 31, 1968, through Dec. 31, 1977, only book value growth managed to stay within hailing distance of the increase in consumer prices as measured by the Consumer Price Index. Earnings growth and dividend growth lagged far behind inflation.

> The conclusion that stocks are a hedge against inflation is questionable, at best.

Consider the following:

	Dec. 31 1968	Dec. 31 1977	Increase
Dow Jones Industrials			
Earnings...........	$57.89	$89.10	53.9%
Dividends.........	31.34	45.10	43.9
Book Value........	521	838	60.8
Consumer Price Index	106.4	186.1	74.9%

In summary, inflation has been a recurring but not constant phenomenon in the U.S. economy and, conventional wisdom notwithstanding, it has not been a good environment for stock market investing. In the last 10 years, the Consumer Price Index rose 91 per cent and during the same period the Dow Jones Industrial Average fell 15 per cent. As a matter of fact, the stock market return has managed to exceed the high annual inflation rates (8 per cent plus) in only one year since 1872. Therefore, the stock market does not appear to be a good inflation hedge. The best time to profit in the stock market is during periods of price stability or even mild deflation.

Taking a Closer Look

27

YEARS OF INFLATION 1872-1979
Includes Annual Stock Market
Performance, Excluding Dividends

Annual Inflation Rate

1%	2%	3%	4%	5%	6%
1872 + 6.9%	1882 − 2.9%	1925 +22.8%	1902 + 1.3%	1941 −15.4%	1881 + 2.8%
1898 +18.6	1887 − 6.5	1934 − 1.1	1903 −18.5	1969 −15.2	1943 +13.8
1914 − 9.0	1888 − 2.4	1935 +37.0	1906 + 3.2		1970 + 4.8
1915 +31.6	1890 −13.6	1958 +34.0	1907 −33.3		1973 −16.6
1926 + 5.1	1897 +12.9	1966 −19.0	1910 −12.3		1976 +17.9
1928 +28.8	1900 +14.1	1967 +15.2	1912 + 2.9		
1940 −12.7	1901 +15.8	1972 +14.6	1937 −32.8		
1950 +17.6	1923 − 2.4		1957 −12.8		
1953 − 3.8	1944 +12.1		1968 + 4.3		
1954 +44.0	1945 +26.7		1971 + 6.1		
1959 +16.4	1952 + 8.4				
1961 +18.7	1956 + 2.3				
1962 −10.8	1960 − 9.3				
1963 +17.0	1965 +10.9				
1964 +14.6					

7%	8%	9%	10%	11%	12%	13%	14% & Over
1880 +19.0%	1916 + 3.4%	1946 − 8.1%	—	1942 + 7.6%	—	1979 + 4.2%	1947 + 2.2% (14)
1899 + 6.5	1948 − 2.1	1975 +38.3		1974 −27.6			1919 +13.1 (15)
1977 −17.3	1951 +14.4	1978 − 3.2					1920 −23.7 (16)
							1917 −30.7 (17)
							1918 +16.1 (18)

YEARS OF DEFLATION 1872-1979
Includes Annual Stock Market
Performance, Excluding Dividends

Annual Deflation Rate

11%	10%	9%	8%	7%	6%
1921 − 7.3%	1932 −19.4%	1931 −46.6%	1894 − 2.9%	—	1878 + 6.3%
					1884 −18.7
					1922 +20.1

5%	4%	3%	2%	1%	0%
1875 − 4.2%	1877 − 9.5%	1908 +37.3%	1873 −13.0%	1892 + 1.4%	1893 −19.8%
1876 −18.0		1930 −28.9	1874 + 3.2	1913 −14.2	1895 + 1.0
1933 +49.5			1879 +43.0	1939 − 3.0	1896 − 2.3
			1883 − 8.7	1949 +12.9	1904 +25.6
			1885 +19.8		1905 +16.0
			1886 + 8.5		1909 +14.3
			1889 + 3.2		1911 + 1.0
			1891 +18.2		1924 +18.6
			1927 +26.3		1929 −10.3
			1938 +28.1		1936 +28.9
					1955 +20.8

Summary Table:
The Six Environments and the Stock Market

Environment	Years	Average Annual Stock Price Change	Compound Annual Growth* (Negative)	Up Market Years	Average Gain	Down Market Years	Average Loss
Extraordinary Inflation (8%-18%)	14	+ 0.3%	− 1.4%	8	+12.4%*	6	− 15.9%
Relatively High Inflation (4%-7%)	20	− 4.6	− 5.8	11	+ 7.5	9	−18.1
Moderate Inflation (2%-3%)	21	+ 8.1	+ 7.1	13	+17.5	8	− 7.2
Stability (1% Inflation- 1% Deflation)	30	+ 9.1	+ 8.0	21	+17.1	9	− 9.5
Moderate Deflation (2%-4%)	13	+ 9.8	+ 7.8	9	+ 20.8	4	−15.0
Extraordinary Deflation (5%-11%)	10	− 2.7	− 5.9	4	+ 8.0	6	− 8.3
The Entire Period The Stock Market	108	+ 4.4%	+ 2.6%	66	+15.0%	42	−14.1%

* Annual percentage gains and declines for all years included in each environment geometrically linked and presented in terms of annual compound positive or (negative) growth rates. Excludes dividends.

Primary Data Table

Year	Inflation (+) Deflation (−)	% Change Stock Market	Year	Inflation (+) Deflation (−)	% Change Stock Market
1872	+ 1%	+ 6.9%	1898	+ 1	+18.6
1873	− 2	−13.0	1899	+ 7	+ 6.5
1874	− 2	+ 3.2	1900	+ 2	+14.1
1875	− 5	− 4.2	1901	+ 2	+15.8
1876	− 5	−18.0	1902	+ 4	+ 1.3
1877	− 4	− 9.5	1903	+ 4	−18.5
1878	− 6	+ 6.3	1904	0	+ 25.6
1879	− 2	+43.0	1905	0	+16.0
1880	+ 7	+19.0	1906	+ 4	+ 3.2
1881	+ 6	+ 2.8	1907	+ 4	− 33.3
1882	+ 2	− 2.9	1908	− 3	+ 37.3
1883	− 2	− 8.7	1909	0	+14.3
1884	− 6	−18.7	1910	+ 4	− 12.3
1885	− 2	+19.8	1911	0	+ 1.0
1886	− 2	+ 8.5	1912	+ 4	+ 2.9
1887	+ 2	− 6.5	1913	− 1	−14.2
1888	+ 2	− 2.4	1914	+ 1	− 9.0
1889	− 2	+ 3.2	1915	+ 1	+ 31.6
1890	+ 2	−13.6	1916	+ 8	+ 3.4
1891	− 2	+18.2	1917	+17	− 30.7
1892	− 1	+ 1.4	1918	+ 18	+16.1
1893	0	−19.8	1919	+15	+13.1
1894	− 8	− 2.8	1920	+16	− 23.7
1895	0	+ 1.0	1921	−11	+ 7.3
1896	0	− 2.3	1922	− 6	+ 20.1
1897	+ 2	+12.9			

Year	Inflation (+) Deflation (−)	% Change Stock Market	Year	Inflation (+) Deflation (−)	% Change Stock Market
1923	+ 2	− 2.4	1952	+ 2	+ 8.4
1924	0	+18.6	1953	+ 1	− 3.8
1925	+ 3	+22.8	1954	+ 1	+44.0
1926	+ 1	+ 5.1	1955	0	+20.8
1927	− 2	+26.3	1956	+ 2	+ 2.3
1928	+ 1	+28.8	1957	+ 4	−12.8
1929	0	−10.3	1958	+ 3	+34.0
1930	− 3	−28.9	1959	+ 1	+16.4
1931	− 9	−46.6	1960	+ 2	− 9.3
1932	−10	−19.4	1961	+ 1	+18.7
1933	− 5	+49.5	1962	+ 1	−10.8
1934	+ 3	− 1.1	1963	+ 1	+17.0
1935	+ 3	+37.0	1964	+ 1	+14.6
1936	0	+28.9	1965	+ 2	+10.9
1937	+ 4	−32.8	1966	+ 3	−19.0
1938	− 2	+28.1	1967	+ 3	+15.2
1939	− 1	− 3.0	1968	+ 4	+ 4.3
1940	+ 1	−12.7	1969	+ 5	−15.2
1941	+ 5	−15.4	1970	+ 6	+ 4.8
1942	+11	+ 7.6	1971	+ 4	+ 6.1
1943	+ 6	+13.8	1972	+ 3	+14.6
1944	+ 2	+12.1	1973	+ 6	−16.6
1945	+ 2	+26.7	1974	+11	−27.6
1946	+ 9	− 8.1	1975	+ 9	+38.3
1947	+14	+ 2.2	1976	+ 6	+17.9
1948	+ 8	− 2.1	1977	+ 7	−17.3
1949	− 1	+12.9	1978	+ 9	− 3.2
1950	+ 1	+17.6	1979	+13	+ 4.2
1951	+ 8	+14.4			

Chapter 4

The Effect of Accelerating and Decelerating Inflation on the Stock Market

Which of the following statements is true?

1. Significant inflation acceleration, 2 per cent or more, is a stock market negative.

2. Significant inflation deceleration, 2 per cent or more, is a stock market positive.

When economic history and stock market performance are rubbed together, the evidence is overwhelming that the stock market performs below average during periods of more than 4 per cent inflation, while in periods of relative price stability or perhaps even mild inflation, market performance is significantly above average.

But what happens to the stock market when inflation is accelerating or decelerating?

To provide some insights into this question, we've isolated all years from 1900 to 1979 in which inflation was 4 per cent and above and in which inflation had accelerated at least 2 per cent from the prior year. We also tracked the stock market performance for these same years. The table below presents the results of the 17 years when inflation was accelerating. The Cowles Commission Index and the Dow Jones Industrial Average were once again used as the stock market proxy.

Seventeen Inflation Acceleration Years: 1900-1979

Year	Inflation Level	Preceding Year Inflation	Change	Stock Market	Net Change in Constant Dollar (Inflation Adjusted)
1902	4%	2%	+ 2%	+ 1.3%	− 2.7%
1906	4	—	+ 4	+ 3.2	− 0.8
1910	4	—	+ 4	−12.3	−16.3
1912	4	—	+ 4	+ 2.9	− 1.1
1916	8	1	+ 7	+ 3.4	− 4.6
1917	17	8	+ 9	−30.7	−47.7
1937	4	—	+ 4	−32.8	−36.8
1941	5	1	+ 4	−15.4	−20.4
1942	11	5	+ 6	+ 7.6	− 3.4
1946	9	2	+ 7	− 8.1	−17.1
1947	14	9	+ 5	+ 2.2	−11.8
1951	8	1	+ 7	+14.4	+ 6.4
1957	4	2	+ 2	−12.8	−16.8
1973	6	3	+ 3	−16.6	−22.6
1974	11	6	+ 5	−27.6	−38.6
1978	9	7	+ 2	− 3.2	−12.2
1979	13	9	+ 4	+ 4.2	− 8.8

Summary: 17 Years

	Nominal Dollars	Constant Dollars
Up Years	8	1
Down Years	9	16
All 17 Years		
Median Annual Performance	− 3.2%	−12.2%
Average Annual Performance	− 7.1%	−15.0%
Hypothetical Annual Compound Loss (17 Years Linked)	− 8.2%	−16.4%

The table shows several interesting things. First, even though the actual up years and down years are almost balanced (eight up, nine down), the losing years were really big losers, declining an average 20 per cent. Also, the years of market advance were marginal at best, averaging 5 per cent. The biggest nominal winner was 1951, which had a 14.4 per cent gain.

When viewed in terms of constant dollars, taking into consideration the dollar erosion from each year's inflation rate, 1951 was the single winning year in the 17 years examined, and that was only a 6.4 per cent gain. Overall, relative investment performance for these inflation acceleration years is miserable when measured in nominal or constant dollars.

The largest nominal loss in inflation acceleration years was 32.8 per cent in 1937 when inflation increased from zero the previous year to 4 per cent. The second biggest nominal loss was 30.7 per cent in 1917 when the inflation rate more than doubled from 8 per cent in 1916 to 17 per cent in 1917. More recently, when inflation almost doubled—from 6 per cent in 1973 to 11 per cent in 1974—the market lost 27.6 per cent.

Rapidly accelerating inflation is a hostile environment for the stock market investor.

Rapidly accelerating inflation, particularly if it is from a level of 4 per cent or more, is a hostile environment for the stock market investor. If the investor can strongly support a conclusion that a current inflation level of 4 per cent or higher will increase by 2 per cent or more in the next 12 months, he should realize he probably has two strikes against him.

Essentially the same procedure has been followed in examining years from 1900 to date when inflation was decelerating. Inflation deceleration years are identified as years in which infla-

Inflation Deceleration Years 1900-1979

Year	Inflation Level	Preceding Year Inflation	Change	Stock Market	Net Change in Constant Dollar (Inflation Adjusted)
1900	+ 2%	7%	− 5%	+14.1%	+12.1%
1904	0	4	− 4	+25.6	+25.6
1908	− 3	4	− 7	+37.3	+40.3
1911	0	4	− 4	+ 1.0	+ 1.0
1913	− 1	4	− 5	−14.2	−13.2
1919	+15	18	− 3	+13.1	− 1.9
1921	−11	16	−27	+ 7.3	+18.3
1938	− 2	4	− 6	+28.1	+30.1
1943	+ 6	11	− 5	+13.8	+ 7.8
1944	+ 2	6	− 4	+12.1	+10.1
1948	+ 8	14	− 6	− 2.1	−10.1
1949	− 1	8	− 7	+12.9	+13.9
1952	+ 2	8	− 6	+ 8.4	+ 6.4
1971	+ 4	6	− 2	+ 6.1	+ 2.1
1975	+ 9	11	− 2	+38.3	+29.3
1976	+ 6	9	− 3	+17.6	+11.6

Summary: 16 Years

	Nominal Dollars	Constant Dollars
Up Years	14	13
Down Years	2	3
All 16 Years		
Median Annual Performance	+13.0%	+10.9%
Average Annual Performance	+13.7%	+11.5%
Hypothetical Annual Compound Gain (16 Years Linked)	+12.9%	+10.6%

tion declined at least 2 per cent from a preceding significant inflation year (4 per cent and above). Sixteen years fit this definition. Note that some high inflation years, such as 1919 (15 per cent) and 1975 (9 per cent), also qualify as inflation deceleration years in that inflation, though still high, was coming down.

We find that 16 years fit our selected criteria, and 14 of these recorded gains in nominal dollars ranging from 38 per cent in 1975 and 37 per cent in 1908 to 6 per cent in 1971. Only 1913 (minus 14 per cent) was a significant losing year. More importantly perhaps, in constant dollars there were only three losing years out of the 16. All in all, these look like pretty good odds.

Comparative Stock Market Investment Results
Periods Studied: 1900–1979
Dividends Excluded

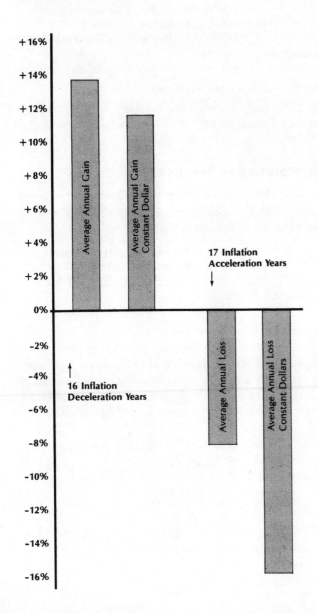

Periods of decelerating inflation
appear to be positive investment
environments even if the actual
level of inflation remains high.

Thus, periods of decelerating inflation appear to be very positive investment environments. And, even though the actual level of inflation may still be high by historic standards, the more important factor is the *declining* trend. Investor recognition of inflation deceleration from levels of 4 per cent and above would appear to be a significant factor, improving the odds of investment success.

Inflation Deceleration in Practice

For example, inflation in 1979, measured by the Consumer Price Index, was 13 per cent. If by the end of 1980, inflation would trail off to 11 per cent, the year would qualify as an inflation deceleration year. Even though 11 per cent is still a very high rate by historic standards, the implications for the market, according to our measurements, could be very positive.

	Year End 1979 Level	Typical Projected Performance	Hypothetical Year End 1980 Level
Dow Jones Industrial Av.	840	+13%	950
S&P 500	108	+13	122

(Excludes dividends, stated in nominal dollars.)

Based on historic performance, the market, as measured by the DJIA, would end at about 950, while the S&P 500 would end at 122.

Inflation Acceleration in Practice

But if inflation in 1980 accelerates to 15 per cent or more from 1979's 13 per cent, thereby qualifying as an inflation acceleration year, how might the stock market perform?

	Year End 1979 Level	Typical Projected Performance	Hypothetical Year End 1980 Level
Dow Jones Industrial Av.	840	− 7%	781
S&P 500	108	− 7	100

(Excludes dividends, stated in nominal dollars.)

Of the 17 years that fit our accelerating inflation criteria, there were nominal gains in eight. But outside of 1951, all were skimpy, and only 1951 recorded a gain in terms of *constant* dollars. So, if you were projecting an inflation rate of 15 per cent or more, by the end of 1980, the indicated strategy would be to avoid the stock market.

Unfortunately, from a practical standpoint this knowledge may not be as valuable as it might appear. The rub is that predicting future inflation, even next year's inflation, is no easy matter. But this is the topic of a later chapter.

Chapter 5

Inflation and Price Earnings Multiples

Which of the following statements is most correct?

1. P/E multiples are lower than normal only in periods of deflation.
2. P/E multiples are lower than normal only in periods of higher inflation.
3. P/E multiples are lower than normal in periods of higher inflation and significant deflation.
4. P/E multiples are lower than normal in periods of price stability.
5. There seems to be no correlation between P/E multiple levels and inflation.

The relationship of the
Consumer Price Index and
common stock valuations
provides useful benchmarks.

As has been demonstrated in previous chapters, the stock market typically performs below average when inflation is 4 per cent or more, and when prices are relatively stable, stock market performance is significantly above average.

To reinforce the view that inflation must be viewed properly as a negative stock market influence (except when inflation is decelerating), an examination should be made of Consumer Price Index (CPI) trends and historic common stock valuations, using annual prevailing normalized price/earnings multiples as the valuation standard. What follows may provide some useful and definitive benchmarks for investors to apply in various inflation environments.

P/E Multiples as Benchmarks

The most widely used tool in security analysis is the price/earnings ratio. This ratio allows the investor to compare the relative value of individual stocks with their earnings. Although the P/E multiple is typically used in comparing individual issues, it also can be used for the stock market as a whole.

The P/E ratio is often a good benchmark to gauge valuations—*and investor psychology.* In its simplest application, the higher the P/E, the more optimistic investors are about the future. In the case of a high P/E for an individual stock, it is usually a reflection of optimism concerning the future growth of earnings. For the market as a whole, a relatively high P/E is a reflection of optimism concerning the future of the economy. Obviously this is an oversimplification, but history has demonstrated that prevailing P/E ratios are more a function of current greed, apprehension and panic than of actual future realized earnings and dividend growth.

Prevailing P/E ratios are more a
function of current greed,
apprehension and panic than of
actual future realized earnings.

At any rate, the historic research clearly indicates that higher levels of inflation bring lower price/earnings valuations in the stock market. There are probably two major reasons why this kind of historical relationship exists.

First, in periods of high inflation corporate earnings often are distorted, larded with inventory profits and the like. Many investors may view this inflation-produced portion of reported earnings as nonrecurring, artificial or "poor quality," or not worthy of a typical P/E multiple.

Second, periods of high inflation reflect an unstable and vulnerable economic environment, which fosters an abnormal degree of investor concern for future economic health and results in a lack of enthusiasm for common stock investing. Lack of confidence results in a lower value being placed on future earnings. As pointed out earlier, the myth that common stocks are a good hedge against inflation is not substantiated historically. Although this credo gained broad acceptance in the 1950s and 1960s, it is far more fiction than fact.

Some might argue a third important reason for this relationship, something along the lines of: Higher inflation means higher interest rates. Higher interest rates mean tougher bond competition for the stock market on a total risk adjusted return basis. So if the stock market is to remain competitive with these higher bond interest rates, it must sell below its typical valuation.

While this factor appears to have been quite important in recent years, the longer term documentation is not all that decisive. For example, our 200-year analysis of inflation and interest rates raises some doubts that higher inflation means higher interest rates. Well...it ain't necessarily so, but more on that whole matter later on.

Comment on Techniques

Comparing P/E multiples based on most recent 12-month earnings is of limited analytical value, especially when the earnings are cyclical in nature. Cyclical earnings must be normalized, smoothed out or averaged, typically over three to five years, before meaningful relative comparisons can be made. Analysis of the raw cyclical data can result in erroneous conclusions.

Analysis of raw cyclical data can result in erroneous conclusions.

In this study we have used a three-year centered average of the earnings (last year, this year, next year) for the market as a whole, using 108 years of data (1872 to 1979). This yields 107 years of annual data without making a 1980 earnings projection. Again the Cowles Commission Index was used for the early years, and the Dow Jones Industrial Average for the more recent years. The years 1931 through 1934 have been excluded from some of the statistical presentations because of their distortion effect. However, data for those years are included in the resource material at the end of this chapter.

Also, it should be noted that the annual P/E data presented is based on the average market index price that prevailed in that particular year. Extreme intra-year highs and lows are not isolated. They are averaged right in with all the other days. Readers should keep in mind the extremes noted in this study are *not* the absolute zeniths and nadirs of market peaks and market bottoms.

What happens to P/E ratios in various inflation/deflation environments?

Let's see what happens to P/E ratios in various inflation/deflation environments.

The table below shows us:

Inflation/Deflation	Years Included	Average P/E	Median P/E
Deflation 6% or more	7	14.7	12.9
Deflation 3% to 5%	6	15.2	14.9
Deflation 2%	10	13.7	13.3
Deflation 1%	5	13.8	14.1
0	11	15.8	13.9
Inflation 1%	14	13.9	13.5
Inflation 2%	14	15.1	14.9
Inflation 3%	7	14.6	15.3
Inflation 4%	10	14.6	14.6
Inflation 5% to 6%	7	13.2	11.7
Inflation 7% to 8%	6	10.7	9.3
Inflation 9% to 11%	5	9.9	9.0
Inflation 12% or more	5	8.9	9.6

As can be seen from the table above and from the aggregate table following, P/E ratios decline steadily once inflation exceeds 4 per cent. Between 6 per cent deflation and 4 per cent inflation, the P/E ratio moves between 14 times and almost 16 times earnings (15.2 times to be precise). At 5 per cent to 6 per cent inflation, it begins to decline steadily, falling below nine times earnings when inflation reaches 12 per cent or more.

What was the median P/E ratio during the 1872-1978 period? The study shows it was 14.1 times earnings, while the average P/E for the period was 14.6 (excluding 1931 through 1934). Bear in mind that the median annual inflation rate for the period was 1.5 per cent and the annual compound rate was 1.8 per cent. Also remember there were 68 years of inflation (1 per cent or more), 28 years of deflation (1 per cent or more) and only 11 years of no change.

When the years of 5 per cent inflation or more are excluded, the median historic P/E for the market advances 3.5 per cent, from 14.1 to 14.6, and the average historic P/E advances 4 per cent from 14.6 to 15.2. See the chart and table below.

Impact Of Inflation On PE Multiples
1872-1978 (1931-34 Ommitted)

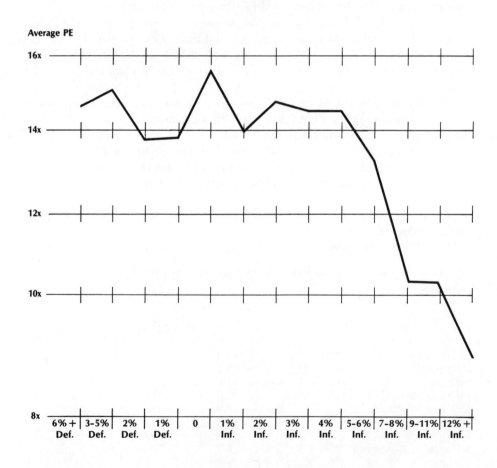

Average Annual P/E (3-Year Earnings Centered)
for the market using Cowles Composite Index
and the Dow Jones Industrials as bases.

	Average P/E	Median P/E
80 Years, Inflation less than 5%	15.2	14.6
7 Years, Inflation 5% to 6%	13.2	11.7
6 Years, Inflation 7% to 8%	10.7	9.3
5 Years, Inflation 9% to 11%	9.9	9.0
5 Years, Inflation 12% Plus	8.9	9.6
103 Years (excludes 1931-34)	14.6	14.1

The highest average P/E ratio occurred in periods of zero inflation. During the 11 years of zero inflation, the market P/E averaged 15.8, though the median was lower at 13.9. The next highest average P/E occurred during periods of 3 per cent to 5 per cent deflation. During the six years that met this criterion, the average P/E was 15.2 and the median was 14.9. This is a relatively small sample, so don't assign much significance to this statistic.

The highest average P/E ratios occurred in periods of zero inflation.

Inflation Earnings Valuation Benchmarks

Evaluation of the data results in the following valuation guidelines. Average data and median data were considered in arriving at these discount benchmarks. Average is arrived at by adding up the individual years and dividing by the number in the sample. Median is the point where half the numbers in the sample are above and half below. This minimizes distortion years.

- *14.5 to 15 times normalized earnings represent the typical market valuation of stocks when inflation is running at an annual rate less than 5 per cent and when deflation exists.*

- *When inflation is in the 5 per cent to 6 per cent zone, a P/E discount of 15 per cent seems appropriate.* Only 7 years of the 108 years studied are in this zone, and, because of this limited experience, one might question the validity of this benchmark. At any rate, the P/E discount calculated using median data is 20 per cent. And, a smaller discount of 13 per cent is indicated when average P/E data are used. Our rule of thumb will be a *15 per cent discount* in this 5 per cent to 6 per cent inflation environment.

- *In the 7 per cent to 8 per cent inflation range, a discount of 33 per cent seems appropriate.* (The P/E discount calculated using median data is 36 per cent, average data indicate a 30 per cent discount.)

- *In the 9 per cent to 11 per cent inflation range, a P/E discount of 36 per cent seems appropriate.* (The P/E discount using median data is 38 per cent; average data indicate a 34 per cent discount.)

- *When inflation blazes at 12 per cent and above, a 38 per cent P/E discount seems appropriate.* A *caveat:* Past history herein provides only five years of experience at these runaway inflation levels, although 1979's 13 per cent inflation gives us a sixth year, and the range in discounts runs from 55 per cent in 1917 to 20 per cent in 1920. As a point of interest, 1979's discount was close to 50 per cent. If this is factored in, this typical discount rises to about 40 per cent.

Common stocks tend to sell at abnormally low price/earnings multiples when inflation flares at 7 per cent and above.

During the past 108 years, common stocks tend to sell at abnormally low price/earnings multiples when inflation is flaring at 7 per cent and above. Inflation in the 5 per cent to 6 per cent range seems to also have a lesser discounting effect. Periods of 4 per cent inflation and below, or deflation periods, seem to have little effect on prevailing P/Es.

As an example, let's make a 1980 stock market appraisal.

Based on historic P/E discounts in various inflation environments, where should the DJIA be selling as this is written? Although they are probably significant, comparative return relationships between stocks and bonds are not taken into consideration, nor are growth prospects or other fundamental considerations. This may be only a starting point.

In the following exercises, which project normal current earnings valuation models for the DJIA, we've employed a three-year centered average of earnings to minimize cyclical earnings distortion. This particular approach to normalizing earnings necessitates making an earnings projection for 1980. This projection is then averaged with 1978's and 1979's actual earnings data. There are many other normalizing techniques, some better, but because this was the approach used in the historic work, we should be consistent.

1978 DJIA earnings	$113.00
1979 earnings	124.00
1980 estimated earnings	100.00
3-year average	$112.33

What if the DJIA sold today at the median P/E multiple calculated for the years in which inflation did not exceed 5 per cent?

P/E 14.6 x 112.33	=	1640 DJIA
Current Level	=	850 DJIA
Indicated gain to typical earnings valuation:		93%

Even with limitations, historic economic relationships still stand as some of the only visible and viable guideposts available.

Of course, the reader should realize the limitations of using historic economic relationships in projecting the future. But even with limitations, these relationships still stand as some of the only visible and viable guideposts available.

The reader also should realize that even though 107 years may seem to be a long time, it is, in reality, a relatively short span in the world's economic history. Unfortunately, the data needed to make the kind of analysis presented here are just not available prior to 1872.

Our conclusion in this particular portion of the study is hardly earthshaking. Most professional investors currently accept and believe inflation brings lower P/E multiples. The useful function here has been to verify this and, to some degree, quantify the level of typical discounts.

So now we are satisfied that these relationships are documented pieces of the puzzle. When fit with the other pieces, it is hoped that a better overall understanding of common stock valuation will take shape. Here are the guidelines suggested by the research as initial steps in the valuation model building process:

- If current inflation levels (or perceived future two-year time horizon inflation levels) are 4 per cent or less, no multiple adjustment from normal (14.6 x normalized earnings) is needed.
- If current or perceived near-term inflation is 5 per cent to 6 per cent, discount 15 per cent from "normal" as a starting point: 0.85 x 14.6 normal P/E = 12.4 inflation adjusted normal P/E.
- If current or perceived near-term inflation is 7 per cent to 8 per cent, discount 33 per cent from "normal" as a starting point: 0.67 x 14.6 normal P/E = 9.8 inflation adjusted normal P/E.
- If current or perceived near-term inflation is 9 per cent to 11 per cent, discount 36 per cent from "normal" as a starting point: 0.64 x 14.6 normal P/E = 9.3 inflation adjusted normal P/E.
- If current or perceived near-term inflation is 12 per cent or more, discount 38 per cent from "normal" as a starting point: 0.62 x 14.6 normal P/E = 9.0 inflation adjusted normal P/E.

In summary, our studies indicate a lower valuation in periods of higher inflation. A 12.4 times earnings may be typical when inflation is in the 5 per cent to 6 per cent range, 9.8 in the 7 per cent to 8 per cent range, 9.3 in the 9 per cent to 11 per cent range, and 9 at 12 per cent inflation and higher. Now we will put these guidelines into practice.

(a) 1979's Consumer Price Index increase was 13 per cent. In this case, a 1011 DJIA would be a normal valuation.

P/E 9 x 112.33   =   1011 DJIA
Current Level   =   850 DJIA
Indicated gain to typical earnings valuation: 19%

(b) If 1980 brought a slight cooling off of inflation to the 9 per cent to 11 per cent zone, things would look a little brighter for common stock valuation:

P/E 9.3 x 112.33   =   1045 DJIA
Current Level   =   850 DJIA
Indicated gain to typical earnings valuation: 23%

(c) But, if 1980 brought an inflation cooldown to the 7 per cent to 8 per cent range, it could be quite a year:

P/E 9.8 x 112.33   =   1101 DJIA
Current Level   =   850 DJIA
Indicated gain to typical earnings valuation: 30%

So, you pay your money and you take your choice. If inflation in 1980 could come down to the 5 per cent to 6 per cent area, the stock market, based on historic relationships, would be over 1400! If inflation falls to the 7 per cent to 11 per cent zone, the current market, based on its earnings relationship, also has 25 per cent to 30 per cent upside potential. And, even if inflation remains at 12 per cent or more, the market, at current levels, is approximately 22 per cent undervalued, applying these guideposts.

But, caution. P/E multiples and inflation are but parts of this equation. Earnings declines from today's normalized levels of $112.33 also can play a part. However, because a three-year average is used, the potential impact of such a decline is substantially reduced. If, for example, 1980's earnings fall 40 per cent to $78 from 1979's $124 earnings, much greater than the 20 per cent decline we have built into our model, the $112.33 normalized earnings estimate used would decline only 7.5 per cent to $104.

One thing is quite clear. A significant decline in the rate of inflation in coming years, down to less than 5 per cent, would imply a mouthwatering degree of upside potential for the stock market, almost 100 per cent above current levels.

Applying these guideposts, the market, at current levels, is approximately 22 per cent undervalued—but caution, P/E multiples and inflation are only parts of the equation.

1872-1978 INFLATION/DEFLATION

	Year	% Inflation	Average P/E	Stock Market Change
12% Plus Inflation:	1917	17%	6.6	− 30.7%
	1918	18	7.0	+16.1
	1919	15	9.7	+13.1
	1920	16	11.8	− 23.7
	1947	14	9.0	+ 2.2
		Average:	8.9	
		Median:	9.6	
9% to 11% Inflation:	1942	11%	10.5	+ 7.6%
	1946	9	13.4	− 8.1
	1974	11	8.7	− 27.6
	1975	9	9.0	+ 38.3
	1978	9	7.7	− 3.2
		Average:	9.9	
		Median:	9.0	
7% to 8% Inflation:	1880	7%	14.2	+19.0%
	1899	7	15.4	+ 6.5
	1916	8	7.6	+ 3.4
	1948	8	8.3	− 2.1
	1951	8	9.5	+14.4
	1977	7	9.2	−17.3
		Average:	10.7	
		Median:	9.3	

	Year	% Inflation	Average P/E	Stock Market Change
5% to 6% Inflation:	1881	6%	15.7	+ 2.8%
	1941	5	11.5	− 15.4
	1943	6	13.9	+ 13.8
	1969	5	15.9	− 15.2
	1970	6	13.9	+ 4.8
	1973	6	11.0	− 16.6
	1976	6	11.3	+ 17.9
		Average:	13.3	
		Median:	11.7	
4% Inflation:	1902	4%	15.3	+ 1.3%
	1903	4	13.2	− 18.5
	1906	4	13.6	+ 3.2
	1907	4	11.5	− 33.3
	1910	4	13.2	− 12.3
	1912	4	14.6	+ 2.9
	1937	4	18.1	·− 32.8
	1957	4	14.7	− 12.8
	1968	4	16.1	+ 4.3
	1971	4	15.5	+ 6.1
		Average:	14.6	
		Median	14.6	
3% Inflation:	1925	3%	9.8	+ 22.8%
	1934	3	24.1*	− 1.1
	1935	3	17.6	+ 37.0
	1958	3	15.0	+ 34.0
	1966	3	15.9	− 19.0
	1967	3	15.6	+ 15.2
	1972	3	13.7	+ 14.6
		Average:	14.6	
		Median:	15.3	
2% Inflation:	1882	2%	15.3	− 2.9%
	1887	2	18.4	− 6.5
	1888	2	17.9	− 2.4
	1890	2	18.1	− 13.6
	1897	2	16.7	+ 12.9
	1900	2	13.2	+ 14.1
	1901	2	14.9	+ 15.8
	1923	2	9.9	− 2.4
	1944	2	14.2	+ 12.1
	1945	2	14.9	+ 26.7
	1952	2	10.3	+ 8.4
	1956	2	14.1	+ 2.3
	1960	2	18.9	− 9.3
	1965	2	14.2	+ 10.3
		Average:	15.1	
		Median:	14.9	

*Excluded from calculation because of distortion.

	Year	% Inflation	Average P/E	Stock Market Change
1% **Inflation:**	1898	1%	14.3	+18.6%
	1914	1	11.7	− 9.0
	1915	1	8.4	+31.6
	1926	1	10.3	+ 5.1
	1928	1	14.2	+28.8
	1940	1	12.8	−12.7
	1950	1	8.1	+17.6
	1953	1	10.3	− 3.8
	1954	1	11.1	+44.0
	1959	1	20.1	+16.4
	1961	1	20.7	+18.7
	1962	1	17.5	−10.8
	1963	1	17.3	+17.0
	1964	1	17.7	+14.6
		Average:	13.9	
		Median:	13.5	
0 **Inflation:**	1893	0	19.2	−19.8%
	1895	0	23.9	+ 1.0
	1896	0	18.1	− 2.3
	1904	0	12.5	+25.6
	1905	0	13.9	+16.0
	1909	0	13.8	+14.3
	1911	0	13.5	+ 1.0
	1924	0	8.6	+18.6
	1929	0	19.1	−10.3
	1936	0	17.4	+28.9
	1955	0	13.7	+20.8
		Average:	15.8	
		Median:	13.9	
1% **Deflation:**	1872	1%	14.1	+ 6.9%
	1892	1	18.2	+ 1.4
	1913	1	13.5	−14.2
	1939	1	16.3	− 3.0
	1949	1	7.0	+12.9
		Average:	13.8	
		Median:	14.1	
2% **Deflation:**	1873	2%	13.0	−13.0%
	1874	2	13.0	+ 3.2
	1879	2	12.6	+43.0
	1883	2	15.7	− 8.7
	1885	2	16.1	+19.8
	1886	2	14.1	+ 8.5
	1889	2	20.0	+ 3.2
	1891	2	13.5	+18.2
	1927	2	11.9	+26.3
	1938	2	7.0	+28.1
		Average:	13.7	
		Median:	13.3	

	Year	% Inflation	Average P/E	Stock Market Change
3% to 5% Deflation:	1875	5%	14.9	− 4.2%
	1876	5	15.9	−18.0
	1877	4	13.1	− 9.5
	1908	3	11.4	+37.3
	1930	3	20.6	−28.9
	1933	5	35.6*	+49.5
		Average:	15.2	
		Median:	14.9	
6% Plus Deflation:	1878	6%	12.5	+ 6.3%
	1884	6	15.3	−18.7
	1894	8	21.1	− 2.8
	1921	11	11.5	+ 7.3
	1922	6	12.9	+20.1
	1931	9	27.7*	−46.6
	1932	10	27.6*	−19.4
		Average:	14.7	
		Median:	12.9	

*Excluded from calculation because of distortion.

Chapter 6

Predicting Future Inflation, That's the Rub

Which of the following statements is most correct?

1. Economists' one-year inflation forecasts are fairly accurate.

2. If there have been three consecutive years of inflation, the probability is over 80 per cent that the next year also will be inflationary.

3. If there have been two consecutive years of increasing inflation, there is over a 70 per cent probability that the next year also will be higher.

4. A good proxy for the next year's inflation rate is this year's inflation rate.

It is clear that inflation has an influence on stock market movements, and that higher levels of inflation affect P/E valuations negatively. Inflation acceleration and deceleration trends also appear to strongly influence stock prices. It follows that if one can get a fix on what the future may bring in terms of inflation or deflation, trend and level, it could be extremely valuable in determining common stock investment strategy.

Look to the Economists?

If the economists could tell us what the future might bring in terms of inflation, our problem would be solved. Unfortunately, the forecasting record of the economic experts, at least in the area of inflation, has left much to be desired. In 1973, only a very small minority of experts anticipated 1974's brutal 11 per cent inflation. The experts' predictions for 1975 and 1976 were not much better. In 1978, most economists again missed the mark, predicting 1978's inflation rate at 5 per cent to 6 per cent, while, in fact, it came in at 9 per cent.

The individual expert predictions of 1979 inflation levels were all over the lot, but typical was probably 9 per cent. This, of course, was considerably shy of the 13.4 per cent rise in the Consumer Price Index. Normally the range of predictions is not this wide, but even in years when there is good consensus, predictions have not worked out very well. In recent years, the record of most economists predicting the next year's inflation rate has been mediocre at best.

The forecasting record of economic experts leaves much to be desired.

Let's examine 1974's forecasts as an example. Some may say this is unfair because OPEC's quadrupling of oil prices was very disruptive. But the increases occurred in the fall of 1973, *before* the 1974 forecasts were made.

Let's look at the record in 1974.

	1974 Median Forecast	1974 Reality	Error
Inflation (CPI)............	6.8%	11.0%	− 4.2
Unemployment...........	5.9%	6.5%	− .6
Real Economic Growth.....	2.2%	(5.6%)	+ 7.8

The economists were wide of the mark in all three categories. The inflation rate was 60 per cent higher than they predicted, unemployment was 10 per cent higher and their predictions for economic growth were wildly optimistic.

Ah! But that is only one year, and a difficult one at that. Is it a fair test? Let us look at the consensus going back to late 1968. Here is the consensus inflation forecast for each year as reported in "Business Week's" annual poll of economists:

Year	GNP Deflation Actual	Business Week Poll Forecast GNP Deflator	Error Over or Under
1969	+ 5.0%	+ 3.5%	− 1.5
1970	+ 5.4	+ 4.2	− 1.2
1971	+ 5.1	+ 3.4	− 1.7
1972	+ 4.1	+ 3.4	− .7
1973	+ 5.8	+ 3.4	− 2.4

Year	GNP Deflation Actual	Business Week Poll Forecast GNP Deflator	Error Over or Under
1974	+ 9.7	+ 6.1	− 3.6
1975	+ 9.6	+ 8.7	− .9
1976	+ 5.2	+ 5.9	+ .7
1977	+ 5.9	+ 5.5	− .4
1978	+ 8.4	+ 6.0	− 2.4

As you can see, the average error during this 10-year period was 1.55 per cent per year. In only four of the 10 years did experts come within 1 per cent of predicting next year's inflation.

The Federal Reserve Bank in Richmond has been conducting a similar study of economists' forecasts using the CPI as a benchmark. Its results have been about the same. The average annual miss was 1.57 per cent per year, although in five of the 10 years the experts were able to come within 1 per cent of predicting next year's inflation.

Year	CPI Actual	Survey Forecast	Error Over or Under
1969	+ 5.4%	+ 3.6%	− 1.8
1970	+ 5.9	+ 4.6	− 1.3
1971	+ 4.3	+ 3.9	− 0.4
1972	+ 3.3	+ 3.1	− 0.2
1973	+ 6.2	+ 3.3	− 2.9
1974	+11.0	+ 6.8	− 4.2
1975	+ 9.1	+ 9.5	+ 0.4
1976	+ 5.8	+ 6.5	+ 0.7
1977	+ 6.5	+ 5.9	− 0.6
1978	+ 9.0	+ 5.8	− 3.2

Economists tend to run in a herd, with uniform—but hardly perfect—predictions.

Steven McNees, vice president of the Federal Reserve Bank of Boston, has attempted to analyze why and how so many economists can be so wrong so often. In recent years, at least, economists have appeared to run in a herd. "The information is too perfect for there to be too much difference between them. Besides, it is safer to be part of the crowd," he says. Well, if the information is so perfect, the results should be better. Uniform? Yes. Perfect? Hardly.

At any rate we cannot depend on the economists to give us an approximate forecast of inflation, at least not next year's inflation.

Statistical Projections

The odds are less than 50-50 that this year's inflation will be repeated next year.

Economists, in making inflation projections, combine many factors, subjective and objective, quantitative and qualitative. The record is not good. One can not merely assume that this year's inflation environment will be repeated next year. The odds are less than 50-50 that it will. What happens if we examine recent past trends and project?

The chart on page 52 presents the history of U.S. inflation and deflation from 1790 to date. The moving average line on that long-term chart gives an impression of persistency and stability for both inflationary and deflationary trends. In 1975 we extensively tested several trend-following approaches in an attempt to predict the following year's inflation. Data from 115 years were examined; 68 of these years were inflationary. Here is a summary of the findings.

Inflation Is Persistent? Consider:

- If this year is an inflationary year, the probability is 76 per cent that next year also will be inflationary, although not necessarily a higher level of inflation.
- If we have had *two consecutive inflationary years,* the probability is 80 per cent the next year also will be inflationary, although not necessarily a higher level of inflation.
- If we have *three consecutive inflationary years,* the probability is 83 per cent the next year also will be inflationary, although not necessarily a higher level of inflation.

So far, so good. Inflation begets inflation. Our analysis also found that noninflationary years are typically followed by more noninflationary years with close to the same frequency as is the case with inflation.

Inflation begets inflation—but the odds are equally good that a noninflationary year will be followed by another noninflationary year.

Inflation Acceleration, Year to Year

If this is an inflation year, what do we know about next year? We know that there is:

- A 45 per cent probability inflation will be higher.
- A 47 per cent probability it will be lower.
- An 8 per cent probability it will be the same.

If we have two consecutive years of increasing inflation, what can we expect of the following year? We can expect:

- A 46 per cent probability of higher inflation.
- A 31 per cent probability of lower inflation.
- A 19 per cent probability of a swing to deflation.
- A 4 per cent probability of no change.

Although historically it appears inflation does perpetuate itself, there is no clear-cut tendency to accelerate on a year to year basis. We cannot say because we have inflation this year it will probably be higher next year. Nor can we say that because inflation has been increasing for two years it will probably increase next year. The statistics show it's less than an even bet it will.

Inflation Stability a Myth?

In the 1960s, economists spoke of permanently "stabilizing" inflation in the 2 per cent to 3 per cent area through the application of various and wondrous economic stabilizers at their command. And, from 1958 through 1967 inflation was "stabilized" in the 1 per cent to 3 per cent zone. Remember? Those were the days when inflation was "good" for the country. This brief period was one of the few times in our country's history that this kind of

The period from 1958 through 1967 was one of the few times in U.S. history that price stability existed.

price stability existed. Should the credit go to the economic tinkerers, or was it a product of the times?

Two other significant periods of price stability in U.S. economic history were 1923 to 1929 (2 per cent inflation/2 per cent deflation range) and 1886 to 1893 (2 per cent inflation/2 per cent deflation range). Both were long before the age of skillful computer-equipped economic navigators.

Year-to-year stability in the rate of inflation historically is most unusual, especially in the upper registers. Still some economists are saying they expect inflation to stabilize in the 6 per cent to 7 per cent area during the next five to 10 years.

Our research found the median volatility swing from one historically high inflation year to the next was 5 per cent above or below. This makes the odds only 50-50 that 1980's inflation rate will even be within five percentage points of 1979's 13 per cent rate, inside a range of 8 per cent to 18 per cent inflation.

Year to year inflation rate volatility accelerates as we move up the inflation ladder.

Year to year inflation rate volatility accelerates as we move up the inflation ladder:

- *Assume inflation is 1 per cent this year.* There is an *87 per cent probability* that next year's rate will be within a range 3 per cent above or below this year's rate (4 per cent inflation/2 per cent deflation range).

- *Assume inflation is 2 per cent this year.* There is a *72 per cent probability* that next year's rate will be within a range 3 per cent above or below this year's rate (1 per cent deflation/5 per cent inflation range).

- *Assume inflation is 3 per cent to 4 per cent this year.* There is a *66 per cent probability* that next year's rate will be within a range 3 per cent above or below this year's rate.

- *Assume inflation is 5 per cent to 8 per cent this year.* There is only a *30 per cent probability* that next year's inflation rate will be within a range 3 per cent above or below this year's rate. Thus, if this year's rate was 7 per cent, there is only a 30 per cent probability next year's inflation rate will fall in the 4 per cent to 10 per cent range.

- *Assume inflation is at 9 per cent or above this year.* There is only a *20 per cent probability* that next year's inflation rate will fall within a range 3 per cent above or below this year's rate. Thus, if this year's inflation rate was 13 per cent, there is an 80 per cent chance next year's inflation will fall *outside* of an already broad 10 per cent to 16 per cent range.

A stabilized rate of inflation on a year to year basis is uncommon. And, based on the record, stabilizing inflation at higher levels, 5 per cent and above, is virtually unprecedented and very likely only a theoretician's pipedream.

Although economic systems may change, man does not—greed and fear and irresponsibility cannot be decycled.

The following may be of interest to some of the more skeptical readers. Some may argue that data of this nature prior to 1935 are of little or no value. We would submit that although economic systems may change, man does not. Greed and fear and irresponsibility cannot be decycled for very long.

The table below shows that for the 36 years since 1862 when inflation was 4 per cent or more, there were only three occasions when the inflation rate the following year was the same. Indeed, less than one-third of the time was the following year's rate within two percentage points. The average swing was 5.4 per cent, with an average upward change of 4.4 per cent and an average downward change of 6.7 per cent. The median increase was 5 per cent and the median decrease was 4 per cent. The chart on the next page graphically plots the history of U.S. inflation and deflation since 1790 and clearly shows how little price stability there has been.

35 Years of 4% and Higher Inflation: 1862-1978

Qualifying Year	Inflation Rate	Following Year's Rate		Raw Difference
1862	18%	18%	Inflation	0%
1863	18	35	Inflation	+ 17
1864	35	1	*Deflation*	− 36
1880	7	6	Inflation	− 1
1881	6	2	Inflation	− 4
1899	7	2	Inflation	− 5
1902	4	4	Inflation	0
1903	4	0		− 4
1906	4	4	Inflation	0
1907	4	3	*Deflation*	− 7
1910	4	0		− 4
1912	4	1	*Deflation*	− 5
1916	8	17	Inflation	+ 9
1917	17	18	Inflation	+ 1
1918	18	15	Inflation	− 3
1919	15	16	Inflation	+ 1
1920	16	11	*Deflation*	− 27
1937	4	2	*Deflation*	− 6
1941	5	11	Inflation	+ 6
1942	11	6	Inflation	− 5
1943	6	2	Inflation	− 4
1946	9	14	Inflation	+ 5
1947	14	8	Inflation	− 6
1948	8	1	*Deflation*	− 9
1951	8	2	Inflation	− 6
1957	4	3	Inflation	− 1
1968	4	5	Inflation	+ 1
1969	5	6	Inflation	+ 1
1970	6	4	Inflation	− 2
1971	4	3	Inflation	− 1
1973	6	11	Inflation	+ 5
1974	11	9	Inflation	− 2
1975	9	6	Inflation	− 3
1976	6	7	Inflation	+ 1
1977	7	9	Inflation	+ 2
1978	9	13	Inflation	+ 4

Summary

	Years	Average Swing	Median Swing
Increases	12	4.4%	5%
Decreases	21	6.7%	4%
Unchanged	3		
	36	5.4%	4%

U.S. Inflation/Deflation
1790 Through 1979

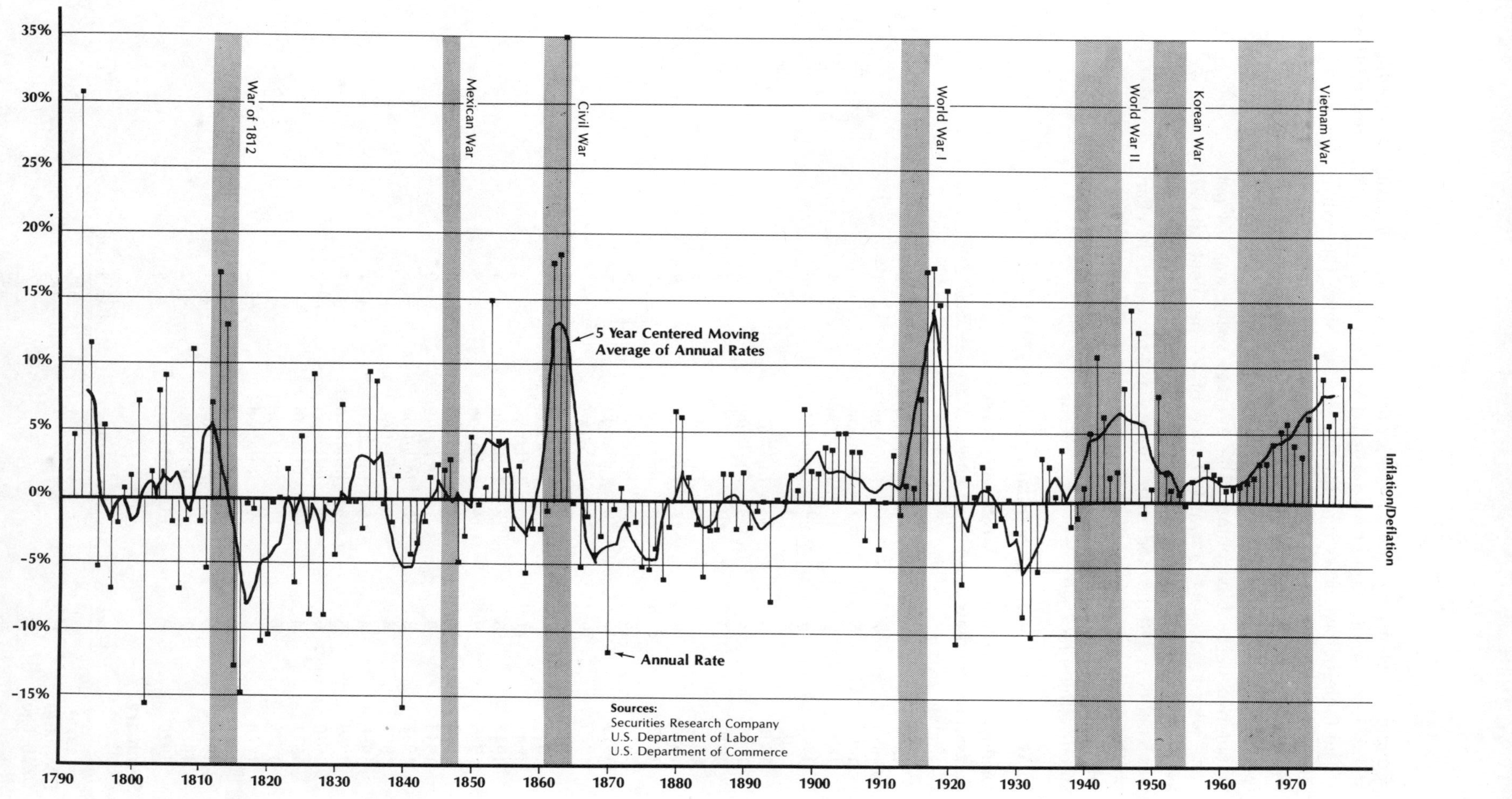

Inflation/Deflation

Vietnam War

Korean War

World War II

World War I

Civil War

Mexican War

War of 1812

5 Year Centered Moving
Average of Annual Rates

Annual Rate

Sources:
Securities Research Company
U.S. Department of Labor
U.S. Department of Commerce

35% 30% 25% 20% 15% 10% 5% 0% -5% -10% -15%

1790 1800 1810 1820 1830 1840 1850 1860 1870 1880 1890 1900 1910 1920 1930 1940 1950 1960 1970

52

Earlier we demonstrated that the best environments for investing in the stock market were periods of price stability or mild deflation. Investing in years of extraordinary inflation or extraordinary deflation brought poor results unless inflation was clearly decelerating. From a practical standpoint, the catch is knowing at the beginning of a particular year what the inflation rate or deflation rate for that year will actually be.

But what would be the effect of investing using the previous year's inflation rate to guide our actions? We have shown that there is little inflation stability over time, but we also have seen the inflation is persistent. For example, we showed earlier in this chapter that if this is an inflationary year, there is a 76 per cent probability that next year also will be an inflationary year. And the chances are about even that it will be an inflation deceleration year. Can we use this in any way?

The charts on the next two pages show us the results. The first presents the median annual stock market gain experienced by investing in particular inflationary and deflationary yearly environments, assuming that the investor knew in advance of each year what the inflation rate would be and invested accordingly. His record is very good if he confined his investing to periods of stability.

The second chart presents comparative investment results, again by inflationary/deflationary environment, but investing one year after the fact. Note the deterioration in performance compared with the first chart.

This performance differential is brought about by the instability of inflation/deflation levels on a year-to-year basis. The second chart seems to indicate better than average investment results are obtained by buying stocks the year following an extraordinary or high inflation year (note the definitions of these are slightly different from those used earlier). However, because of the relatively small number of years in the sample—only seven years of extraordinary inflation in the 103 years examined—and because of the wide variance in annual data, we are not suggesting this as a strategy. While this research covered 1872 through 1974, the addition of the last five years does not significantly change the results.

To summarize:

If this year's environment is:	The odds next year's environment will be the same are:
Extraordinary Deflation (5%-13%)	38%
Moderate Deflation (2%-4%).....	16
Price Stability (1% Inf.-1% Def.)..	35
Moderate Inflation (2%-3%).....	23
High Inflation (4%-8%).........	17
Extraordinary Inflation (9% +)....	45

So, even though our work indicates there is a demonstrable correlation between annual stock market movements and the annual rate of inflation or deflation, this revelation, although helpful to the investor, does not qualify as an investment panacea. It is not a magic key to successful investment strategy

103 Years of Investing (1872-1974)
In Six Inflationary/Deflationary Environments

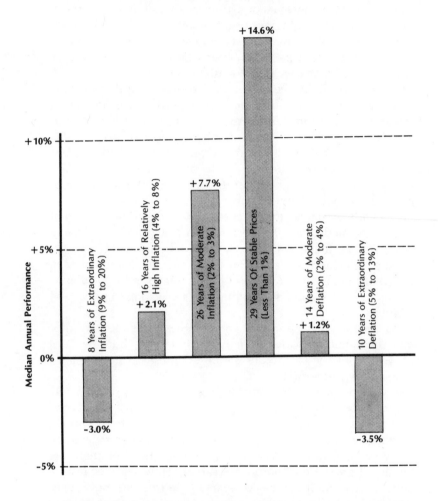

This chart presents an approximation of theoretical investment results achieved by an investor who owned stocks only in the years that qualified by their annual inflation or deflation rates for a particular environment. In reality, of course, the years were not consecutive. Also, it is highly unlikely that any investor would be able to consistently predict actual annual inflation or deflation rates for each year on January 1st of that year.

Still, the calculations are an effective way to demonstrate the relative investment attractiveness of each environment. Dividends are not included.

because it depends on one's ability to predict inflation or deflation levels one year in advance. Predicting next year's inflation, especially when inflation is currently high, can be as difficult as predicting the stock market itself.

Economists have had a poor batting average in predicting inflation, even next year's rate. This is especially true when inflation is in the upper registers.

However, extrapolating next year's inflation rate merely by using past trends also is not very reliable, especially when inflation is at relatively high levels.

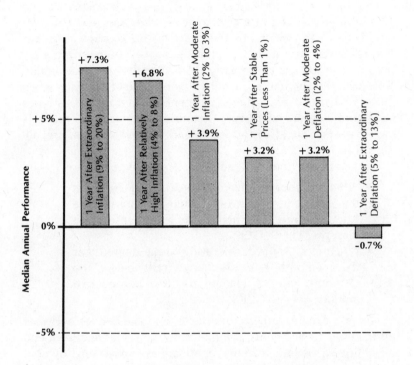

This chart presents a theoretical approximation of investment results achieved owning stocks the year following a particular inflation or deflationary environment.

Results are quite different than those recorded in the previous chart primarily because of the lack of inflation/deflation continuity from one year to the next.

This chart seems to indicate better than average investment results are obtained by buying stock the year following an extraordinary or high inflation year (like 1975). But because of the relatively small number of years in the sample (only seven years of extraordinary inflation can be used) and because of the wide variance in annual data, we are not suggesting this as a strategy.

Our work demonstrates that inflation, or deflation for that matter, tends to persist on a year to year basis. But projecting accelerating or decelerating year to year trends, merely employing past data, is of questionable value.

A Useful Technique

However, there is some hope. We are now employing a variety of tools to measure inflation acceleration and deceleration for the CPI, PPI (Wholesale Price Index) and GNP Deflator, as well as several other inflation measures. Past testing indicates some of these have been quite successful in determining shifts in inflation momentum and also calling major stock market turning points. Three-month, six-month and 12-month rates of change have been related to one another in a variety of ways. While

Yet several tools have been quite successful in determining shifts in inflation momentum and also in calling major stock market turning points.

there is probably no magic mechanical formula, our research strongly indicates a solid relationship between inflation direction and stock market movements, at least when inflation is running at 3 per cent and above.

The following chart is an example of this. It shows the six- and 12-month annualized rate of change for the Consumer Price Index. The period covered by the chart is 1962 through 1978, but the research also includes other relatively high inflationary periods, the 1940s and the early 1950s. Results are quite similar. Note that this momentum work appears to be of no value when inflation is running less than 3 per cent or 4 per cent. This tends to confirm earlier conclusions that inflation in its lower registers has no observable effect on stock market movements or prevailing valuations.

The operating rules applied in the following chart are:

- When inflation is accelerating to the degree that the six-month rate of change is above the 12-month rate of change for two consecutive months: SELL STOCKS.
- When inflation is decelerating to the degree that the six-month rate of change falls below the 12-month rate of change for two consecutive months: BUY STOCKS.

This is a simple, rather crude technique and it does not work all the time. Refinements, using other time frames and front end weighting of the data, can be beneficial, as can the employment of inflation indices other than CPI. The Wholesale Index, however, appears to be too volatile, erratic and perhaps distorted to be of much help other than as a lead warning device. While this kind of analysis can be incorrect at times, it can be quite helpful. We doubt very much if there is any one right formula, but this momentum work does appear to be a useful tool.

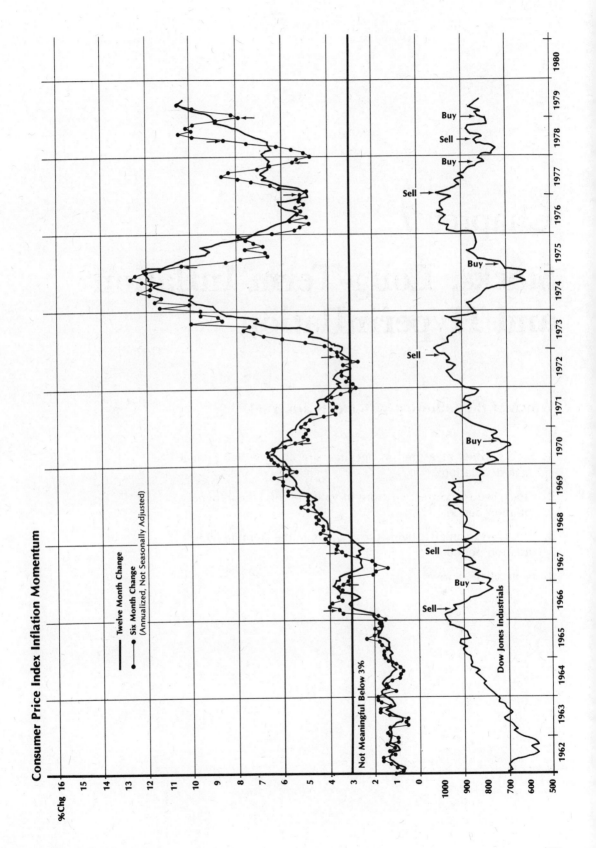

Consumer Price Index Inflation Momentum

Twelve Month Change

Six Month Change
(Annualized, Not Seasonally Adjusted)

Not Meaningful Below 3%

Dow Jones Industrials

57

Chapter 7

Stocks, Long-Term Inflation and Hyperinflation

Which of the following statements are true?

1. Stocks, when measured in decades, are an effective hedge against inflation.
2. Stocks were an effective store of value in the French hyperinflation period.
3. Stocks were an effective store of value in the German hyperinflation period.
4. None of the above.

The poor performance of the stock market during the past decade, a period of unusually high inflation for the U.S., has quashed much of the stocks-are-a-hedge-against-inflation talk. However, quite a few experts still maintain that:

Not all experts touting stocks as a hedge against inflation have been quashed.

1. On a really long-term basis, stocks are a hedge against inflation erosion. "Long-term" in this context seems to mean 20 years or longer.
2. While the stock market might not be a hedge against the kind of inflation experienced in the last decade, it would probably provide protection in a hyperinflation environment.

In this, the concluding chapter devoted to the stock market and inflation, these two hypotheses will be critically examined.

Are Stocks Really a Long-Term Inflation Hedge?

Not long ago, a Ph.D. in Economics, after studying some of our inflation/stock market work, wrote me a letter. "Your studies are thorough and interesting but surely you cannot deny that stocks on a long-term basis serve as an effective hedge against inflation." He then cited several 10 to 20-year periods in which the stock market and the Consumer Price Index (CPI) seemed to be moving in unison. His conclusion was that stock market performance to a significant degree reflects the rate of inflation.

The chart below comparing the Dow Jones Industrial Average performance with the CPI in nine 10-year periods (1930 to date)

**Ten-Year Periods of Change
1930-1978**

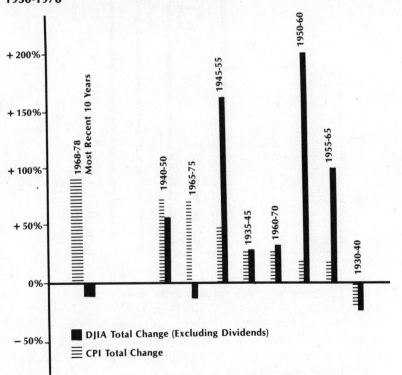

■ DJIA Total Change (Excluding Dividends)
☰ CPI Total Change

Although the market far
outperforms inflation in periods
of low inflation, the opposite is
true in periods of significant
inflation.

certainly does not substantiate this claim. In the three highest inflationary periods, market performance trailed inflation,
especially in the most recent 10-year period. Some hedge! Only
in the 1935 to 1945 period and the 1960 to 1970 period did the
stock market and inflation track fairly well. In periods of low inflation, or mild deflation (1950-60 and 1955-65), the market far
outperformed inflation. In periods of significant inflation
(1968-78, 1940-50 and 1965-75) the opposite was true.

Two of the three bonanza periods for the market were 1950 to
1960 and 1955 to 1965, periods of relative price stability.

Now let's look at the seven 20-year periods.

**Twenty-Year Periods Of Change
1930–1978**

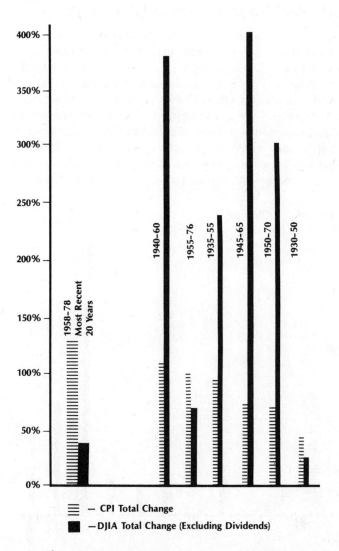

≡ — CPI Total Change
■ —DJIA Total Change (Excluding Dividends)

In the most recent 20-year period, stocks also have lagged
behind the inflation rate. In the other 20-year comparison
periods there seems to be no real correlation between the degree
of inflation and DJIA performance.

In an earlier chapter it was stated that stock market perform- ance reflected the degree of earnings dividend and book value growth more closely than it did inflation. And, when examining the nine 10-year periods on a correlation basis, this seems to be true. The closest statistical correlation is dividend growth, then book value growth, earnings growth and finally in last place was inflation.

"But, wait," the hard core stocks-are-an-inflation-hedge believer might say. "Don't earnings and dividend growth in nominal terms actually reflect inflation, moving up with the in- flation rate?" Not necessarily.

Earnings and dividends don't necessarily move up with the inflation rate.

Here are the data for the most recent 10-year periods exa- mined:

	CPI	Earnings Increase	Dividend Increase	DJIA Change
1965-1975	up 71%	up 41%	up 31%	down 14%
1968-1978	up 100%	up 85%	up 58%	down 17%

It seems management has not, at this point anyway, mastered the art of being able to bring higher inflation down to the bottom line or increasing dividend payments to keep up with inflation, although in the more recent period there appears to be some im- provement. The time could come when this can be achieved. Then again, it may not.

Now it's true, examining the 20-year chart, that on a long-term basis the stock market has usually appreciated faster than the dollar has eroded. In five of the seven 20-year periods presented on the last chart this was the case. But doesn't it make more sense to see this as a reflection of real growth in the U.S. economy, earnings, dividends and book value?

If inflation persists in the U.S. economy during the next 10 years and real corporate earnings also increase, it is very likely stocks will go up. If, however, real economic growth stagnates and earnings trail inflation, then stock prices will not keep pace with inflation. Real earnings are the prime mover of stock prices over the long term, not inflation.

Real earnings, not inflation, are the prime mover of stock prices over the long term.

Stocks a Hyperinflation Hedge in the U.S.?

In early 1980 several well-known and respected market strat- egists again began using the old stocks-as-a-hyperinflation-hedge concept to explain a burst of strength in the market. The explana- tion was that stocks are running on the upside because many in- vestors believe the nation is headed for hyperinflation and stocks are the way to protect against the feared ravages.

Our historical studies of inflation lead us to seriously question the basic tenet that stocks would serve as an investment hedge against hyperinflation. Let's examine in some detail the German hyperinflation of the 1920s. This is the commentator's favorite example of stocks as a hyperinflation hedge. The French case history will be discussed later.

Hyperinflation—the German Experience

First, the bare German facts. From July, 1919, to November, 1923, the wholesale price index in Germany rose from 339 to

The German hyperinflation
experience was a wild and
woolly ride.

If the investor did not lose his
nerve, stocks could have worked
out as an inflation hedge.

72,000,000,000, and stock prices went up a bit more percentagewise, rising from 100 to 24,000,000,000 in the same period. A wonderful inflation hedge, right? This is the hyperinflation hedge so often cited. But, let's back up to January, 1918, and take a closer look.

The stock index in real terms (adjusted for inflation) was very erratic, falling from an adjusted index level of 100 in January, 1918, to an adjusted index level below 5 in October, 1922. This was a fall in real terms of more than 95 per cent in less than five years. At that point, stocks as a hedge against hyperinflation were not really working well.

Then came a huge jump in stock prices. From October, 1922, to November, 1923, the inflation-adjusted stock index moved up more than 500 per cent in real terms. This wild burst put common stocks back on course as an inflation hedge for the whole period. So in November, 1923, the inflation-adjusted stock index actually had gained 12 per cent in real terms from its July, 1919, level, the period cited by hyperinflation hedge advocates.

In this particular time frame, stocks did, in a sense, act as a store of value for this part of the hyperinflation period, although it was a wild and woolly ride. Any investor who happened to sell out prior to that spectacular move in the last 12 months was a big loser. Still, if the investor did not lose his nerve (a 95 per cent decline in real terms is a bit unsettling), stocks could have worked out as an inflation hedge *in that specific period*.

Here is some background. World war had broken out in 1914 and the value of the German mark declined moderately through the fall of 1917. Then a recovery set in, rallying from a low of 13.2¢ gold to 20.7¢ gold in January, 1918. For six months the mark held, but the decline took hold again and by February, 1919, it broke below 10¢. By February, 1920, it was quoted at 1¢ gold. By 1923, the mark was essentially worthless. In November, 1923, the mark was replaced by the Rentenmark, then after the reorganization of the Reichsbank in October, 1924, the Rentenmark was replaced by the Reichsmark, with a par value of 23.8¢ gold.

On the following pages are eight-year graphs tracking the gold value of German stocks, the mark and commodities from January, 1918, to January, 1925, as calculated by *Axe Houghton* in a 1951 economic study. This does not record the intra-year highs or lows.

German Hyperinflation Investment Results (Gold Value)

	January 1918 through January 1923	January 1918 through January 1925
German Currency	100% Loss	100% Loss
German Stocks	96% Loss	64% Loss
Commodities	51% Loss	21% Loss

Other — Not Experiencing Hyperinflation

Gold	0% Loss	0% Loss
British Stocks	3% Gain	19% Gain
U.S. Stocks	29% Gain	58% Gain
U.S. Bonds	6% Gain	10% Gain

German Investment Results
(Gold Value)

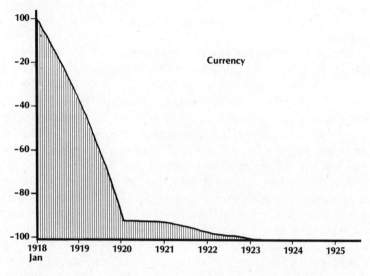

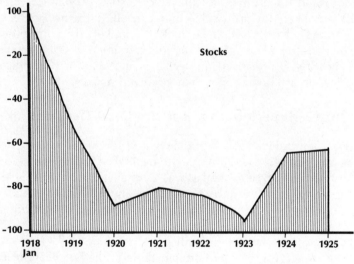

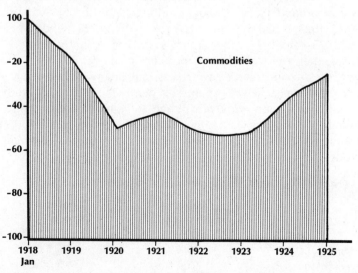

Does the wild German experience in any way justify a pacifying conclusion that stocks will act as a store of at least some value in a future hyperinflationary period? Before even entertaining this possibility, the investor should also look beyond the statistics.

Why did the German stock market, adjusted for inflation, leap ahead in 1923? In November, 1923, the government allowed owners of real assets to retain title and ownership, with the claims against these assets, in effect, cancelled. Thus, companies owning factories and land were saved. Then, because these companies were producing tangible goods, they could quickly acquire the new stable currency and were in a position to prosper handsomely. Investors quickly recognized this.

Would this history repeat itself? In the aftermath of another raging epidemic of hyperinflation in the U.S. or elsewhere in the world, what would be the likelihood of capitalists and property owners again being treated so favorably? Or for that matter, would capitalism and private ownership even survive?

Today it would seem that this kind of bushel basket hyperinflation would bring down not only the existing economic system, but the political system as well.

Today it would seem that this kind of bushel basket hyperinflation would bring down not only the existing economic system, but very likely the political system as well. In the new order rising from such destruction we think it is unlikely the corporations and capitalists would get the favored treatment this time around, as they clearly received in Germany in 1923. For that matter, capitalism as known today may not even survive.

France—Hyperinflation But Not Total Devastation

Now let's take a look at France in essentially the same period. The hyperinflation was not as extreme. France did not lose World War I and was not punished as was Germany. Nor did France lose a large amount of territory as did Germany. Moreover, the allies did not impose serious economic and political restrictions on that nation. Thus, stocks faired a shade better in hyperinflation. They were not, however, a hedge.

French stocks fared a shade better, but they were not a hedge against hyperinflation.

The French franc, after holding stable in the last years of the war at around 19¢ gold, began falling in the spring of 1919. By April, 1920, it had fallen to 6¢; it rose to 9¢ in 1922, and fell to 4¢ in 1926. In 1927, the franc stabilized slightly under 4¢. Altogether, the franc lost 78 per cent of its value from 1919 to 1927. It did not become worthless, but prices still went up 400 per cent over a six-year span. This qualifies as hyperinflation.

Following is an eight-year graph tracking the gold value of French stocks, the franc and commodities from January, 1919, through 1928. Data are again derived from the *Axe Houghton* study.

French Hyperinflation Investment Results (Gold Value)

	January 1919 through January 1921	January 1919 through January 1926
French Currency	65% Loss	79% Loss
French Stocks	63% Loss	63% Loss

French Investment Results
(Gold Value)

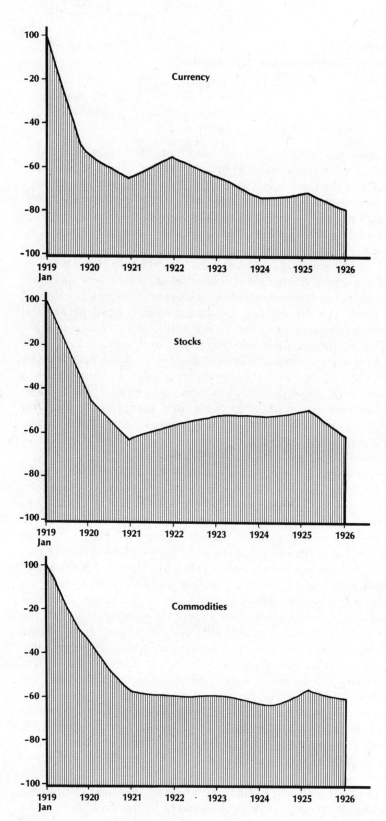

65

	January 1918 through January 1923	January 1918 through January 1925
French Bonds	69% Loss	80% Loss
Commodities	59% Loss	62% Loss
Other—Not Experiencing Hyperinflation		
Gold	0% Loss	0% Loss
British Stocks	36% Loss	26% Gain
U.S. Stocks	12% Loss	92% Gain
U.S. Bonds	16% Loss	10% Gain

One can clearly see that between January, 1919, and January, 1921, French stocks were no inflation hedge. They lost almost as much as the currency. Even in the longer period, 1919 through 1926, they were a poor inflation hedge. While currency was losing 79 per cent of its value, stocks were losing 63 per cent.

One difficulty in examining whether stocks are a hyperinflation hedge is the limited data available.

One difficulty encountered in critically examining the stocks-as-a-hyperinflation-hedge thesis is the limited data available. In the musty annals of economic history, there are numerous instances where the individual countries were experiencing hyperinflation, but few instances where there was also a stock market existing. The French and German instances cited herein and some fragmentary data from a few Latin American countries are about all the serious researcher has to work with.

At this point, the Latin American data available appear to be inconclusive. It is probably the dynamic real economic growth in these now emerging nations that has caused these Latin American stock markets to outperform the inflation rates, not any intrinsic characteristics of stocks as an inflation hedge. Without real economic growth, these stock markets would in all probability fall far behind inflation. Real earnings are the prime mover of stock prices over the long-term...not inflation.

All in all, the French and German instances discussed here certainly do not provide much comfort for those who continue to believe stocks might be a hedge against hyperinflation.

Western world politics, including those of the U.S., have moved far to the left since the early 1920s, when hyperinflation brought the German economic system to its knees. The Chairman Maos and Fidel Castros of the world could very well emerge from such a new hyperinflation castastrophe as the powers, the new order. Socialism, communism, and the state could be running the show. Capitalism and private enterprise might well end up being discredited and blamed. Favored treatment as in Germany? Most unlikely, in our view. Survival? Even that is at least questionable.

When all things are considered, common stocks as a hyperinflation hedge may be only a cruel fiction.

Thus, when all things are considered, common stocks as a hyperinflation hedge may be only a cruel fiction. Judging from the tables and graphs herein an investor who firmly believes hyperinflation is the future course might be best off gritting his teeth and taking on a load of gold, even at these barbaric prices. Note that even commodities did not function all that well as store of value.

In the French and German experiences, investing outside the afflicted nations did work effectively in the past. But in the future could the investor accurately anticipate the relatively stable nations? Then also one has to question if *any* Western nation could be a bastion of safety if the dominant economic power of the world, the U.S., crumbled in a quake of hyperinflation. The after-shock could be devastating, even in the Swiss Alps. And then one final problem. Moving capital out of the hyperinflation plagued nation might be exceedingly difficult once the tremors are clearly recognized.

Chapter 8

Inflation (Deflation) and Interest Rates—It's Not Supposed to Be That Way

Which of the following statements are true?

1. Historically bond yields are higher in years of price stability than in years of deflation.
2. Historically bond yields are higher in years of deflation than in years of inflation.
3. Historically short-term rates are lower in years of inflation than in years of deflation.
4. Historically short-term rates have an average of being higher than long-term yields.

Everyone knows inflation brings high interest rates...government officials, economists, fixed income managers, stockbrokers, corporate executives, the man on the street. We are all aware of this truism. And the higher the inflation, the higher the interest rates. Who would argue with that?

Investment people also know there is actually a measurable direct relationship between prevailing long-term rates and the rate of inflation, the real rate of interest. We also know that accelerating inflation means higher interest rates and decelerating inflation strongly implies lower interest rates. Who would argue with that?

The impact of inflation on interest rates varies as one progresses up the yield curve to longer maturities and, of course, we also know that short-term interest rates are typically lower than long-term rates.

Today, the preceding axioms are broadly accepted. They have come to be viewed as truisms, unchallenged, undisputed common knowledge. Most of us, because this thinking is so universally accepted, assume that historic financial data convincingly confirm these beliefs. We don't view these axioms as theory, we view them as fact. Billions of dollars are committed every year on these assumptions.

Surprisingly, long-term economic history does not strongly support these accepted truisms, and, in some cases history appears to contradict what most of the investment business has come to believe as indisputable fact.

Obviously, what occurred in the past is not a rubber stamp for the future. Conditions change and what worked yesterday does not always work tomorrow. Relationships that existed then may not exist now. Our purpose is not to disprove these broadly accepted investment axioms, but we do want to make the reader aware that these truisms have not always been true. *They are not natural laws.* This does not mean one should become an atheist on the subject, only a skeptical agnostic. If we can shake your faith, open your eyes, you may avoid some unpleasant future investment traps. Blind faith may be comforting today, but if unwarranted, it can get you in a mess of trouble down the road.

The statistics, tables and charts that follow are derived from a series of historic financial data covering almost 200 years of short- and long-term interest rates and consumer prices in the U.S. and England. The sources and the annual data employed are presented elsewhere in this chapter. It is believed that basic data are as accurate and reliable as any available. The sources are noted on the tables. Internal calculations based on this data were made with diligence and care.

Long-Term Interest Rates...The First Cut

High inflation means high interest rates, while price stability and deflation are accompanied by lower interest rates. Right? Wrong!

The first simple test of this truism was classifying 188 years of average annual yields for quality long-term U.S. bonds back to

Investment people accept as fact the relationship between prevailing interest rates and the rate of inflation.

History does not support the accepted truisms and, in some cases, appears to contradict what most of the investment business accepts as indisputable fact.

Long-term interest rates—"It's not supposed to be that way."

1792. The annual yields were then separated into the three following environments (based on annual changes in the CPI).

1. **Inflation Years:** Years in which the CPI was up 1.6 per cent or more.
2. **Stable Years:** Years in which the CPI was up or down 1.5 per cent or less.
3. **Deflationary Years:** Years in which the CPI declined 1.6 per cent or more.

The results of this classification are below:

		High Quality Long-Term Bonds	
		Average Yield	Median Yield
89 Inflation Years	(47%)	4.94	4.87
42 Stable Years	(22%)	4.19	4.25
57 Deflation Years	(31%)	5.07	5.01
188 Years	100%	4.81	4.83

As can be seen from the table above, long-term interest rates have typically been 10 to 15 basis points higher in deflationary years than in inflationary years. In the 57 deflationary years shown above, the average yield was 5.07 per cent, while in the inflationary years, it was only 4.94 per cent. Stable years had the lowest average yields, 4.19 per cent.

"It's not supposed to be that way."
— WILLIE NELSON

Short-term Interest Rates…The First Cut

The first test here involved classifying 149 years of average annual returns on prime commercial paper, four- to six-month paper or a reasonable proxy, back to 1831. These yields were then separated and averaged in the same three environments, again based on annual changes in the CPI.

Again, we defined inflation years as those in which the CPI was up 1.6 per cent or more. Stable years were those in which the CPI was up or down 1.5 per cent or less, and deflation years were those in which the CPI was down 1.6 per cent or more.

The results are tabulated below:

		High Quality Short-Term Paper	
		Average Yield	Median Yield
71 Inflation Years	(48%)	5.49	5.40
39 Stability Years	(26%)	4.83	4.69
38 Deflation Years	(26%)	6.30	5.45
148 Years	100%	5.50	5.28

Again, this approach showed that short-term rates have been higher in deflationary years than in inflationary years. Indeed, the difference in average returns was almost 80 basis points in favor of the deflationary years. Once again, the stable years showed the lowest interest rates, as expected. But the surprise is the relationship between the inflationary and deflationary years.

"It's not supposed to be that way."

— WAYLON JENNINGS (Willie's friend)

Short-term interest rates — "It's not supposed to be that way."

Long-Term — Short-Term Rates
1831-1979

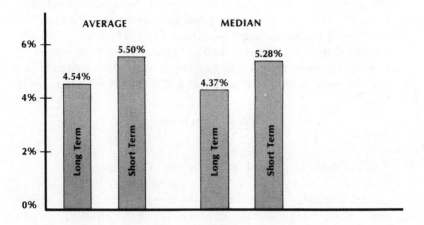

Long-Term By Environment
1791-1979

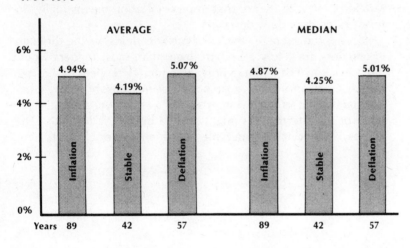

Short-Term By Environment
1831-1979

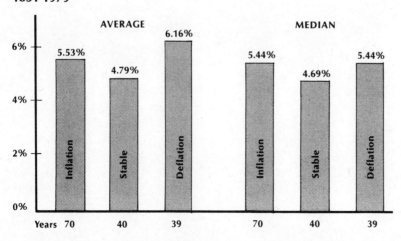

There is a third surprise for many readers. Short-term rates historically have been higher than long-term rates on both an average and a median basis. If we look at the period from 1831 through 1979, where both long and short rates are available, we find that the average short-term rate was 5.50 per cent and the median short-term rate was 5.28 per cent. The average long-term rate for the same period was 4.54 per cent, 96 basis points lower and the median long-term rate was 4.37 per cent, 91 basis points lower.

	Short Rates	Long Rates	Difference
Average	5.50%	4.54%	− .96
Median	5.28%	4.37%	− .91

While most of this will be discussed in considerable detail in other chapters, a couple of observations may be made here:

First, this meat axe division of the historic yield data is admittedly crude. Simple annual rates of inflation or deflation can and have fluctuated widely from year to year and some kind of smoothing of inflation data is appropriate. However, in this simple form the data seem to contradict today's accepted interest rate/inflation rate theory that implies inflation means higher interest rates than does deflation.

Second, the average yields and median yields for the three environments are likely all much lower than most readers would have thought. The average prevailing long-term yield of 4.81 per cent for the entire 188 year period seems absurdly low when compared to current levels. Also the average yield of 5.50 per cent for short-term rates might seem a bit on the low side. This will be covered in considerable detail in another chapter.

The data seem to contradict today's accepted interest rate/inflation rate theory that implies inflation means higher interest rates than does deflation.

Chapter 9

Interest Rates, Inflation and Deflation

Which of the following statements are true?

1. Long-term interest rates historically have tended to move up at about the same rate as inflation accelerates.
2. Long-term interest rates tend to fall in strong deflationary periods.
3. Short-term interest rates tend to fall in strong deflationary periods.
4. Short-term interest rate levels appear to be influenced more by business cycle considerations than by inflation or deflation.

That first cut was disturbing, but don't completely throw out the inflation/interest rate dogma yet. A more careful analysis of the historic data, while not supporting much of the inflation/interest rate theory which is currently in vogue, does reveal it is not all wrong.

Long-Term Interest Rates...A Second Cut

The analysis that follows covers the same 188 years of U.S. inflation and deflation as measured by the CPI. This time the CPI data are smoothed via a three-year centered average of annual rates. The same 188 years of average annual interest rates for high quality, long term, fixed income securities are employed.

Inflation environments of 4 per cent and above historically been accompanied by higher than average long-term interest rates.

This more careful analysis indicates—to some extent at least—that inflation environments of 4 per cent and above historically have been accompanied by higher than average long-term interest rates. However, the relationship is a far cry from what most economists and fixed income investment professionals currently believe. The analysis also indicates that higher deflation levels also are accompanied by higher than average levels of long-term rates.

The following tables and charts detail the findings. Note one table and one chart exclude the very low long-term interest rates of 1939 to 1950 from calculations. In this period it can be argued that nonmarket circumstances unnaturally restrained interest rates. First, World War II held down interest rates and an excess profits tax put a ceiling on dividends. Then the Treasury and the Federal Reserve Bank Board cooperatively kept interest rates pegged. During this time the entire government market was supported by the federal reserve banks, fixing long government bonds at 2.5 per cent and three-month Treasury bills at 0.38 per cent. This pegging agreement lasted until the spring of 1951. During this period of artificial rates there were significant bursts of inflation.

No matter which way you slice the cake, the same conclusions can be drawn.

Some might argue that U.S. long-term rates prevailing in that period, averaging below 2.9 per cent in our data base, are unrealistic, artificially depressed by the U.S. government. The other side of the argument is that there have been other circumstances of "artificially" depressed interest rates in this country's history, as well as England's and Europe's. And, no matter what the reason, no matter what extraneous forces were present, that's the way it was. All the data should, therefore, be included. While personally favoring this latter position, we will present the data both ways, but the same conclusions can be drawn no matter which way the cake is sliced.

Looking now at the tables and charts, we can see that whether we include or exclude the 1939 to 1950 "artificial" years, the average interest rate when inflation exceeded 4 per cent was above 5 per cent, while in years of relative price stability it did not top 4.75 per cent. However, in years of price deflation the interest rate on long-term bonds again increased, peaking at a 5.7 per cent rate in years of more than 6 per cent deflation. The charts reveal this symmetry clearly.

It is also clear from the tables that the average interest rate has trailed the inflation rate significantly. For example, in the 14 years when inflation exceeded 9 per cent, the average interest rate on long-term bonds was only 6.09 per cent. If we exclude the years which some regard as artificial, then this average interest rate rises only to 6.36 per cent.

Inflation/ Deflation Environment	Years	Long-Term Interest Rates		Years	Excluding 1939-1950 As Artificial Years	
		Average	Median		Average	Median
Inflation 9% +	14	6.09%	5.50%	13	6.36%	5.52%
Inflation 6-8%	14	5.05	5.07	10	6.02	5.39
Inflation 4-5%	17	5.25	6.01	15	5.61	6.02
Inflation 2-3%	29	4.08	3.93	26	4.25	3.98
Inflation 1%	28	4.22	4.28	27	4.28	4.32
0	19	4.68	4.52	19	4.68	4.52
Deflation 1%	18	4.61	4.62	17	4.72	4.77
Deflation 2-3%	22	5.09	5.24	22	5.09	5.24
Deflation 4-5%	15	4.96	4.81	15	4.96	4.81
Deflation 6% +	11	5.70	5.75	11	5.65	5.75
	187	4.81%	4.82%	175	4.95%	4.93%

Average Long-Term Interest Rates
By Inflation/Deflation Environments

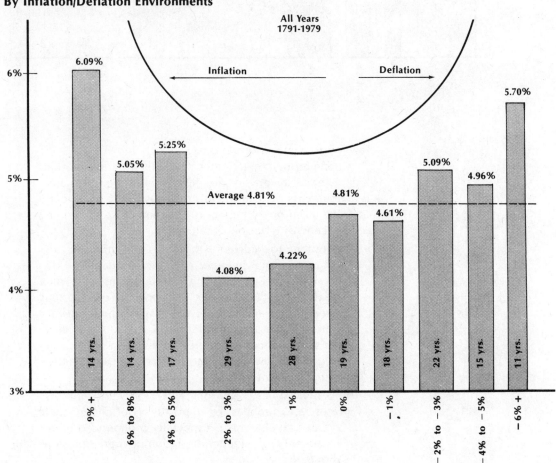

Average Long-Term Interest Rates
By Inflation/Deflation Environments

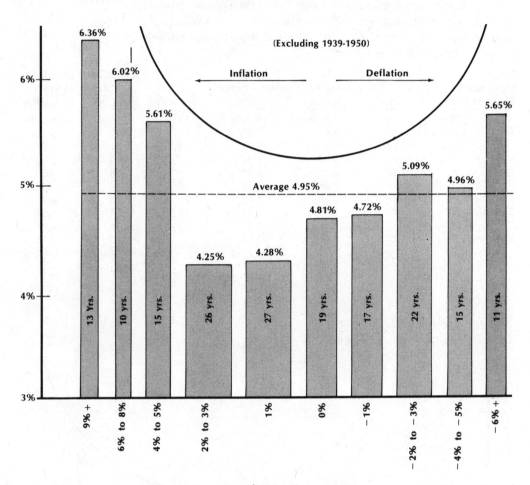

Now, on to some observations:

- Long-term interest rates typically rise above their average levels in the higher inflation rate environments of 4 per cent and above, but historically the inflationary impact is less than close to keeping pace with inflation acceleration.

- Counter to current thought, in inflation environments of 6 per cent and above, long-term rates do not typically reflect the rate of inflation plus "real interest" of 2 per cent to 3 per cent. Our research reveals in the 28 years where the three-year centered average of inflation exceeded 6 per cent, the average nominal interest rate was, in most cases, actually below the inflation rate itself, a negative real rate of interest.

- In deflationary environments, long-term interest rates also appear to typically rise above their average levels. This is especially pronounced in environments of steeper deflation, 6 per cent and above.

- The best environment for relatively low long-term yields appears to be a stable to modestly inflationary environment. As was demonstrated earlier, this same conclusion also holds true for the stock market.

Why do rates seem to rise at both ends of the spectrum — at higher inflation levels and higher deflation levels — while remaining relatively low in the middle? One explanation might be that these extremes represent periods of severe economic problems. Investments during these periods, even in top quality corporate bonds, appear to involve a higher level of risk. Thus, they must provide higher potential returns to be attractive. In higher deflation periods, the risk is usually depression, while in higher inflation periods the risk is twofold, loss of purchasing power and the possibility of economic collapse. Periods of relative price stability, on the other hand, also are typically periods of economic stability and prosperity.

Rates seem to rise at both ends of the spectrum, while remaining relatively low in the middle.

Short-Term Interest Rates...A Second Cut

Let's take a look now at the short-term interest rate history. This analysis covers the years between 1831 and 1979, examining historic short-term rates in eight separate inflationary and deflationary environments. We used the Consumer Price Index to define the periods, but unlike the preceding treatment of long-term rates these annual inflation data are not averaged or smoothed. We feel that four to six-month short rates are most validly analyzed against shorter term inflationary or deflationary conditions.

Again we present the data in two ways. The first includes all years; the second excludes the 1939 to 1950 period to eliminate possible distortions from this "artificial" period.

Once again, you can see that interest rates are lowest in periods of relative price stability and then generally rise as the inflation rate or deflation rate increases. However, with short-term rates the symmetry is not as smooth as in the case of long-term rates. The short-term interest rate trails the inflation rate. The average rate in periods of very high inflation (10 per cent or

Interest rates are lowest in periods of relative price stability and then rise as the inflation rate or deflation rate increases.

Summary Table

Inflation/Deflation Environment	Short-Term Rates			Short-Term Rates (Excluding 1939-1950)		
	Years	Average	Median	Years	Average	Median
Inflation 10% +	12	6.27%	5.84%	10	7.35%	6.69%
Inflation 6-9%	17	5.61	5.36	14	6.61	5.86
Inflation 3-5%	21	5.32	5.55	20	5.56	5.64
Inflation 2%	20	5.23	5.00	18	5.47	5.24
Stability 1% inflation 1% deflation	40	4.79	4.52	36	5.21	4.80
Deflation 2-3%	21	6.57	5.62	21	6.57	5.62
Deflation 4-5%	8	6.60	5.89	8	6.60	5.89
Deflation 6% +	10	4.94	4.81	10	4.94	4.81

Short-Term Rates (Median Rates)
1831-1979

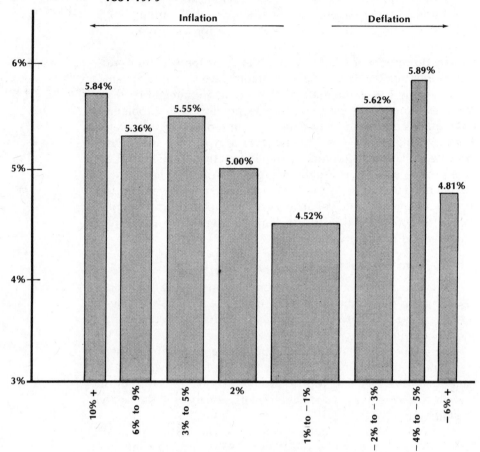

more) was only 6.27 per cent including all years, and 7.35 per cent excluding the "artificial" years.

Again some observations:

- Short-term rates typically rise somewhat above their average levels in higher inflation environments, but far less than one might expect. This work again indicates that interest rates, this time short-term rates, do not keep pace with accelerating inflation.

- Counter to current theory, history does not substantiate the hypothesis that interest rates reflect the rate of inflation plus "real interest" of even 1 per cent to 2 per cent. In the 29 years tabulated, where inflation was 6 per cent and above, the average short-term interest rate, even in nominal terms, was below the inflation rate, again a negative real rate of interest.

- As with long-term rates, deflation, except at levels of 6 per cent or more, also seems to be accompanied by higher short-term interest rates. However, unlike the long-term rate correlation, short rates fell significantly in the higher deflationary years. This

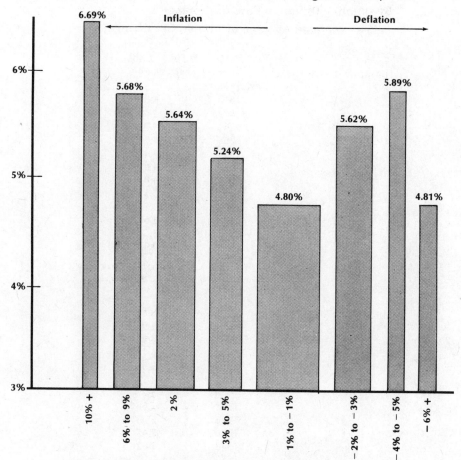

Short-Term (Median Rates)   **1831-1979** (Excluding 1939-1950)

Inflation ← | → Deflation

- 6.69% (10% +)
- 5.68% (6% to 9%)
- 5.64% (2%)
- 5.24% (3% to 5%)
- 4.80% (1% to –1%)
- 5.62% (–2% to –3%)
- 5.89% (–4% to –5%)
- 4.81% (–6% +)

may be a function of slackening short-term demand for funds. These 10 high deflation years also tended to be recession or business contraction years. In this environment, the demand for short-term funds is at a low ebb.

- As with longer term rates, there seems to be some evidence that periods of relative price stability are a favorable environment for short-term rates.

All things considered, inflation does not necessarily have controlling impact on short-term rates. It appears that business cycle pressures, with expanding and contracting demand for credit, have a significantly greater impact on short-term rates than do inflation/deflation or price stability. Also, it seems that the perceived economic credit risk factor does not play the important role it does with longer term rates. Short-term credit instruments, because of the very limited time horizons, do not seem to have much variation in risk premiums.

In summary then, it appears that neither long-term nor short-term interest rates keep pace with inflation, though both tend to move in the same direction as inflation. However, both increase with deflation except that short-term rates begin to decline again when the deflation rate reaches 6 per cent or more.

Business cycle pressures have significantly greater impact on short-term interest rates than do inflation/deflation or price stability.

Average Annual Long-Term Bond Yields
By Inflation/Deflation Rate Environments
(3-Year Centered Average of Annual CPI Change)

	Year	% Inf.	Yield
Inflation 9% or Higher:	1793	15%	5.48%
	1794	11	5.90
	1813	12	6.30
	1862	11	5.52
	1863	23	4.77
	1864	17	4.83
	1917	14	4.41
	1918	17	4.82
	1919	16	4.84
	*1947	10	2.57
	1974	9	8.53
	1975	9	8.66
	1978	10	8.80
	1979	11	9.65
	14 Years		6.09% **Average Yield**
			5.50% **Median Yield**
Inflation 6% to 8%:	1812	6%	6.12%
	1836	6	4.96
	1853	7	4.99
	1854	7	5.13
	1865	8	5.51
	1916	8	4.10
	1920	6	5.27
	1942	7	2.66
	1943	6	2.55
	1946	8	2.45
	1948	7	2.82
	1973	7	7.36
	1976	7	8.59
	1977	7	8.20
	14 Years		5.05% **Average Yield**
			5.07% **Median Yield**
Inflation 4% to 5%:	1795	4%	6.02%
	1805	5	6.38
	1814	5	7.64
	1835	5	4.83
	1852	5	4.98
	1861	4	6.45
	1881	5	3.70
	1900	4	3.31
	*1941	5	2.59
	*1945	4	2.54
	1951	4	2.90
	1952	4	3.03
	1968	4	6.01
	1969	5	6.78
	1970	5	7.88
	1971	4	7.23
	1972	5	7.06
	17 Years		5.25% **Average Yield**
			6.01% **Median Yield**

*Possible distortion (see text)

	Year	% Inf.	Yield
Inflation 2% to 3%:	1800	3%	6.94%
	1832	2	5.00
	1834	2	4.87
	1837	2	4.95
	1845	2	5.16
	1846	3	5.50
	1851	2	5.08
	1880	3	4.02
	1882	2	3.62
	1898	3	3.26
	1899	3	3.24
	1901	3	3.28
	1902	3	3.34
	1903	3	3.55
	1906	2	3.65
	1911	2	3.93
	1915	3	4.18
	1935	2	3.44
	1936	2	3.11
	*1944	3	2.54
	*1949	2	2.68
	*1950	3	2.62
	1956	2	3.35
	1957	3	3.93
	1958	2	3.81
	1959	2	4.37
	1965	2	4.43
	1966	2	5.13
	1967	3	5.47
	29 Years		4.08% **Average Yield**
			3.93% **Median Yield**
Inflation 1%	1808	1%	5.96%
	1810	1	5.82
	1826	1	4.56
	1830	1	4.90
	1831	1	4.95
	1844	1	5.16
	1855	1	5.16
	1856	1	5.10
	1887	1	3.80
	1888	1	3.69
	1889	1	3.51
	1904	1	3.57
	1905	1	3.51
	1907	1	3.92
	1910	1	3.87
	1912	1	3.95
	1913	1	4.14
	1924	1	4.51
	1925	1	4.50
	1937	1	3.12
	1938	1	2.90
	*1940	1	2.70
	1953	1	3.27
	1960	1	4.39
	1961	1	4.32
	1962	1	4.32

*Possible distortion (see text)

	Year	% Inf	Yield	
	1963	1%	4.23%	
	1964	1	4.36	
	28 Years		4.22%	**Average Yield**
			4.28%	**Median Yield**
Unchanged:	1799		7.42%	
	1806		6.14	
	1811		5.95	
	1824		4.52	
	1828		4.72	
	1838		5.01	
	1847		5.77	
	1850		5.31	
	1873		5.58	
	1875		5.07	
	1891		3.84	
	1896		3.50	
	1908		3.90	
	1909		3.78	
	1914		4.11	
	1926		4.36	
	1934		3.83	
	1954		2.97	
	1955		3.10	
	19 Years		4.68%	**Average Yield**
			4.52%	**Median Yield**
Deflation 1%:	1797	1%	7.40%	
	1822	1	4.98	
	1823	1	5.00	
	1829	1	4.77	
	1833	1	4.87	
	1848	1	5.71	
	1849	1	5.31	
	1872	1	5.36	
	1879	1	4.22	
	1886	1	3.81	
	1890	1	3.68	
	1892	1	3.72	
	1897	1	3.33	
	1921	1	5.16	
	1927	1	4.18	
	1928	1	4.19	
	1929	1	4.47	
	*1939	1	2.77	
	18 Years		4.61%	**Average Yield**
			4.62%	**Median Yield**
Deflation 2% to 3%:	1796	2%	6.30%	
	1798	3	7.56	
	1801	3	6.44	
	1802	2	6.02	
	1803	2	6.16	
	1807	3	6.08	
	1821	3	4.93	
	1827	3	4.61	
	1843	2	5.03	
	1857	3	5.19	

*Possible distortion (see text)

Year	%Def.	Yield
1860 %	2	5.57 %
1866	2	5.50
1867	3	5.34
1868	3	5.28
1874	3	5.47
1883	2	3.63
1884	3	3.62
1885	3	3.98
1893	3	3.73
1894	3	3.62
1895	3	3.46
1923	2	4.51

22 Years   5.09% **Average Yield**
            5.24% **Median Yield**

Deflation 4% to 5%:

Year	%Def.	Yield
1817	5%	5.86%
1818	4	5.78
1825	4	4.52
1839	5	5.21
1842	4	6.07
1858	4	5.03
1859	5	4.81
1870	5	5.44
1871	4	5.32
1876	5	4.59
1877	5	4.45
1878	4	4.34
1922	5	4.49
1930	4	4.31
1933	4	4.19

15 Years   4.96% **Average Yield**
            4.81% **Median Yield**

Deflation 6% +:

Year	%Def.	Yield
1804	6%	6.29%
1809	11	5.85
1815	6	7.30
1816	9	7.25
1819	7	5.90
1820	7	5.16
1840	6	5.07
1841	9	5.75
1869	6	5.37
1931	7	4.15
1932	8	4.61

11 Years   5.70% **Average Yield**
            5.75% **Median Yield**

**Average Annual Short-Term Interest Rates
By Annual Inflation/Deflation Environments**

(no smoothing — actual annual CPI change used)

	Year	% Inf.	Yield
Inflation 10% or higher:	1853	15%	10.25%
	1862	17	5.32
	1863	18	5.65

*Possible distortion (see text)

Year	% Inf.	Yield
1864	35 %	7.36 %
1917	17	5.07
1918	17	6.02
1919	15	5.37
1920	16	7.50
*1942	11	0.66
*1947	14	1.03
1974	11	9.87
1979	13	11.11

12 Years   6.27%   **Average Yield**
           5.84%   **Median Yield**

Inflation 6% to 9%:

Year	% Inf.	Yield
1831	7%	6.12%
1835	9	7.00
1836	9	18.00
1880	6	5.23
1881	6	5.36
1899	7	4.15
1916	8	3.84
1943	6	0.69
1946	8	0.81
1948	8	1.44
1951	8	2.16
1970	6	7.72
1973	6	8.15
1975	9	6.33
1976	6	5.35
1977	6	5.60
1978	9	7.50

17 Years   5.61%   **Average Yield**
           5.56%   **Median Yield**

Inflation 3% to 5%:

Year	% Inf.	Yield
1845	3%	4.71%
1847	3	9.59
1850	5	8.04
1854	4	10.37
1902	4	5.81
1903	4	6.16
1906	4	6.25
1907	4	6.66
1910	4	5.72
1912	3	5.41
1934	3	1.02
1937	4	0.94
*1941	5	0.54
1957	4	3.81
1958	3	2.46
1966	3	5.55
1967	3	5.10
1968	4	5.90
1969	5	7.83
1971	4	5.11
1972	3	4.69

21 Years   5.32%   **Average Yield**
           5.55%   **Median Yield**

*Possible distortion (see text)

	Year	% Inf.	Yield
Inflation 2%:	1839	2%	12.58%
	1844	2	4.87
	1846	2	8.33
	1855	2	8.92
	1857	2	11.56
	1882	2	5.64
	1887	2	5.73
	1888	2	4.92
	1890	2	5.62
	1897	2	3.50
	1900	2	5.71
	1901	2	5.40
	1923	2	5.07
	1925	2	4.02
	1935	2	0.76
	*1944	2	0.73
	1945	2	0.75
	1952	2	2.33
	1960	2	3.85
	1965	2	4.38
	20 Years		5.23% **Average Yield**
			5.00% **Median Yield**

	Year	% Inf.	Yield
Stability +1% inflation to 1% deflation:	1832	0%	6.25%
	1833	0	7.83
	1837	0	14.25
	1851	0	9.66
	1852	1	6.33
	1861	− 1	6.70
	1865	0	7.77
	1867	− 1	7.32
	1871	− 1	6.89
	1872	1	8.63
	1892	− 1	4.10
	1893	0	6.78
	1895	0	2.83
	1896	0	5.82
	1898	1	3.83
	1904	0	5.14
	1905	0	5.18
	1909	0	4.69
	1911	0	4.75
	1913	− 1	6.20
	1914	1	5.47
	1915	1	4.01
	1924	0	3.98
	1926	1	4.34
	1928	− 1	4.85
	1929	0	5.85
	1936	0	0.75
	*1939	− 1	0.59
	*1940	1	0.56
	*1949	− 1	1.48
	*1950	1	1.45
	1953	1	2.52
	1954	0	1.58

*Possible distortion (see text)

Year	% Inf.	Yield
1955	0	2.18
1956	1	3.31
1959	1	3.97
1961	1	2.97
1962	1	3.26
1963	1	3.55
1964	1	3.97

40 Years   4.79% **Average Yield**
               4.52% **Median Yield**

Deflation 2% to 3%:

Year	% Inf.	Yield
1834	− 2%	14.70%
1838	− 2	9.04
1842	− 3	8.08
1843	− 2	4.41
1849	− 3	10.25
1856	− 2	8.83
1859	− 2	6.14
1860	− 2	7.31
1869	− 3	9.66
1873	− 2	10.27
1874	− 2	5.98
1879	− 2	5.14
1883	− 2	5.62
1885	− 2	4.05
1886	− 2	4.77
1889	− 2	4.85
1891	− 2	5.46
1908	− 3	5.00
1927	− 2	4.11
1930	− 2	3.59
1938	− 2	0.81

21 Years   6.57% **Average Yield**
               5.98% **Median Yield**

Deflation 4% to 5%:

Year	% Inf.	Yield
1841	− 4%	6.80%
1848	− 5	15.10
1866	− 5	6.33
1868	− 4	7.28
1875	− 5	5.44
1876	− 5	5.13
1877	− 4	5.01
1933	− 5	1.73

8 Years   6.60% **Average Yield**
              5.88% **Median Yield**

Deflation: 6%:

Year	% Inf.	Yield
1840	−16%	7.75%
1858	−11	4.81
1870	−11	7.23
1878	− 6	4.82
1884	− 6	5.21
1894	− 8	3.04
1921	−10	6.62
1922	− 6	4.52
1931	− 9	2.64
1932	−10	2.73

10 Years   4.46% **Average Yield**
              4.81% **Median Yield**

*Possible distortion (see text)

Representative High Grade Long-Term Interest Rates
Average Annual Rates
1790 - 1979

Year	Annual Inflation/ Deflation	Interest Rate	
1790	NA%	5.85%	Foreign loan made to U.S. government
1791	NA	5.54	Average foreign loans made to U.S. government
1792	+ 4.7	5.05	Foreign loan made to U.S. government
1793	+30.6	5.48	Interpolated
1794	+11.5	5.90	Foreign loan made to U.S. government
1795	− 5.2	6.02	Interpolated
1796	+ 5.5	6.30	Interpolated
1797	− 6.9	7.40	Interpolated
1798	− 1.9	7.56	Federal government bonds
1799	+ 0.3	7.42	Federal government bonds
1800	+ 1.9	6.94	Federal government bonds
1801	+ 7.4	6.44	Federal government bonds
1802	−15.5	6.02	Federal government bonds
1803	+ 2.0	6.16	Federal government bonds
1804	+ 8.0	6.29	Federal government bonds
1805	+ 7.3	6.38	Federal government bonds
1806	− 1.7	6.14	Federal government bonds
1807	− 6.9	6.08	Federal government bonds
1808	− 1.8	5.96	Federal government bonds
1809	+11.3	5.85	Federal government bonds
1810	− 1.7	5.82	Federal government bonds
1811	− 5.2	5.95	Federal government bonds
1812	+ 7.3	6.12	Federal government bonds
1813	+17.0	6.30	Federal government bonds
1814	−13.0	7.64	Federal government bonds
1815	−12.8	7.30	Federal government bonds
1816	−14.7	7.25	Federal government bonds
1817	− 0.3	5.86	Federal government bonds
1818	− 0.7	5.78	Federal government bonds
1819	−10.8	5.90	Federal government bonds
1820	−10.2	5.16	Federal government bonds
1821	− 0.4	4.93	New England municipals (U.S. debt no longer significant)
1822	+ 0.4	4.98	Interpolated
1823	+ 2.2	5.00	New England municipals
1824	− 6.4	4.52	New England municipals
1825	+ 4.6	4.52	New England municipals
1826	− 8.7	4.56	Interpolated
1827	+ 9.5	4.61	New England municipals
1828	− 8.7	4.72	Interpolated
1829	−0−	4.77	New England municipals
1830	− 4.3	4.90	New England municipals
1831	+ 7.0	4.95	Interpolated
1832	−0−	5.00	New England municipals
1833	−0−	4.87	New England municipals (no federal debt at all)
1834	− 2.3	4.87	New England municipals
1835	+ 9.5	4.83	New England municipals
1836	+ 8.7	4.96	New England municipals
1837	− 0.4	4.95	New England municipals
1838	− 1.6	5.01	New England municipals
1839	+ 1.6	5.21	New England municipals

Year	Annual Inflation/ Deflation	Interest Rate	
1840	− 15.7 %	5.07 %	New England municipals
1841	− 4.3	5.75	Federal government average new issue
1842	− 3.5	6.07	Federal government average market yield
1843	− 1.6	5.03	Federal government average market yield
1844	+ 1.6	4.85	Federal government average market yield
1845	+ 2.6	5.16	Federal government average market yield
1846	+ 2.1	5.50	Federal government average market yield
1847	+ 3.0	5.77	Federal government average market yield
1848	− 4.9	5.71	Federal government average market yield
1849	− 2.6	5.31	New England municipals
1850	+ 4.7	5.31	New England municipals
1851	− 0.5	5.08	New England municipals
1852	+ 1.0	4.98	New England municipals
1853	+15.0	4.99	New England municipals
1854	+ 4.4	5.13	New England municipals
1855	+ 2.1	5.16	New England municipals
1856	− 2.1	5.10	New England municipals
1857	+ 2.5	5.19	New England municipals
1858	−10.6	5.03	New England municipals
1859	− 2.3	4.81	New England municipals
1860	− 2.3	5.57	Federal government bonds
1861	− 0.9	6.45	Federal government bonds
1862	+17.8	5.52	Highest grade corporates (RR)
1863	+18.4	4.77	Highest grade corporates (RR)
1864	+35.2	4.83	Highest grade corporates (RR)
1865	− 0.5	5.51	New England municipals
1866	− 5.1	5.50	New England municipals
1867	− 1.3	5.34	New England municipals
1868	− 4.1	5.28	New England municipals
1869	− 2.9	5.37	New England municipals
1870	−11.5	5.44	New England municipals
1871	− 0.7	5.32	New England municipals
1872	+ 0.7	5.36	New England municipals
1873	− 2.0	5.58	New England municipals
1874	− 1.7	5.47	New England municipals
1875	− 5.2	5.07	New England municipals
1876	− 5.4	4.59	New England municipals
1877	− 3.8	4.45	New England municipals
1878	− 6.0	4.34	New England municipals
1879	− 2.1	4.22	New England municipals
1880	+ 6.5	4.02	New England municipals
1881	+ 6.1	3.70	New England municipals
1882	+ 1.9	3.62	New England municipals
1883	− 1.9	3.63	New England municipals
1884	− 5.8	3.62	New England municipals
1885	− 2.1	3.98	Highest grade corporates (RR)
1886	− 2.1	3.81	Highest grade corporates (RR)
1887	+ 2.1	3.80	Highest grade corporates (RR)
1888	+ 2.1	3.69	Highest grade corporates (RR)
1889	− 2.1	3.51	Highest grade corporates (RR)
1890	+ 2.1	3.68	Highest grade corporates (RR)
1891	− 2.1	3.84	Highest grade corporates (RR)
1892	− 0.8	3.72	Highest grade corporates (RR)
1893	−0−	3.73	Highest grade corporates (RR)
1894	− 7.6	3.62	Highest grade corporates (RR)

Year	Annual Inflation/ Deflation	Interest Rate	
1895	−0− %	3.46 %	Highest grade corporates (RR)
1896	− 0.4	3.50	Highest grade corporates (RR)
1897	+ 1.8	3.33	Highest grade corporates (RR)
1898	+ 0.9	3.26	Highest grade corporates (RR)
1899	+ 6.7	3.24	30-year prime corporates
1900	+ 2.1	3.31	30-year prime corporates
1901	+ 2.0	3.28	30-year prime corporates
1902	+ 4.0	3.34	30-year prime corporates
1903	+ 3.9	3.55	30-year prime corporates
1904	−0−	3.57	30-year prime corporates
1905	−0−	3.51	30-year prime corporates
1906	+ 3.7	3.65	30-year prime corporates
1907	+ 3.6	3.92	30-year prime corporates
1908	− 3.4	3.90	30-year prime corporates
1909	−0−	3.78	30-year prime corporates
1910	+ 3.6	3.87	30-year prime corporates
1911	−0−	3.93	30-year prime corporates
1912	+ 3.5	3.95	30-year prime corporates
1913	− 1.0	4.14	30-year prime corporates
1914	+ 1.3	4.11	30-year prime corporates
1915	+ 1.0	4.18	30-year prime corporates
1916	+ 7.6	4.10	30-year prime corporates
1917	+17.4	4.41	30-year prime corporates
1918	+17.5	4.82	30-year prime corporates
1919	+14.9	4.84	30-year prime corporates
1920	+15.8	5.27	30-year prime corporates
1921	−10.7	5.16	30-year prime corporates
1922	− 6.3	4.49	30-year prime corporates
1923	+ 1.8	4.51	30-year prime corporates
1924	+ 0.2	4.51	30-year prime corporates
1925	+ 2.5	4.50	30-year prime corporates
1926	+ 1.0	4.36	30-year prime corporates
1927	− 1.9	4.18	30-year prime corporates
1928	− 1.3	4.19	30-year prime corporates
1929	−0−	4.47	30-year prime corporates
1930	− 2.5	4.31	30-year prime corporates
1931	− 8.8	4.15	30-year prime corporates
1932	−10.3	4.61	30-year prime corporates
1933	− 5.1	4.19	30-year prime corporates
1934	+ 3.4	3.83	30-year prime corporates
1935	+ 2.5	3.44	30-year prime corporates
1936	+ 0.1	3.11	30-year prime corporates
1937	+ 3.6	3.12	30-year prime corporates
1938	− 1.9	2.90	30-year prime corporates
1939	− 1.4	2.77	30-year prime corporates
1940	+ 1.0	2.70	30-year prime corporates
1941	+ 5.0	2.59	30-year prime corporates
1942	+10.7	2.66	30-year prime corporates
1943	+ 6.2	2.55	30-year prime corporates
1944	+ 1.7	2.54	30-year prime corporates
1945	+ 2.3	2.54	30-year prime corporates
1946	+ 8.5	2.45	30-year prime corporates
1947	+14.4	2.57	30-year prime corporates
1948	+ 7.8	2.82	30-year prime corporates
1949	− 1.0	2.68	30-year prime corporates

Year	Annual Inflation/ Deflation	Interest Rate	
1950	+ 1.0%	2.62%	30-year prime corporates
1951	+ 7.9	2.90	30-year prime corporates
1952	+ 2.2	3.03	30-year prime corporates
1953	+ 0.8	3.27	30-year prime corporates
1954	+ 0.5	2.97	30-year prime corporates
1955	− 0.4	3.10	30-year prime corporates
1956	+ 1.5	3.35	30-year prime corporates
1957	+ 3.6	3.93	30-year prime corporates
1958	+ 2.7	3.81	30-year prime corporates
1959	+ 0.8	4.37	30-year prime corporates
1960	+ 1.6	4.39	30-year prime corporates
1961	+ 1.0	4.32	30-year prime corporates
1962	+ 1.1	4.32	30-year prime corporates
1963	+ 1.2	4.23	30-year prime corporates
1964	+ 1.3	4.36	30-year prime corporates
1965	+ 1.7	4.43	30-year prime corporates
1966	+ 2.9	5.13	30-year prime corporates
1967	+ 2.9	5.47	30-year prime corporates
1968	+ 4.2	6.01	30-year prime corporates
1969	+ 5.4	6.78	30-year prime corporates
1970	+ 5.9	7.88	30-year prime corporates
1971	+ 4.3	7.23	30-year prime corporates
1972	+ 3.3	7.06	30-year prime corporates
1973	+ 6.2	7.36	30-year prime corporates
1974	+11.0	8.53	30-year prime corporates
1975	+ 9.1	8.66	30-year prime corporates
1976	+ 5.7	8.59	30-year prime corporates
1977	+ 6.5	8.20	30-year prime corporates
1978	+ 9.0	8.80	30-year prime corporates
1979	+13.4	9.65	30-year prime corporates

SHORT-TERM INTEREST RATES
1831-1979

Year	Annual Inflation/ Deflation	Average Short-Term Rate Commercial Paper*
1831	+ 7.0%	6.12%
1832	− 0 −	6.25
1833	− 0 −	7.83
1834	− 2.3	14.70
1835	+ 9.5	7.00
1836	+ 8.7	18.00
1837	− 0.4	14.25
1838	− 1.6	9.04
1839	+ 1.6	12.58
1840	−15.7	7.75
1841	− 4.3	6.80
1842	− 3.5	8.08
1843	− 1.6	4.41

* 1831-1856 Bigelow's Boston first-class commercial paper 3 to 6 month.

1857-1899 New York City choice commercial paper 2 to 3 month.

1900-1978 Prime commercial paper 4 to 6 month.

Year	Annual Inflation/ Deflation	Average Short-Term Rate Commercial Paper
1844	+ 1.6 %	4.87 %
1845	+ 2.6	4.71
1846	+ 2.1	8.33
1847	+ 3.0	9.59
1848	− 4.9	15.10
1849	− 2.6	10.25
1850	+ 4.7	8.04
1851	− 0.5	9.66
1852	+ 1.0	6.33
1853	+15.0	10.25
1854	+ 4.4	10.37
1855	+ 2.1	8.92
1856	− 2.1	8.83
1857	+ 2.5	11.56
1858	−10.6	4.81
1859	− 2.3	6.14
1860	− 2.3	7.31
1861	− 0.9	6.70
1862	+17.8	5.32
1863	+18.4	5.65
1864	+35.2	7.36
1865	− 0.5	7.77
1866	− 5.1	6.33
1867	− 1.3	7.32
1868	− 4.1	7.28
1869	− 2.9	9.66
1870	−11.5	7.23
1871	− 0.7	6.98
1872	+ 0.7	8.63
1873	− 2.0	10.27
1874	− 1.7	5.98
1875	− 5.2	5.44
1876	− 5.4	5.13
1877	− 3.8	5.01
1878	− 6.0	4.82
1879	− 2.1	5.14
1880	+ 6.5	5.23
1881	+ 6.1	5.36
1882	+ 1.9	5.64
1883	− 1.9	5.62
1884	− 5.8	5.21
1885	− 2.1	4.05
1886	− 2.1	4.77
1887	+ 2.1	5.73
1888	+ 2.1	4.91
1889	− 2.1	4.85
1890	+ 2.1	5.62
1891	− 2.1	5.46
1892	− 0.8	4.10
1893	− 0 −	6.78
1894	− 7.6	3.04
1895	− 0 −	2.83
1896	− 0.4	5.82
1897	+ 1.8	3.50
1898	+ 0.9	3.83
1899	+ 6.7	4.15
1900	+ 2.1	5.71

Year	Annual Inflation/ Deflation	Average Short-Term Rate Commercial Paper
1901	+ 2.0 %	5.40 %
1902	+ 4.0	5.81
1903	+ 3.9	6.16
1904	– 0 –	5.14
1905	– 0 –	5.18
1906	+ 3.7	6.25
1907	+ 3.6	6.66
1908	– 3.4	5.00
1909	– 0 –	4.69
1910	+ 3.6	5.72
1911	– 0 –	4.75
1912	+ 3.5	5.41
1913	– 1.0	6.20
1914	+ 1.3	5.47
1915	+ 1.0	4.01
1916	+ 7.6	3.84
1917	+ 17.4	5.07
1918	+ 17.5	6.02
1919	+ 14.9	5.37
1920	+ 15.8	7.50
1921	– 10.7	6.62
1922	– 6.3	4.52
1923	+ 1.8	5.07
1924	+ 0.2	3.98
1925	+ 2.5	4.02
1926	+ 1.0	4.34
1927	– 1.9	4.11
1928	– 1.3	4.85
1929	– 0 –	5.85
1930	– 2.5	3.59
1931	– 8.8	2.64
1932	– 10.3	2.73
1933	– 5.1	1.73
1934	+ 3.4	1.02
1935	+ 2.5	0.76
1936	+ 0.1	0.75
1937	+ 3.6	0.94
1938	– 1.9	0.81
1939	– 1.4	0.59
1940	+ 1.0	0.56
1941	+ 5.0	0.54
1942	+ 10.7	0.66
1943	+ 6.2	0.69
1944	+ 1.7	0.73
1945	+ 2.3	0.75
1946	+ 8.5	0.81
1947	+ 14.4	1.03
1948	+ 7.8	1.44
1949	– 1.0	1.48
1950	+ 1.0	1.45
1951	+ 7.9	2.16
1952	+ 2.2	2.33
1953	+ 0.8	2.52
1954	+ 0.5	1.58
1955	– 0.4	2.18
1956	+ 1.5	3.31
1957	+ 3.6	3.81

Year	Annual Inflation/ Deflation	Average Short-Term Rate Commercial Paper
1958	+ 2.7%	2.46%
1959	+ 0.8	3.97
1960	+ 1.6	3.85
1961	+ 1.0	2.97
1962	+ 1.1	3.26
1963	+ 1.2	3.55
1964	+ 1.3	3.97
1965	+ 1.7	4.38
1966	+ 2.9	5.55
1967	+ 2.9	5.10
1968	+ 4.2	5.90
1969	+ 5.4	7.83
1970	+ 5.9	7.72
1971	+ 4.3	5.11
1972	+ 3.3	4.69
1973	+ 6.2	8.15
1974	+11.0	9.87
1975	+ 9.1	6.33
1976	+ 5.7	5.35
1977	+ 6.5	5.60
1978	+ 9.0	7.80
1979	+13.4	11.11

Chapter 10

Today's "Real" Rate of Interest Theory May Be Tomorrow's Myth

Is the following statement true or false?

All those respected economic experts are wrong about the existence of a "real" rate of interest.

Late in 1978, one of the leading interest rate experts in the U.S., an officer of one of the largest investment banking and brokerage firms, wrote a detailed commentary reflecting some of the most advanced thinking on "real" interest rates.

The commentator will remain nameless for reasons which will become apparent later in this chapter. Below are a series of quotes from that commentary, each of which is followed by comments by this author. Readers should not construe the following as taking some cheap shots at this individual, but it is important to point out that the thinking he expresses on the subject of "real" interest rates is essentially the same as that of a large and rapidly growing mass of economic and monetary experts.

Common economic thinking on real interest rates may not necessarily be true.

> **Quote:** "Market, or nominal rates of interest are comprised of two components: the real rate of interest and the expected rate of inflation."

Based on history, this dogmatic statement of what the writer obviously believes to be indisputable fact may not be true, except, perhaps, over short periods of time. At any rate, he could have at least qualified this with a "maybe" or a "perhaps."

> **Quote:** "Over long periods of time the real interest rate tends toward stability, so many rates of interest typically fluctuate around changes in market inflation expectations."

As we shall show in this chapter, outside of one period, we could find no time in which "the real interest rate tends toward stability."

We could find no time in which the real interest rate tends toward stability.

> **Quote:** "Using statistical observations dating back to 1955, the mean rate of interest on government bonds registers 2.1 per cent with a standard error of 0.9 per cent. Thus, real government bond rates have generally fluctuated during the past 23 years in a 1.2 per cent to 3 per cent range."

Most economic and monetary experts think economic history started around 1954. The "real" interest advocates find this especially convenient because earlier data do not support their position.

> **Quote:** "Assuming for the moment that the real rate is stable (an assumption not always correct), the key to forecasting money rates lies in projecting the expected rate of inflation and then simply adding about 2 per cent."

Well, this time at least he hedged himself a bit on the stability of the real rate. Now, on to a simple key to forecasting money rates.

> **Quote:** "There are, in our view, two principal influences on the expected inflation rate: observance of past rates of inflation over a period of about five years, as well as an assessment of the anticipated inflation rate for the next year or so."

Few experts have had much luck
recently in anticipating correctly,
and a simple one-year projection
of recent history does not work
very well either.

As we will show in the following chapter, the results of the past-five-year approach are not exactly encouraging. As for assessing the anticipated inflation rate for the next year, this could be done by taking a consensus, but keep in mind, few experts have had much luck recently in anticipating correctly, and a simple one-year projection of recent history does not work very well either.

Quote: "A number of investors, however, often make the mistake of ignoring past inflation history."

So do a lot of commentators, economic experts and academicians, including this particular money market economist.

Quote: "Taking present circumstances as an example, consumer prices this fall appear to be rising at an annual rate of about 10 per cent, thus suggesting a 12 per cent government bond rate. The actual bond rate, however, is currently 8.88 per cent. So, the line of reasoning goes, perhaps the market is telling us that inflation is really headed much lower, along with bond rates as well. This reasoning places far too much emphasis on the near term, and ignores a more substantial piece of history."

The entire concept of "real" rate
of interest is more myth than
reality.

Look who is chiding whom about ignoring a "more substantial piece of history." Our long-term work, using either three-or five-year moving averages of past inflation as proxies for future inflation shows that the entire concept of "real" rate of interest is more a myth than reality.

But let us take a look at the research in detail.

"Real" Rates of Interest: It Ain't Necessarily So

Professional investors, economists, politicians, businessmen and bankers now accept the theory of a "real" rate of interest. The "real" rate of interest is arrived at by subtracting the inflation rate from the quoted (nominal) interest rate. Thus, if nominal interest rates are 9 per cent and the current inflation rate is 6 per cent, then the real interest rate would be 3 per cent. The rationale behind this theory of "real" interest is that inflation erodes the value of a dollar, so a lender who lends money for five years at 6 per cent is a real loser if inflation over that five years runs at 7 per cent, or even only 6.5 per cent. In effect, the lender actually has lost money at a rate of 1 per cent or 0.5 per cent per year. Obviously, this is not good business.

Therefore, if a lender expects inflation to run at 7 per cent during the next five years, he should charge interest of 10 per cent. This would give him a "real" rate of interest (that is, a real return) of 3 per cent per year.

This all seems to make sense from the lender's standpoint. The theory of "real" interest rates has been around for a long time, at least in academic circles. Professional fixed-income investors, underwriters and bond issuers began focusing on the concept in the last decade or so.

One of the primary reasons for this awareness was a chart that regularly appeared in Monetary Trends, a monthly publication of the Federal Reserve Bank of St. Louis. This bank was and is a leader in espousing monetary theory, and its weekly and monthly publications are among the most widely read reports in the investment world.

The chart below first appeared on the back cover of Monetary Trends where it was immediately apparent to a reader, and it "proved" to many professionals, that the theory of "real" interest rates was fact. Perhaps it was some kind of natural law. The chart shows market interest rates climbing steadily from about 4.5 per cent at the beginning of 1965 to a peak of about 8.5 per cent in 1970, with a few fluctuations along the way, and then settling at about 7.4 per cent through 1972 and 1973. Through all of this, the adjusted yield (the market yield less the annual rate

The Federal Reserve Bank of St. Louis has been a leader in espousing monetary theory.

Yields On Highest-Grade Seasoned Corporate Bonds

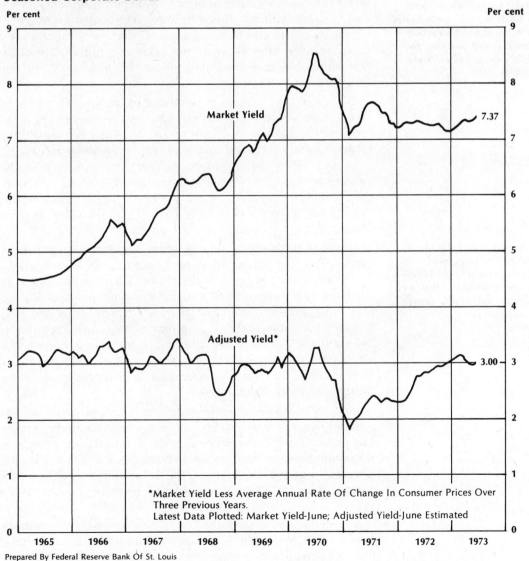

*Market Yield Less Average Annual Rate Of Change In Consumer Prices Over Three Previous Years.
Latest Data Plotted: Market Yield-June; Adjusted Yield-June Estimated

Prepared By Federal Reserve Bank Of St. Louis

of change in consumer prices over the three previous years) hovered fairly consistently around 3 per cent, with one plunge as low as 2 per cent at the beginning of 1971. This apparent historic documentation, combined with the appealing rational underlying theory, led to an almost universal acceptance.

Admittedly, the chart is impressive. The adjusted yield or "real" rate of interest has remained remarkably stable in the period covered. The approach very neatly rationalized and, perhaps, justified the high rates of the late 1960s and 1970s, rates that were unprecedented for most living investors.

This writer was introduced to the world of investments in 1960. Back then no professionals, except perhaps a few on the lunatic fringe, believed long-term high grade bonds could ever, in their lifetime, yield more than 6 per cent. But the 6 per cent barrier was broken in 1968. It was a new world and there just had to be an explanation, a rationale. Rates kept going up, moving through 7 per cent in the next two years, then 8 per cent. But "real" interest rate theory could explain it all. Lenders, of course, were very pleased with this thesis because it provided an excellent defense against consumer and political charges of usury and excessive profits. After all, when the inflation erosion of the dollar was subtracted, their "real" return was only a skimpy 2 per cent to 3 per cent.

But one of the problems encountered in applying the theory of "real" interest rates to a current situation is determining what the inflation adjustment factor should be. The key is really the future inflation rate, and that may not be the same as past experience. The St. Louis Fed, in its chart calculation, used the average annual rate of inflation, as measured by the CPI, over the previous three years as a proxy for expected future rates. But this did not fit very well in 1974 and 1975, so the statistics were rejuggled.

Theorists maintain the proper inflation rate adjustment is the expected rate of future inflation. Few, however, are willing to stick their necks out and actually predict future inflation, and as we have seen, economists also have a very poor record for predicting inflation, even one year in advance. Thus, the past typically continues to serve as a proxy for the future. Factoring in 1974 and 1975, it was found the past inflation rate/interest rate correlation fits better if a five-year average of past inflation is used instead of a three-year average as a proxy for expected inflation. But more on that later.

First, let's take a look at the long-term history of "real" interest volatility year to year. In the following chart, the deflation rate has been added to the nominal interest rate during periods of deflation because the dollar becomes worth more in such periods. In periods of inflation, the inflation rate has been subtracted from the nominal interest rate to determine the "real" rate.

As can clearly be seen, the "real" rate of interest is far more volatile than perceived. Even when inflation and deflation have been smoothed with a three-year average, the swings have run

Lenders are very pleased with the thesis of "real" interest rates because it provides an excellent defense against consumer and political charges of usury and excessive profits.

Theorists maintain the proper inflation rate adjustment is the expected rate of future inflation, but few are willing to stick their necks out and actually predict future inflation.

"Real" Interest 1791-1909
Long-Term Interest Rates
Adjusted For Inflation/Deflation

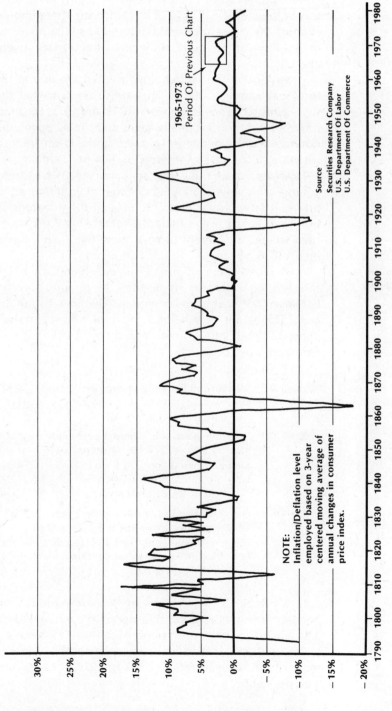

NOTE:
Inflation/Deflation level
employed based on 3-year
centered moving average of
annual changes in consumer
price index.

1965-1973
Period Of Previous Chart

Source
Securities Research Company
U.S. Department Of Labor
U.S. Department Of Commerce

The "real" rate of interest is far more volatile than perceived, even when inflation and deflation have been smoothed.

from a positive 17 per cent to a negative 18 per cent. During the Civil War inflation, for example, the "real" rate of interest plunged to a minus 18 per cent. Similarly, it plunged to minus 12 per cent in the World War I inflation and then climbed to more than 12 per cent in the 1930s. On two other occasions, early in the history of the nation, the "real" interest rate rose to more than 15 per cent.

There have been 10 periods of negative "real" interest, ranging from one year to 10 years in duration. But the relative stability of "real" interest from the mid-1950s through 1969 is unique. And, this is the statistical base of evidence most commonly used to support the concept of real interest. No similar extended period of stability can be found in the almost 200 years covered by the chart.

If we look at the table below, we can see that at first glance the "real" rate of interest appears to be just what the experts say—about 3 per cent. Between 1792 and 1979, the median long-term bond rate was 4.84 per cent, and the average annual inflation rate was 1.5 per cent. Subtracting the latter from the former we get a "real" rate of interest of 3.34 per cent.

However, if we take the academician's first approach and assume a three-year moving average of inflation as the appropriate inflation adjustment factor, and if we include only inflation years (years where the inflation rate is 2.5 per cent or more), then we get a different picture. Now the "real" interest rate is minus 0.36 per cent.

If we look at high inflation years, the picture is even gloomier.

If we look at high inflation years only (years when the inflation rate is 5.5 per cent or more), then the picture is even gloomier because the "real" rate of interest declines to minus 3.44 per cent. This is not very helpful to those who maintain there is a constant "real" rate of interest and that it hovers between 2 per cent and 3 per cent.

1792 - 1979	Median Annual Long-Term Bond Rate.....	4.84%
	Less: Average Annual Inflation Rate.......	(1.50%)
	"Real" Rate of Interest.............	3.34%
1792 - 1979	Inflation years only where 3-year centered moving average is 2.5% or more.	
	Median Annual Long-Term Bond Rate.....	4.84%
	Less: Median Annual Inflation Rate.......	(5.20%)
	"Real" Rate of Interest.............	−0.36%
1792 - 1979	High inflation years only where 3-year centered moving average is 5.5% or more.	
	Median Annual Long-Term Bond Rate.....	5.06%
	Less: Median Annual Inflation Rate.......	(8.50%)
	"Real Rate of Interest.............	−3.44%

If we look at the history in 30-year periods, the picture becomes even more confusing because the '"real" interest rate was highest in the earliest periods (in the 1792 to 1821 and 1822 to 1851 periods). It then declined continuously, except that in the most recent 30-year period, 1950 to 1979, it edged up again to 1.66 per cent.

Years	Average Long-Term Bonds	Compounded Annual Inflation Rate	Real Rate of Return
By 30-Year Periods:			
1792 - 1821	6.24%	0.65%	5.59%
1822 - 1851	5.06	− 0.36	5.42
1852 - 1881	5.07	1.02	4.05
1882 - 1911	3.62	0.36	3.26
1912 - 1941	4.06	1.39	2.67
1942 - 1971	3.81	3.43	0.38
Most Recent 30 Years:			
1950 - 1979	5.48%	3.82%	1.66%
By 15-Year Periods:			
1792 - 1806	6.36%	2.90%	3.46%
1807 - 1821	6.13	− 1.56	7.69
1822 - 1836	4.80	0.71	4.09
1837 - 1851	5.32	− 1.42	6.74
1852 - 1866	5.24	4.26	0.98
1867 - 1881	4.90	− 2.12	7.02
1882 - 1896	3.68	− 1.15	4.83
1897 - 1911	3.56	1.90	1.66
1912 - 1926	4.49	4.11	0.38
1927 - 1941	3.64	− 1.26	4.90
1942 - 1956	2.80	4.18	− 1.38
1957 - 1971	5.11	2.69	2.42
Most Recent 15 Years:			
1965 - 1979	7.15%	5.66%	1.49%

Breaking history into 15-year periods gives more erratic results with the real rate reaching a high of 7.69 per cent in the 1807 to 1821 period and a low of minus 1.38 per cent in the 1942 to 1956 period.

How then, do the experts conclude that the "real" interest rate is stable over time? It depends on when you look at it.

It is almost as though economic history started in 1954, the year most of the monetary experts' "long term" charts begin. The question is, is this a result of laziness or inadequate data? Perhaps it is that the earlier data failed to support their "theory" with any degree of consistency.

The concept of a "real" rate of interest is widely held, but it does not appear to be a natural law. It is not a truism that has prevailed forever. Like many investment concepts and theories, sometimes it works and sometimes it doesn't.

Although the concept of a "real" rate of interest is widely held, it does not appear to be a natural law.

These observations are not completely justified by data presented so far and there are several questions that need to be answered. For example, what are the results if deflationary periods are omitted? (More than a few observers are convinced deflation can never occur again.) What are the results if a different time frame measure of inflation is employed? What are the results of a similar examination of short-term rates? And lastly, has the economic system reached such a high level of sophistication and control that the record of the ancient past (before 1954) means nothing? The following exhibits and the next chapter examine these questions.

"Real" Interest Only in Periods of Inflation

The table below groups years into inflationary periods. For example, there have been 28 years since 1790 when inflation ranged between 0.5 per cent and 1.4 per cent. In these 28 years, the "real" interest rate averaged 3.27 per cent. In the 17 years when inflation ranged between 1.5 per cent and 2.4 per cent, the nominal interest rate averaged 4.15 per cent while the "real" rate declined to an average of 2.14 per cent. As the inflation rate increases, the "real" interest rate declines steadily, until at an inflation rate of more than 7.5 per cent (17 years) the nominal interest rate averages 5.72 per cent, but the "real" interest rate is minus 6.69 per cent!

Real Interest Rates on Long-Term Bonds
(3-year centered average inflation)

Inflation Environment	Years	Nominal Rate Average	Nominal Rate Median	Real Rate Average	Real Rate Median
7.5% +	17	5.72	5.48	−6.69	−5.88
5.5 - 7.4	13	5.30	5.13	−1.14	−0.84
3.5 - 5.4	15	5.27	6.01	0.81	1.28
2.5 - 3.4	15	3.98	3.55	1.03	0.62
1.5 - 2.4	17	4.15	4.37	2.14	2.43
0.5 - 1.4	28	4.25	4.28	3.27	3.07

The chart on the following page presents annual "real" interest rates for those years in which the three-year average of inflation was 2.5 per cent or higher. This eliminates deflation distortion as well as periods of relative price stability. All qualifying inflation years, 1793 through 1979, are included, 60 years in all. An additional 45 years of mild inflation, ranging from 0.5 per cent to 2.4 per cent, are included in the appendix to this chapter. But it was felt these data were actually more representative of an economic condition of relative price stability.

The chart shows that the volatility of "real" interest rates in periods of inflation is similar to the volatility in the all encompassing chart on Page 99. There have been 28 years of positive "real" interest inflation environments and 32 years of negative "real" interest. In only eight out of the 60 years the "real" interest rate exceeded 2 per cent, less than 14 per cent of the time. Again in this display, the only period of reasonable consistency appears to be the more recent period through 1977. This display also supports another earlier conclusion. If the theory espousing a continuing, relatively stable level of "real" interest rates is some form of natural law, Moses must have brought it down from the mountain on a stone tablet sometime in the early 1950s.

If the theory espousing a continuing, relatively stable level of "real" interest rates is some form of natural law, Moses must have brought it down from the mountain in the early 1950s.

Taking a closer look, the chart on page 104 recasts the annual "real" interest rate data into specific inflation environments. Four environments were selected with approximately the same number of years falling in each environment. Environment I includes years in which the three-year average of inflation was 7.5

**Real Long-Term Interest Rates
in 2.5% Plus Inflation Years**

(Using 3-Year Centered Average
of CPI as Inflation Proxy)

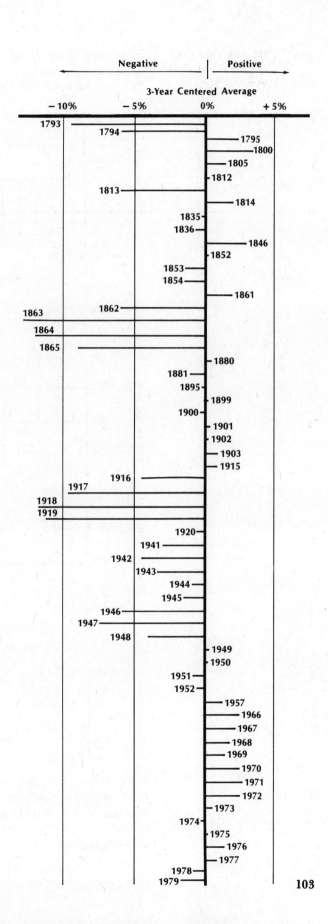

103

Real Long-Term Interest Rate In Inflation Years
(3-Year Centered Average)

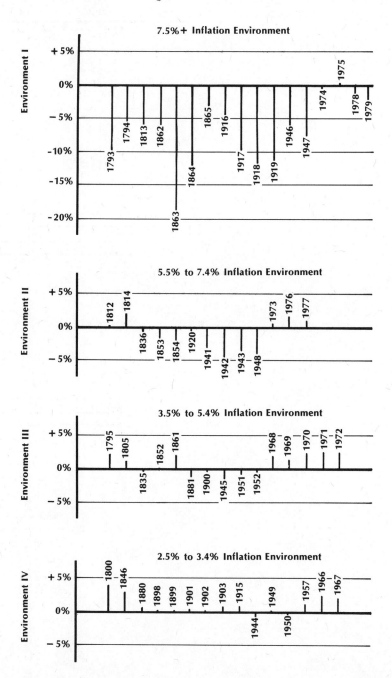

per cent or higher, environment II was the 5.5 per cent to 7.4 per cent range, environment III was 3.5 per cent to 5.4 per cent and environment IV was 2.5 per cent to 3.4 per cent.

Observations

The conclusions are immediately obvious: The higher the inflation rate the less likely a positive "real" rate of interest is to be achieved. Further, the 2 per cent to 3 per cent "real" rate of interest rule of thumb has never prevailed with inflation above 5.5 per cent, though it did come close in 1976. If investors strongly believed that long-term quality bonds are priced in terms of nominal rates, which would return a "real" rate of 2 per cent to 3 per cent plus compensation for anticipated erosion of the dollar through inflation, they had better think again because "it ain't necessarily so," not if a three-year average of past inflation is used as a proxy for future inflation. Even in periods of relatively mild inflation—2.5 per cent to 3.4 per cent,—the "real" interest rate was only 1 per cent or less in 10 of 15 years.

In another chapter we run the same test applying the now more popular five-year average of past inflation as the proxy for anticipated inflation. This works a little better but not much.

B. Moderate Inflation

Inflation Environment	Number of Years	Positive Real Rates		Negative Real Rates			
		2% +	0.1% - 2%	0% - 2%	2.1% - 4%	4.1% - 6.0%	6% +
3.5% - 5.4%	15	4	5	6	0	0	0
2.5% - 3.4%	15	4	10	1	0	0	0
	30	8	15	7	0	0	0

2.5% - 5.4% Inflation

% of years real interest positive 2% or more...............	27%
% of years real interest positive 0.1% to 2%..............	50%
% of years positive real rate..................	77%
% of years real interest 0 to negative 2%.................	23%
% of years real interest negative 2.1% to negative 4%......	0
% of years real interest negative 4.1% to negative 6%......	0
% of years real interest negative 6% or more..............	0
% of years negative real rate..................	23%

2.5% to 5.4% Inflation

Average real interest rate:	0.92%
Median real interest rate:	0.75%

Real Interest Rates on Long-Term Bonds
(3-year centered average inflation)

	Year	Percent Inflation	Nominal Long-Term Rate	Real Rate
Inflation 7.5% + :	1793	15.1	5.48	− 9.62
	1794	11.4	5.90	− 5.50
	1813	12.4	6.30	− 6.10
	1862	11.4	5.52	− 5.88
	1863	23.5	4.77	−18.73
	1864	16.8	4.83	−11.97
	1865	8.5	5.51	− 2.99
	1916	8.5	4.10	− 4.40
	1917	14.1	4.41	− 9.69
	1918	16.6	4.82	−11.78
	1919	16.0	4.84	−11.16
	1946	8.3	2.45	− 5.85
	1947	10.2	2.57	− 7.63
	1974	8.8	8.53	− 0.27
	1975	8.6	8.66	+ 0.06
	1978	9.6	8.80	− 0.80
	1979	11.1	9.65	−1.35
	17 Years		5.72 Avg. Rate	− 6.69 Avg. "Real" Rate
			5.48 Median	− 5.88 Median
Inflation 5.5% - 7.4%:	1812	6.0	5.12	+ 0.12
	1814	5.7	7.64	+ 1.94
	1836	5.8	4.96	− 0.84
	1853	6.6	4.99	− 1.61
	1854	7.0	5.13	− 1.87
	1920	5.9	5.27	− 0.63
	1941	5.5	2.59	− 2.91
	1942	7.2	2.66	− 4.54

Year	Per Cent Inflation	Nominal Long-Term Rate		Real Rate
1943	6.1	2.55		− 3.55
1948	6.9	2.82		− 4.08
1973	6.8	7.36		+ 0.56
1976	7.1	8.59		+ 1.49
1977	7.1	8.20		+ 1.10
13 Years		5.30	Avg. Rate	− 1.14	Avg. "Real" Rate
		5.13	Median	− 0.84	Median

Inflation 3.5% - 5.4%:

Year	Per Cent Inflation	Nominal Long-Term Rate		Real Rate
1795	3.7	6.02		2.32
1805	5.1	6.38		1.28
1835	5.2	4.83		− 0.37
1852	4.9	4.98		0.08
1861	4.5	6.45		1.95
1881	4.8	3.70		− 1.10
1900	3.6	3.31		− 0.29
1945	4.1	2.54		− 1.56
1951	3.7	2.90		− 0.80
1952	3.6	3.03		− 0.57
1968	4.2	6.01		1.81
1969	5.2	6.78		1.58
1970	5.2	7.88		2.68
1971	4.5	7.23		2.73
1972	4.6	7.06		2.46
15 Years		5.27	Avg. Rate	0.81	Avg. "Real" Rate
		6.01	Median	1.28	Median

Inflation 2.5% - 3.4%:

Year	Per Cent Inflation	Nominal Long-Term Rate		Real Rate
1800	3.1	6.94		3.84
1846	2.6	5.50		2.90
1880	3.4	4.02		0.62
1898	3.1	3.26		0.16
1899	3.2	3.24		0.04
1901	2.7	3.28		0.58
1902	3.3	3.34		0.04
1903	2.6	3.55		0.95
1915	3.3	4.18		0.88
1944	3.4	2.54		− 0.86
1949	2.5	2.68		0.18
1950	2.6	2.62		0.02
1957	2.6	3.93		1.33
1966	2.5	5.13		2.63
1967	3.3	5.47		2.17
15 Years		3.98	Avg. Rate	1.03	Avg. "Real" Rate
		3.55	Median	0.62	Median

Inflation 1.5% - 2.4%:

Year	Per Cent Inflation	Nominal Long-Term Rate		Real Rate
1826	1.5	4.56		3.06
1832	2.3	5.00		2.70
1834	2.3	4.87		2.57
1837	2.1	4.95		2.85
1845	2.1	5.16		3.06
1851	1.7	5.08		3.38
1882	2.0	3.62		1.62
1906	2.4	3.65		1.25
1911	2.3	3.93		1.63
1924	1.5	4.51		3.01
1935	2.3	3.44		1.14
1936	2.4	3.11		0.71

	Year	Per Cent Inflation	Nominal Long-Term Rate		Real Rate	
	1940	1.5	2.70		1.20	
	1956	1.6	3.35		1.75	
	1958	2.4	3.81		1.41	
	1959	1.7	4.37		2.67	
	1965	2.0	4.43		2.43	
	17 Years		4.15	**Avg. Rate**	2.14	**Avg. "Real" Rate**
			4.37	**Median**	2.43	**Median**
Inflation 2.5% - 1.4%:	1808	0.6	5.96		5.36	
	1810	1.3	5.82		4.52	
	1830	0.8	4.90		4.10	
	1831	0.8	4.95		4.15	
	1844	0.9	4.85		3.95	
	1850	0.5	5.31		4.81	
	1855	1.4	5.16		3.76	
	1856	0.8	5.10		4.30	
	1887	0.7	3.80		3.10	
	1888	0.7	3.69		2.99	
	1889	0.7	3.51		2.81	
	1904	1.3	3.57		2.27	
	1905	1.2	3.51		2.31	
	1907	1.2	3.92		2.72	
	1910	1.2	3.87		2.67	
	1912	0.8	3.95		3.15	
	1913	1.3	4.14		2.84	
	1925	1.2	4.50		3.30	
	1926	0.5	4.36		3.86	
	1937	0.9	3.12		2.22	
	1938	0.8	2.90		2.10	
	1953	1.1	3.27		2.17	
	1955	0.5	3.10		2.60	
	1960	1.1	4.39		3.29	
	1961	1.3	4.32		3.02	
	1962	1.1	4.32		3.22	
	1963	1.2	4.23		3.03	
	1964	1.4	4.36		2.96	
	28 Years		4.25	**Avg. Rate**	3.27	**Avg. "Real" Rate**
			4.28	**Median**	3.07	**Median**

Chapter 11

Are You Still a Disciple of "Real" Interest Rate Theory?

Which of the following statements are true?

Historically the concept of "real" interest rates:

1. Works better with short-term interest rates than long-term rates.

2. Appears to work very well when a five-year past inflation rate is used in the equation to represent inflationary expectations.

3. Appears to work somewhat better applying the five-year past inflation rate to long-term rates.

Using Five-Year Averages

The preceding analysis employs three-year averages of the Consumer Price Index as a proxy for expected inflation in arriving at "real" interest. In the past this was the common methodology. Our research actually used a three-year *centered* average of inflation (last year, this year and next year). This, if anything, should have improved the correlation because we had the hindsight advantage of including one year of future inflation in establishing the expectation rate.

Many economists have shifted to a five-year average of past inflation as a proxy for predictions.

But common practice has changed since this original research was carried out several years ago. Now many money market economists and analysts have shifted focus from a three-year to a five-year average of past inflation as a proxy for inflationary expectations. This adjustment fits 1974 and 1975 more neatly into the equation. This may be hindsight curve fitting, but to be consistent with the common practice today, our data were rerun using the five-year approach.

The table below shows the results using the five-year approach for different inflation environments. It is quickly evident that the "real" interest rate has been in the 2 per cent to 3 per cent range only when the inflation rate has been less than 2.4 per cent, though it was close when inflation was between 2.5 per cent and 3.4 per cent. In all other inflation environments, the "real" rate was less than 1 per cent, or negative.

Real Interest Rates on Long-Term Bonds
(Five-Year Centered Average of Inflation)

Inflation Environment	Years	Nominal Rate Average	Nominal Rate Median	Real Rate Average	Real Rate Median
9.0%	8	6.20	5.39	− 5.52	− 6.68
7.5 - 8.9	4	6.17	5.82	− 2.46	− 2.73
6.5 - 7.4	5	6.01	7.40	− .85	0.10
5.5 - 6.4	8	4.51	3.70	− 1.37	− 2.01
4.5 - 5.4	8	5.32	5.72	0.42	0.64
3.5 - 4.4	9	4.77	5.16	0.85	0.99
2.5 - 3.4	12	4.98	4.96	1.97	1.99
1.5 - 2.4	24	4.29	4.01	2.36	1.97
0.5 - 1.4	22	4.20	4.05	3.16	3.07

But let's take a closer look. The first chart that follows presents the "real" interest rate for all years where inflation averages were at 2.5 per cent and above. As might be expected, the five-year approach smooths things out somewhat, and statistically knocks six years out of the study base.

Some Observations

The five-year approach uncovers a period of "real" interest rate inconsistency not observed in the three-year approach.

The five-year approach also uncovers a period of "real" interest rate consistency that was not observable using the three-year approach. This is found in the inflation years from 1813 to 1857. However, in this entire period, while 51 per cent of the years recorded positive "real" rates of interest, only 21 per cent had "real" rates of 2 per cent or higher.

Real Long-Term Interest Rates
In Inflation Years

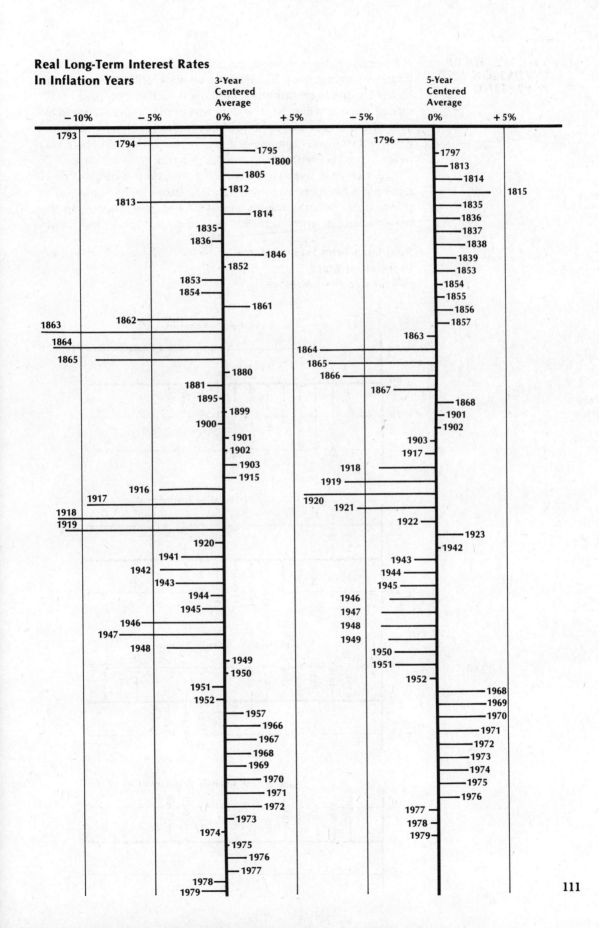

111

Even when the five-year approach is broken down into the four infation environments (chart below), it is still clear that the higher the inflation rate the less likely it is that a positive "real" rate of interest will exist. The data reveal that a "real" rate in excess of 2 per cent was achieved only once (1974) in the 25 years when inflation was running at 5.5 per cent or higher. There was never a positive real rate at the 7.5 per cent inflation level.

The five-year approach also confirms that negative "real" rates have been common throughout history and at times quite substantial, being as low as minus 19 per cent. Indeed, in the years when inflation was 5.5 per cent or higher, the "real"

**Real Long-Term Interest Rates
in Inflation Years**
(5-Year Centered Average)

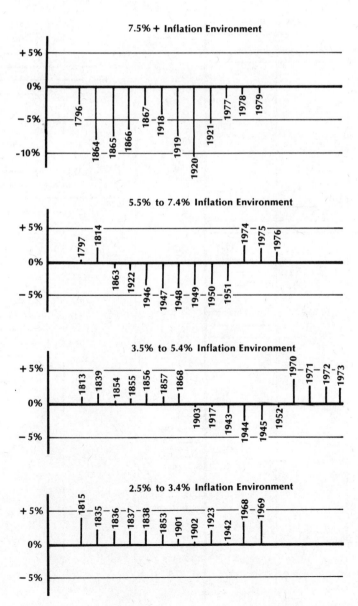

interest rate was positive in only 20 per cent of the years. Obviously, then, the "real" rate was negative for 80 per cent of the years when inflation ran above 5.5 per cent.

Real Interest Rates in Higher Inflation Environments
(Five-Year Centered Average of Inflation)

Inflation Environment	Number of Years	Positive Real Rates		Negative Real Rates			
		2% +	0.1% - 2% +	0% - 2%	2.1% -4%	4.1% - 6.0%	6% +
7.5% +	12	0	0	3	3	1	5
5.5% -7.4%	13	1	4	2	6	0	0
	25	1	4	5	9	1	5

5.5% + Inflation

% of years real interest positive 2% or more.............. 4%
% of years real interest positive 0.1% to 2%.............. 16

     % of years positive real rate.................. 20%

% of years real interest 0 to negative 2%................. 20%
% of years real interest negative 2.1% to negative 4%...... 36%
% of years real interest negative 4.1% to negative 6%...... 4%
% of years real interest negative 6% or more.............. 20%

     % of years negative real rate................ 80%

5.5% + Inflation

Average real interest rate: − 2.77%
Median real interest rate: − 3.00%

Things look better when we consider the years of mild inflation, those where the inflation rate was between 2.5 per cent and 5.4 per cent. In these instances the "real" interest rate was 2 per cent or more in 34 per cent of the years and was positive for a total of 79 per cent of the years. The average "real" interest rate for these years was 1.19 per cent and the median was 1.48 per cent, compared to minus 2.77 per cent and minus 3.00 per cent for the higher inflation years. Still, looking at all 54 years in which inflation exceeded 2.5 per cent average real interest rate was minus 0.59 per cent and the median was only + 0.48 per cent. The tables at the end of this chapter provide a breakdown of inflation by year for each inflationary environment.

The interest rate looks better when we consider the years of mild inflation.

Real Interest Rates in Moderate Inflation Environments
(Five-Year Centered Average of Inflation)

Inflation Environment	Number of Years	Positive Real Rates		Negative Real Rates			
		2% +	0.1% - 2% +	0% - 2%	2.1% - 4%	4.1% - 6.0%	6% +
3.5% - 5.4%	17	4	7	4	2	0	0
2.5% - 3.4%	12	6	6	0	0	0	0
	29	19	13	4	2	0	0

2.5% to 5.4% Inflation

% of years real interest positive 2% or more.............. 34%
% of years real interest positive 0.1% to 2%.............. 45

     % of years positive real rate.................. 79%

2.5% to 5.4% Inflation (contin.)

% of years real interest 0 to negative 2%. 14%
% of years real interest negative 2.1% to negative 4%. 7
% of years real interest negative 4.1% to negative 6%. 0
% of years real interest negative 6% or more. 0
                                                                  _____
        % of years negative real rate. 21%

2.5% - 5.4% Inflation

Average real interest rate: +1.19%
Median real interest rate: +0.50%

TOTAL Inflation 2.5% or More (54 Years):
       Average   =   −0.59
       Median   =   +0.48

Now, with the facts and statistics in hand, let us go back to the market letter writer quoted in Chapter 10. Again, we are not attacking this particular writer, but his thinking is representative of the economic and monetary consensus that exists today.

> **Quote:** "Investors are not particularly concerned with each monthly jiggle in the inflation rate, but instead seek some indications of the permanent or underlying inflation rate, as perhaps evidenced by price movements measured over five-year periods. With this process in mind current bond yields make much more sense and highlight the steady increase in inflation measured over five-year periods."

A cursory examination shows the futility of using a five-year moving average of past inflation to project future inflation.

Our long-term work, using a five-year moving average of past inflation to project future inflation, has a very poor batting average over the years. The chart in this chapter presents a five-year average of past inflation as well as annual rates going back 187 years. A cursory examination will show the futility of this approach except for the last decade or so.

> **Quote:** "From 1969 to 1974 consumer prices ranged between 4 percent and 5.5 percent, and accordingly government bond rates generally ranged between 6 percent and 7.5 percent. In 1974, however, 5-year price movements jumped to a 6 percent to 7 percent range, and bond rates rose well above 8 percent. The 5-year price benchmark hovered around 6.5 percent during 1975 and 1976, and although yields eased temporarily to a quarterly average rate around 7.5 percent, it was clear that expectations of abnormally high inflation were firmly and correctly embedded in market thinking."

While not being familiar with this particular commentator's approach in the early 1970s, this was the period when many experts abandoned the three-year average of inflation and moved to a five-year average because it "fit" better.

> **Quote:** "By late 1976 the five-year underlying inflation rate began to rise again, passing through 7 per cent on its way to 8 per cent by the fall

quarter of 1978. With consumer prices measured over 20 quarter periods generally bumping around 7.5 per cent over the past two years, it is not surprising that bond yields have jumped from 7.5 per cent in late 1976 to nearly 9 per cent in late 1978. Applying our rule of thumb: 7.5 per cent underlying (expected) inflation plus 2 per cent real return equals 9.5 per cent money rate on government bonds, and recent market developments are moving in a fashion consistent with the model's predicted outcome."

There is that old rule of thumb again, that natural law that seems to have gone into effect in 1954, but was nonexistent prior to that time. And, even the thumb's effectiveness since 1954 depends on what kind of average of past inflation was being used to approximate the inflation expectation.

Traditional rules of thumb depend on what kind of average of past inflation is used to approximate the inflation expectation.

Here is one of those "long-term" charts again, tracking all the way back to the beginning of economic history, 1954. Inflation is

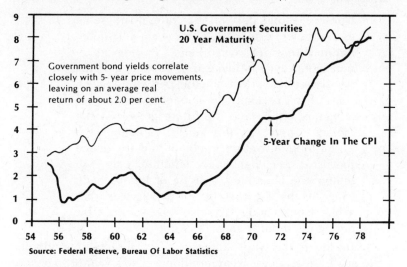

Source: Federal Reserve, Bureau Of Labor Statistics

portrayed with a five-year annual rate of change in the CPI, but even with this new modification, the "rule of thumb" 2 per cent difference between the two lines (the real rate) has not been maintained very well in recent years.

Quote: "Two problems remain. First, as mentioned earlier, real rates are not always stable. In fact, a study of empirical evidence suggests that when rising inflation is correctly anticipated, the money rate of interest rises by less than the rise in inflation, thus allowing for only a partial adjustment for real rates."

Hey, wait a minute. At one point, as noted in Chapter 10, it was said that "over long periods of time the real interest rate tends toward stability," although later this was hedged as being not always correct. Then there is that statement about "when rising inflation is correctly anticipated." Our earlier survey of experts' predictions on this shows consistent errors of over 1.5 per cent even one year out, more in recent years. Just who are these people who have been correctly anticipating even sometimes? Now what's this about "partial adjustment for real rates?"

> **Quote:** "This occurs in part because the demand for real money balances declines during periods of hyperinflation, as can be seen by a look at real bond rates since 1974, averaging only around 1 per cent."

Have real bond rates averaged 1 per cent since 1974? What has happened to the 2 per cent "rule of thumb"? For four years, this hasn't been working quite like it is supposed to, even with the revised application of a five-year moving average of inflation instead of the three-year average.

Perhaps in the next few years, if interest rates do not move "in a fashion consistent with the model's predicted outcome," some enterprising analyst will come up with a new formula that in hindsight fits, say, a five-year front-end weighted average of past inflation.

> **Quote:** "Second, past inflation rates do not serve as a sufficient explanation for the anticipated inflation rate a year or so hence. Price expectations are heavily influenced by economic policy decisions made in Washington, particularly decisions that are likely to impact the thrust of monetary policy and the future growth of the money supply. In this regard, although the Carter Administration is committed to reduce the Fiscal Year 1980 budget deficit to "only" $30 billion, the liberal-left uprising of the Kennedy wing of the Democratic Party suggests that White House budget resolve may soften a bit during the months ahead."

So the key to this whole approach from a practical standpoint is to qualitatively guess what inflation will be a year or so hence. I thought this was so simple. Now it comes down to evaluating economic policy decisions, monetary policy, future money supply growth and politics. Why didn't you say so in the first place?

"Real" Interest and Short-Term Rates

The concept of "real" interest rates usually is applied to long-term interest rates. Data relating to short-term rates (average annual rates for four to six-month prime commercial paper or equivalent) dating back to 1831 have been accumulated and are presented elsewhere in this book. Therefore it was decided to compare the short-term interest rates with the rate of inflation.

Comparing apples with apples, the annual average short-term rate was run against the annual inflation rate. Smoothing the inflation rate across several years is not appropriate when the credit instrument has a life of six months or less.

The chart that follows presents the real rate of interest for 53 inflation years (2.5 per cent or more) from 1831 to date. The next

In the next few years, if interest rates do not follow the model, some enterprising analyst will come up with a new formula.

Although short-term interest rates cannot be smoothed across several years, they can be compared with the rate of inflation.

Real Short-Term Interest Rates
in Inflation Years

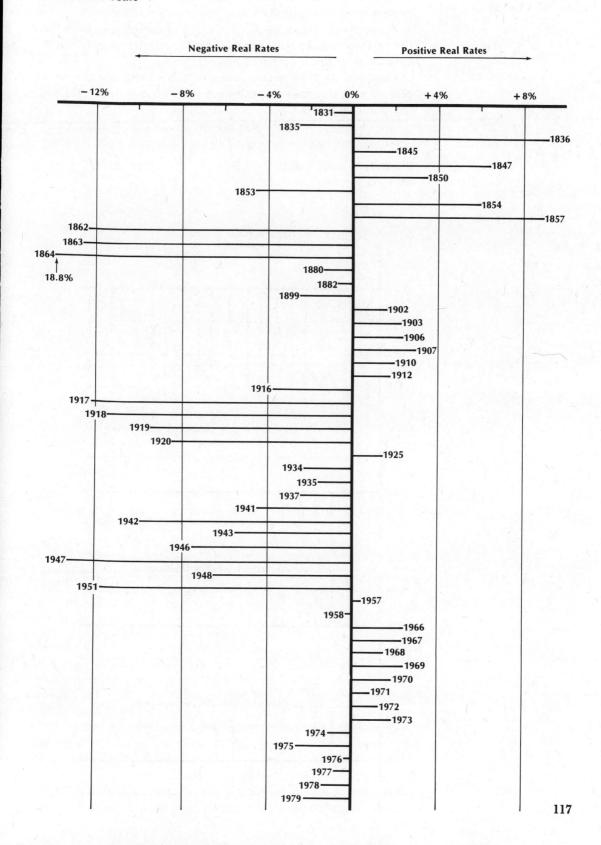

117

chart breaks the same data down in the same four inflation environments used earlier, but this time it is based on existing annual rates of inflation.

As can be seen from the first chart, 22 of the inflation years (42 per cent) recorded positive "real" short-term interest rates, but in only 13 years did it exceed 2 per cent.

The 1966 to 1973 period and the early 1900s are the only periods with a consistent positive real return, but since 1973 the real short-term rate has become negative.

Thus, trying to analyze short-term rates using the concept of "real" return appears to be a frustrating proposition. Inflation

**Short Term Real Rates
by Inflation Environment**

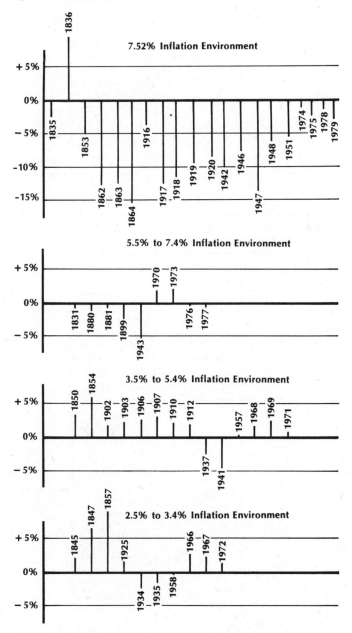

appears to have even less influence on short rates than on long rates. Business cycle considerations are far more important, and the concept of "real" interest rates has little obvious application in short-term money market investing.

The breakdown of "real" short-term rates by inflation environment (on the preceding chart and in the table below) demonstrates that short rates very rarely match inflation rates in inflation environments of 5.5 per cent or more. This occurred in only three of 29 years recorded. In only one year did the "real" rate of interest rise to more than 2 per cent.

Short-term rates very rarely match inflation rates in inflation environments of 5.5 per cent or more.

Short-Term Annual Real Interest Rates in Higher Inflation Environments

Inflation Environment	Number of Years	Positive Real Rates		Negative Real Rates			
		2% +	0.1% - 2% +	0% - 2%	2.1% - 4%	4.1% - 6.0%	6% +
7.5% +	20	1	0	2	3	2	11
5.5% - 7.4%	9	0	2	5	1	1	0
	29	1	2	7	4	3	11

5.5% + Inflation

% of years real interest positive 2% or more..............	3%
% of years real interest positive 0.1% to 2%..............	7
% of years positive real rate.................	10%
% of years real interest 0 to negative 2%..................	24%
% of years real interest negative 2.1% to negative 4%......	17
% of years real interest negative 4.1% to negative 6%......	10
% of years real interest negative 6% or more..............	39
% of years negative real rate.................	90%

5.5% + Inflation

Average real interest rate:	− 5.37%
Median real interest rate:	− 4.26%

Short-Term Annual Real Interest Rates in Moderate Inflation Environments

Inflation Environment	Number of Years	Positive Real Rates		Negative Real Rates			
		2% +	0.1% - 2% +	0% - 2%	2.1% - 4%	4.1% - 6.0%	6% +
3.5% - 5.4%	14	7	5	0	1	1	0
2.5% - 3.4%	10	5	2	2	1	0	0
	24	12	7	2	2	1	0

2.5% - 5.4% Inflation

% of years real interest positive 2% or more..............	50%
% of years real interest positive 0.1% to 2%..............	29
% of years positive real rate.................	79%
% of years real interest 0 to negative 2%..................	8%
% of years real interest negative 2.1% to negative 4%......	8
% of years real interest negative 4.1% to negative 6%......	4
% of years real interest negative 6% or more..............	0
% of years negative real rate.................	21%

Average real interest rate:	+ 1.76%
Median real interest rate:	+ 2.01%

TOTAL Inflation 2.5% or More (53 Years):

Average	=	− 2.14
Median	=	− 0.89

In years when inflation was more than 5.5 per cent, the average real rate of interest was minus 5.37 per cent. The median rate was minus 4.26 per cent. In years when inflation was between 2.5 per cent and 5.4 per cent, the average "real" interest rate was 1.76 per cent and the median "real" rate was 2.01 per cent. For all years when inflation was in excess of 2.5 per cent, the average "real" rate of interest was minus 2.14 per cent and the median rate was minus 0.89 per cent.

In summary, there seems to be little longer term evidence supporting or even suggesting the conclusion that market or nominal rates of interest (long or short term) are historically intrinsically comprised of two components: the real rate of interest and a quantifiable expected rate of inflation.

The relative stability of "real" interest rates from the mid-1950s through 1969 appears to be a rarity and should not be relied upon in future years.

Further, the relative stability of "real" interest from the mid-1950s through 1969 appears to be a rarity and should not be relied upon in future years.

Many of today's authorities on interest rates can be validly criticized for their dogmatic attitudes, their failure to engage in historic supportive research and their propensity to juggle the facts and time frames to support their conclusions.

In periods of higher inflation, the currently popular quantitative formulas used to justify and explain existing nominal rates have rarely worked at all.

The entire concept of an intrinsic "real" rate of interest has been almost blindly accepted by most investors, economists and now politicians as economic fact. Few have bothered to critically examine or even question the validity of this concept. The experts are being taken at face value, just as was the case with the "stocks are an inflation hedge" doctrine.

Even though the concept of an intrinsic "real" interest rate appears to be theory and not fact, it will continue to be an important consideration in long-term fixed-income markets.

Even though the concept of an intrinsic "real" rate appears to be theory and not fact, it will continue to be an important consideration in the long-term fixed-income markets for years to come. If enough people, especially those who control the investment of massive amounts of capital, believe this is an economic truism, they will act accordingly. When sailors thought the world was flat, they sailed as if it was.

The past chapters are not intended to be a definitive, landmark rebuttal of the "real" rate theory. Rather, we hope the discussion may stimulate further sophisticated critical analysis of the concept. While bits and pieces of the study may be validly attacked, it is still clear that no undisputable evidence exists to substantiate the existence of an intrinsic "real" rate of interest. And for literally billions of dollars to be invested annually based on the supposed existence of such a rate, based on the shaky evidence that does exist, borders on the incredible.

It is equally amazing that the academicians in this nation continue to teach this concept in the economics departments and business schools, without so much as a qualification. It's the gospel, to be accepted without question. John Maynard Keynes was once quoted as saying "history is for undergraduates." Maybe that's the problem.

To investors, pension officers, corporations and professional portfolio managers we close with this warning, combining two well worn quotes: "Ignorance may well be bliss," but keep in mind, "it ain't necessarily so." In future years the "real" rate of interest may go the way of other once mighty investment myths.

Real Interest Rates on Long-Term Bonds
(Five-Year Centered Average of Inflation)

	Year	Per Cent Inflation	Nominal Long-Term Rate		Real Rate	
Inflation 9.0% +	1864	12.8%	4.83		− 7.97	
	1865	13.2	5.51		− 7.69	
	1866	12.2	5.50		− 6.70	
	1919	11.5	4.84		− 6.66	
	1920	14.6	5.27		− 9.33	
	1921	10.4	5.16		− 5.24	
	1978	9.1	8.80		− 0.30	
	1979	9.4	9.65		− 0.25	
	8 Years		+ 5.28	Avg. Yld.	− 5.52	Avg. "Real" Rate
			+ 5.21	Median	− 6.68	Median
Inflation 7.5% to 8.4%	1796	8.8	6.30		− 2.50	
	1918	8.7	4.82		− 3.88	
	1867	8.3	5.34		− 2.96	
	1977	7.7	8.20		− 0.50	
	4 Years		+ 6.17	Avg. Yld.	− 2.46	Avg. "Real" Rate
			+ 5.82	Median	− 2.73	Median
Inflation 6.5% to 7.4%	1797	7.3	7.40		+ 0.10	
	1947	6.5	2.57		− 3.93	
	1948	6.8	2.82		− 3.98	
	1975	6.7	8.66		+ 1.98	
	1976	7.0	8.59		+ 1.59	
	5 Years		+ 6.01	Avg. Yld.	− 0.85	Avg. "Real" Rate
			+ 7.40	Median	+ 0.10	Median
Inflation 5.5% to 6.4%	1814	5.7	7.64		+ 1.94	
	1863	5.7	4.77		− 0.93	
	1922	5.5	4.49		− 1.01	
	1946	5.8	2.45		− 3.35	
	1949	6.3	2.68		− 3.62	
	1950	6.0	2.62		− 3.38	
	1951	5.9	2.90		− 3.00	
	1974	6.1	8.53		+ 2.43	
	8 Years		+ 4.51	Avg. Yld.	− 1.37	Avg. "Real" Rate
			+ 3.70	Median	− 2.01	Median
Inflation 4.5% to 5.4%	1813	5.4%	6.30		+ 0.90	
	1854	4.8	5.13		+ 0.38	
	1917	5.1	4.41		− 0.69	
	1944	4.8	2.54		− 2.26	
	1945	5.1	2.54		− 2.56	
	1971	4.5	7.23		+ 2.73	
	1972	4.6	7.06		+ 2.46	
	1973	5.0	7.36		+ 2.36	
	8 Years		+ 5.32	Avg. Yld.	+ 0.42	Avg. "Real" Rate
			+ 5.72	Median	+ 0.64	Median

	Year	Per Cent Inflation	Nominal Long-Term Rate		Real Rate	
Inflation 3.5% to 4.4%	1839	3.5	5.21		+ 1.71	
	1855	4.3	5.16		+ 0.86	
	1856	3.9	5.10		+ 1.70	
	1857	4.2	5.19		+ 0.99	
	1868	3.8	5.28		+ 1.48	
	1903	3.7	3.55		− 0.15	
	1943	4.2	2.55		− 1.65	
	1952	3.5	3.03		− 0.47	
	1970	4.2	7.08		+ 3.68	
	9 Years		+ 4.77	Avg. Yld.	+ 0.42	Avg. "Real" Rate
			+ 5.16	Median	+ 0.99	Median
Inflation 2.5% to 3.4%	1815	3.2	7.30		+ 4.10	
	1835	2.7	4.83		+ 2.13	
	1836	3.1	4.96		+ 1.86	
	1837	3.0	4.95		+ 1.95	
	1838	2.7	5.01		+ 2.31	
	1853	3.4	4.99		+ 1.59	
	1901	2.7	3.28		+ 0.58	
	1902	3.1	3.34		+ 0.24	
	1923	2.5	4.51		+ 2.01	
	1942	2.6	2.66		+ 0.06	
	1968	2.6	6.01		+ 3.41	
	1969	3.4	6.78		+ 3.38	
	12 Years		+ 4.98	Avg. Yld.	+ 1.97	Avg. "Real" Rate
			+ 4.96	Median	+ 1.99	Median
Inflation 1.5% to 2.4%	1805	1.8	6.38		+ 4.58	
	1807	2.0	6.08		+ 4.08	
	1809	1.8	5.85		+ 4.05	
	1812	1.8	6.12		+ 4.32	
	1847	1.5	5.77		+ 4.27	
	1883	2.0	3.63		+ 1.63	
	1899	1.8	3.24		+ 1.44	
	1900	2.2	3.31		+ 1.11	
	1904	2.4	3.57		+ 1.17	
	1905	2.0	3.51		+ 1.51	
	1906	2.3	3.65		+ 1.35	
	1907	2.2	3.92		+ 1.72	
	1914	1.5	4.11		+ 2.61	
	1916	2.4	4.10		+ 1.70	
	1938	1.7	2.90		+ 1.20	
	1953	2.1	3.27		+ 1.17	
	1954	2.4	2.97		+ 0.57	
	1955	2.2	3.10		+ 0.90	
	1958	1.6	3.81		+ 2.21	
	1959	1.6	4.37		+ 2.77	
	1960	1.9	4.39		+ 2.39	
	1962	1.5	4.32		+ 2.82	
	1966	1.6	5.13		+ 3.53	
	1967	2.0	5.47		+ 3.47	
	24 Years		+ 4.29	Avg. Yld.	+ 2.36	Avg. "Real" Rate
			+ 4.01	Median	+ 1.97	Median

	Year	Per Cent Inflation	Nominal Long-Term Rate		Real Rate
Inflation 0.5% to 1.4%	1808	1.2%	5.96		+ 4.76
	1816	1.2	7.25		+ 6.05
	1833	0.5	4.87		+ 4.37
	1848	0.8	5.71		+ 4.91
	1884	1.3	3.62		+ 2.32
	1908	0.7	3.90		+ 3.20
	1909	0.7	3.78		+ 3.08
	1910	1.4	3.87		+ 2.47
	1911	0.7	3.93		+ 3.23
	1912	0.7	3.95		+ 3.25
	1913	1.2	4.14		+ 2.94
	1915	1.0	4.18		+ 3.18
	1927	0.7	4.18		+ 3.48
	1937	1.0	3.12		+ 2.12
	1939	0.7	2.77		+ 2.07
	1941	1.2	2.59		+ 1.39
	1956	0.9	3.35		+ 2.45
	1957	1.2	3.93		+ 2.73
	1960	2.0	4.39		+ 2.39
	1963	1.2	4.23		+ 3.03
	1964	1.3	4.36		+ 3.06
	1965	1.3	4.43		+ 3.13
22 Years			+ 4.20	Avg. Yld.	+ 3.16 Avg. "Real" Rate
			+ 4.05	Median	+ 3.07 Median

Short-Term Real Rates in Inflation Years

	Year	Per Cent Inflation	Interest Rate	Real Rate
Inflation 7.5% +	1835	9.5%	7.00	− 2.50
	1836	8.6	18.00	+ 9.30
	1853	15.0	10.25	− 4.75
	1862	17.8	5.32	− 12.48
	1863	18.4	5.65	− 12.85
	1864	35.2	7.36	− 27.84
	1916	7.6	3.84	− 3.76
	1917	17.4	5.07	− 12.33
	1918	17.5	6.02	− 11.48
	1919	14.9	5.37	− 9.53
	1920	15.8	7.50	− 8.30
	1942	10.7	0.66	− 10.04
	1946	8.5	0.81	− 7.69
	1947	14.4	1.03	− 13.37
	1948	7.8	1.44	− 6.36
	1951	7.9	2.16	− 5.74
	1974	11.0	9.87	− 1.13
	1975	9.1	6.33	− 2.77
	1978	9.0	7.50	− 1.50
	1979	13.4	11.11	− 2.29
20 Years				− 7.37 Average
				− 7.03 Median

	Year	Per Cent Inflation	Interest Rate	Real Rate	
Inflation 5.5% to 7.40%	1831	7.0	6.12	− 0.88	
	1880	6.5	5.23	− 1.27	
	1881	6.1	5.36	− 0.74	
	1899	6.7	4.15	− 2.55	
	1943	6.2	0.69	− 5.51	
	1970	5.9	7.72	+ 1.82	
	1973	6.2	8.15	+ 1.95	
	1976	5.7	5.35	− 0.35	
	1977	6.5	5.60	− 0.09	
	9 Years			− 0.94	Average
				− 0.88	Median
Inflation 3.5% to 5.4%	1850	4.7	8.04	+ 3.34	
	1854	4.4	10.37	+ 5.97	
	1902	4.0	5.81	+ 1.81	
	1903	3.9	6.16	+ 2.26	
	1906	3.7	6.26	+ 2.55	
	1907	3.6	6.66	+ 3.06	
	1910	3.6	5.72	+ 2.12	
	1912	3.5	5.41	+ 1.91	
	1937	3.6	0.94	− 2.66	
	1941	5.0	0.54	− 4.46	
	1957	3.6	3.81	+ 0.21	
	1968	4.2	5.90	+ 1.70	
	1969	5.4	7.83	+ 2.43	
	1971	4.3	5.11	+ 0.81	
	14 Years			+ 1.50	Average
				+ 2.02	Median
Inflation 2.5% to 3.4%	1845	2.6	4.71	+ 2.11	
	1847	3.0	9.59	+ 6.59	
	1857	2.5	11.56	+ 9.06	
	1925	2.5	4.02	+ 1.52	
	1934	3.4	1.02	− 2.38	
	1935	2.5	0.76	− 1.74	
	1958	2.7	2.46	− 0.24	
	1966	2.9	5.55	+ 2.65	
	1967	2.9	5.10	+ 2.20	
	1972	3.3	4.69	+ 1.39	
	10 Years			+ 2.12	Average
				+ 1.82	Median

Chapter 12

Productivity and Inflation

Which of the following statements are true?

1. U.S. productivity growth may not be as poor as the statistics indicate.

2. Productivity tends to improve in the late stages of business expansion.

3. From 1970 to 1977, Italy had a better record of productivity growth than Japan.

4. One of the most significant reasons underlying the lagging U.S. productivity growth is the great influx of women and younger workers into the labor force.

5. The banking and insurance industries have enviable records of productivity improvement.

Previous chapters have stated the problem: Inflation is bad for the economy, and it is bad for the investor. The stock market, historically, has been a poor hedge against inflation, especially higher levels of inflation such as we have experienced in the past several years. Further, one cannot look to "real" interest rates on fixed-income investments for protection against inflation. As we have shown, there is no such thing as an immutable "real" rate of interest. The "real" rate has been negative far too often to be relied upon for protection. What then is an investor to do in this environment? Where lies a possible solution?

At least part of the solution to the economy's inflation problem and the investor's inflation problem lies in increased productivity. Productivity improvement can go a long way in offsetting the impact of the government policies and the external forces which have infected the economy with the virus of inflation, but it cannot eradicate the virus by itself.

Similarly, productivity, as we will show, may well be the watchword for the investor who wishes to at least protect himself or herself in an inflationary environment. Almost every development in an economy favorably affects someone. The trick is to identify who the problems will favor, and productivity is the key.

Part of the solution to the economy's inflation problem and the investor's inflation problem lies in increased productivity.

Defining Productivity

In recent years, economists, politicians and corporate executives have become increasingly aware of the link between productivity and inflation. The widening gap between workers' pay and workers' output is felt by many to be a significant structural cause of today's inflation. The commonly used definition of productivity is output per man hour, although there are also measures of energy productivity and capital productivity.

Simply put, if a person on an assembly line today is turning out 110 bleeps in an eight hour shift, compared to 100 last year, his or her productivity has increased 10 per cent. If a typist in a typing service now produces an average of 55 letters a day compared to 50 last year, his or her productivity has also increased 10 per cent.

Now, if the bleep maker or the typist gets a 10 per cent pay increase, but also increases output by 10 per cent there is no inflationary effect, theoretically. The labor cost per unit of output remains the same. However, if output increases fall short of wage increases, there is trouble. Now perhaps management can reduce other nonlabor costs of doing business which would offset the higher cost of labor and would allow overall out-the-door cost per bleep or per letter to remain the same. Conceivably management might absorb these higher labor costs per unit, reducing profits. But because management and investors usually are not too keen about this alternative, an attempt is made to raise prices, compensating for the increased costs. Sometimes, if the competition is intense or if users find cheaper substitutes, the price increases don't stick, but management can be expected to give it the old college try. This then is cost-push inflation. If pro-

If output increases fall short of wage increases, there is trouble.

ductivity gains do not match wage increases, it's typically bad news on the inflation front.

In 1978, productivity for all workers in the U.S. rose about 1 per cent, while wages increased about 10 per cent. Theoretically, for management to maintain the status quo on margins, and if nonlabor costs also increased 10 per cent, the price of the goods or services sold also would have to rise 9 per cent to 10 per cent. Labor costs now approximate two-thirds of production costs in the U.S., so even if nonlabor costs do not increase at all, prices on manufactured goods would have to increase 6 per cent to 7 per cent to maintain the status quo.

The common statistics concerning productivity per man hour, overall and by industry, are not as precise as they might seem. The calculations are not based on the actual units produced per worker per hour. While an intense study at an individual plant or production line may get down to this, it is not feasible in the broader measurements. Instead, the broader productivity measures are arrived at by dividing total sales (adjusted by some approximation of inflation) by man hours worked. If the approximation of price increases for a particular industry or the aggregate is not valid, the inflation adjustment will be wrong and so will the productivity calculation.

> Broad productivity measures are arrived at by dividing total sales by man hours worked.

If as some critics say, the inflation indices have been consistently overstating inflation by 1 per cent or 2 per cent per year (more in 1979), productivity would in turn be understated by 1 per cent or 2 per cent per year. These potential inflation price index flaws are dealt with elsewhere in this book, but keep this in mind when reading this and the following chapter. Productivity gains are getting smaller, there is little doubt about that, but the situation may not be quite as horrible as the statistics and data seem to indicate.

Nevertheless, no matter what flaws are present, wages in the U.S. and most other countries have been increasing in the last decade at a much faster rate than output per hour. Now, especially because other nonlabor manufacturing costs such as government regulation, electricity, fuel and raw materials are rising as fast as or faster than labor costs, the manufacturer or service provider is under even more intense pressure to raise prices. This, of course, means the actual cost of living goes up for the consumer workers, causing the workers to seek even greater increases in wages just to "hold their own." One of the routes off this ascending spiral staircase of inflation is to somehow increase output per man hour, pulling it even with, or even ahead of, the inflation rate. Clearly then, at least one of the keys to resolving the U.S. inflation dilemma is improving productivity.

The Big Productivity Slide

Lagging productivity growth is one of this nation's most urgent and challenging economic problems. The rate of productivity growth in the U.S. during the last decade has slowed alarmingly. By our calculations, factoring in 1979, the five-year average of productivity gains is now only 1 per cent per year for the non-

> The rate of productivity growth in the U.S. during the last decade has slowed alarmingly.

farm business sector. Inflation, during the same period, is running at 8 per cent plus per year. This is shown in the chart below. As can be seen, productivity gains have declined steadily from better than 3.5 per cent per year in the mid-1960s to about 1 per cent. The data for 1979, not included on this chart, have taken the line down again.

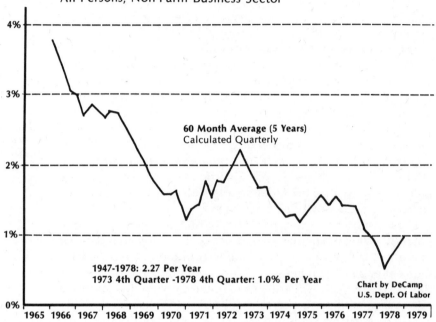

Recent Productivity Trends
All Persons, Non-Farm Business Sector

If we analyze the quarter to quarter changes in productivity from 1968 through 1979, as reported by the U.S. Department of Labor, we find that in 22 of the last 48 quarters (46 per cent) no productivity gains were recorded. And, in 17 of these quarters (35 per cent) productivity actually declined significantly. This is shown in the bar graph on the next page. Productivity declined in all four quarters of 1979.

It's true that productivity typically declines in economic recessions and often backs off in the very late stages of an expansion. But it is most distressing to see deteriorating productivity coming in the mild stages of an economic recovery, as it has been doing in this last cycle.

The U.S.: At the Bottom of the List

There is another side to this slow rate of productivity growth. If other countries have more rapid productivity growth, their industrial sector becomes more competitive relative to ours. During the last decade, the U.S. is tied for last place among the industrial nations in productivity gains. It shares last place with Britain, which is so often maligned as the prime example of a nation with antiquated plants, bureaucratic burdens and unmotivated work forces. The next graph shows the rankings. Belgium is on

The U.S. is tied for last place among industrial nations in productivity gains.

Eleven-Year Productivity Record: 1968-1978

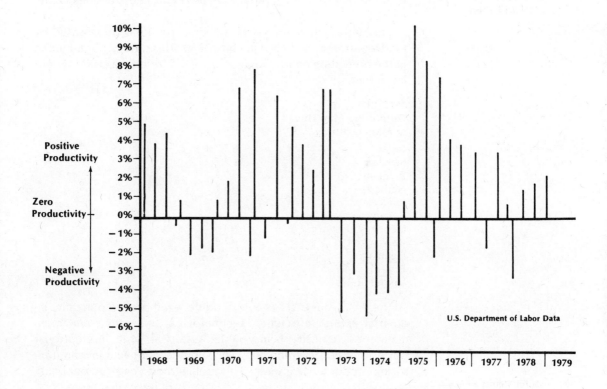

Positive Productivity

Zero Productivity

Negative Productivity

U.S. Department of Labor Data

1968 | 1969 | 1970 | 1971 | 1972 | 1973 | 1974 | 1975 | 1976 | 1977 | 1978 | 1979

International Productivity Comparisons
(Output Per Hour In Manufacturing)
1967-1977

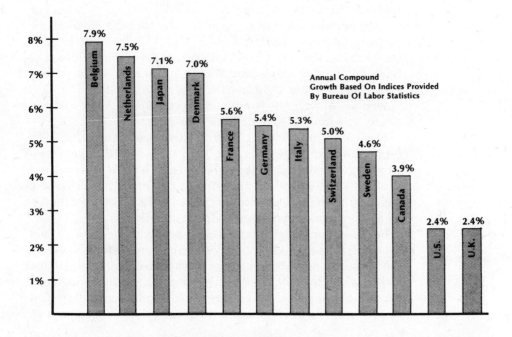

Annual Compound
Growth Based On Indices Provided
By Bureau Of Labor Statistics

Belgium 7.9%
Netherlands 7.5%
Japan 7.1%
Denmark 7.0%
France 5.6%
Germany 5.4%
Italy 5.3%
Switzerland 5.0%
Sweden 4.6%
Canada 3.9%
U.S. 2.4%
U.K. 2.4%

top with a 7.9 per cent rate of productivity gain, followed by Holland (7.5 per cent), Japan (7.1 per cent) and Denmark (7 per cent).

The table below shows the rankings for 1978, as released by the Department of Labor in early 1980. This data is not included in the preceding chart. Obviously the U.S. relative position is not improving.

1977-1978
Output Per Man Hour
In Manufacturing

Japan	+ 7.9%
Sweden	+ 5.7
Belgium	+ 5.7
Netherlands	+ 5.1
France	+ 4.9
Canada	+ 4.7
Germany	+ 3.6
Italy	+ 2.9
Denmark	+ 1.9
Britain	+ 1.8
United States	+ 0.6

The U.S., once the world's prime example of dynamic industrial growth efficiency, technological innovation and management superiority, is in trouble. Almost all of its international trade competitors stand head and shoulders above it in manufacturing productivity growth. This means their costs are declining relative to those of U.S. industry. They are becoming more competitive on world markets relative to the U.S. and their products are becoming more competitive even in the U.S.

The costs for almost all U.S. trade competitors on the international scene are declining relative to U.S. industry.

Industry by Industry

If we examine U.S. productivity gains for 15 manufacturing industries between 1960-1974 (the most recent data available) and compare them with the gains in those industries made by our major competitors (Germany, Japan and the United Kingdom), the problem becomes startlingly clear. The U.S. ranks last in 12 of the 15 categories and second to last in the remaining three. The table on the next page provides the grisly details. In not one category does the U.S. lead in productivity gains. The only categories in which it is not last are textiles, lumber and furniture, and fabricated metal products.

This saga of the slide in U.S. productivity gains should not be a revelation to most readers, but its full extent and implications must be recognized if it is to be reversed. If it is not reversed, it is likely this nation will be cursed with continued high inflation, high unemployment, a cascading dollar, reduced corporate profits and uncompetitive American products.

If the U.S. continues to lag in productivity gains, it will become steadily less competitive in world markets.

If the nation continues to lag in productivity gains, it will become steadily less competitive in world markets and even in the domestic market. The nation's balance-of-payments deficit will grow and the dollar will decline in foreign exchange markets, causing our imported necessities, such as oil, to cost more and thereby pushing inflation up further. Not only will continued in-

	United States	United Kingdom	Germany	Japan 1960-72
All Manufacturing Industries.................	2.7*	4.1	5.8	9.8
Food and Tobacco...........................	3.0*	3.3	5.0	6.4
Textile Mill Products.......................	4.6	6.0	6.8	4.4*
Apparel and Leather Goods..................	2.9*	3.7	4.4	3.5
Lumber and Furniture.......................	3.8	3.6*	6.7	4.2
Paper and Printing.........................	2.3*	3.0	5.4	8.9
Chemicals and Allied Products...............	4.5*	7.1	9.2	14.0
Petroleum and Coal Products.................	3.6*	7.0	8.5	14.9
Rubber and Miscellaneous Manfactures........	2.4*	4.6	6.7	7.7
Stone, Clay, Glass and Concrete Products......	1.4*	4.9	5.7	7.5
Primary Metals.............................	1.2*	2.4	5.4	12.2
Fabricated Metal Products...................	2.0	1.8*	4.4	9.6
Machinery, Except Electrical.................	1.7*	4.2	2.8	11.8
Electrical Equipment and Supplies.............	5.0*	5.4	6.5	12.3
Transportation Equipment...................	2.6*	2.8	4.5	12.6
Instruments and Related Products.............	2.7*	6.6	4.7	8.2

*Indicates worst.

flation affect investments in the stock and bond markets directly, but market prices for U.S. stocks and bonds must be affected as U.S. companies lose competitive positions in world and domestic trade.

Productivity must be a key concern of investors and everyone concerned about the impact of inflation on the nation. The bottom line of all of this is that the falling U.S. productivity growth rate is a serious national problem demanding immediate attention. It is an integral part of the inflation problem.

The U.S. Productivity Slide: Why?

Barry Bosworth, former director of the Council on Wage and Price Stability, stated that by the end of 1978, U.S. productivity gains for the year "would be awfully close to zero." He went on to say that economists aren't certain why productivity has dropped from its previous levels. "We just don't have the explanation of why productivity growth in this country has been so slow in this past decade," Bosworth told the Joint Economic Committee of Congress.

The explanation is multifaceted. Here are the identifiable factors this writer has come across in researching the subject. We will classify them in four categories:

A. Significant

B. Probably Significant

C. Maybe Significant

D. Surely Significant: The Washington Effect

Readers should keep in mind this writer hardly qualifies as a productivity expert. But, because productivity trends and inflation are more than casually related, an assessment of this nature is important in any analysis of inflation.

Productivity increases in the service area are more difficult to come by than in the manufacturing area.

American business is hurting itself with an ever-increasing Chiefs-to-Indians ratio.

First, Some Major Reasons for the Productivity Slide:

• Seventy per cent of all jobs in the U.S. are now "service" jobs, compared to 49 per cent in 1956. Productivity increases in the service areas are more difficult to come by than in the manufacturing area. It's not just a matter of new machines (how do you make a barber more efficient?). Most managers have never viewed the service industry with the same rationality they have manufacturing. *The industrialization of the service industry is in its infancy.*

• American industry is spending less on research and development. Currently total r&d spending is 13 per cent below the 1968 peak, and, in order for r&d expenditures to make up the same portion of GNP as they did in 1968, they would have to be increased 50 per cent from current levels. *The result is probably a slowdown in technological innovation.*

• Capital spending for new plant and equipment has slowed, with capital stock per worker growing since 1957 at 1.3 per cent a year (constant dollars), compared with 1.8 per cent in 1948 to 1957. Perhaps as important is that in recent years much of the capital spending has been earmarked for environmental and occupational safety considerations, not for improved efficiency. In 1977, it was estimated that 10 per cent of total capital spending was in these "nonproductive" areas.

• *Capital spending continues to slow down as corporate planners become even more uncertain about the economic future and the implications of high inflation.* From 1956 to 1966, according to the American Productivity Center, industrial investment equaled 3.8 per cent of the GNP. More recently it has been running less than 1 per cent of the GNP.

• The U.S. industrial plant and equipment complex is older than most of our international competitors, and, as pointed out earlier, replacement is slowing down. A 30-year-old steel mill is just not as efficient as a 10-year-old steel mill. In 1966, the U.S. plant and equipment complex averaged 15.5 years of age. In 1976, the average age was up to 17.5 years, clear evidence of our lagging capital investment. Currently in Japan the average age of the plant and equipment complex is under 10 years, while in Germany it is approximately 10 to 12 years. *Among our major competitors only the United Kingdom now has a more antiquated plant and equipment complex.*

• American business, especially larger companies, is hurting itself with an ever increasing Chiefs-to-Indians ratio. Too many supervisors, too many supervisors supervising the supervisors and too many supervisors supervising the supervisors supervising the supervisors. The ratio of management personnel to production employees, be they in a plant or an office, should be going down with the new technology available. It is not. The growing business bureaucracy is not only expensive in itself, but in many cases impedes output and retards improvement and change. To often it is counterproductive.

- *During the last 10 years, there has also been a large increase in the percentage of workers who are required in nonproductive jobs.* As one president of a major corporation said: "OSHA, EEOC, and all the government red tape, regulation and bureaucracy require hundreds, no, thousands of jobs that didn't even exist a few years ago." General Motors now employs 25,000 people, spending more than $1 billion dollars a year to comply with government regulations. Another corporation averages 8,800 reports to 18 different agencies each year. It's expensive for small businesses as well...87 different federal agencies now regulate the small businessman. In addition, the number of man hours required for crime and security protection has grown rapidly in recent years.

- *As a nation's industrial complex matures, productivity growth declines.* Quantum gains in productivity come in the early stages of a nation's industrial development. As an example: South Korean productivity is leaping ahead 10 per cent to 12 per cent per year currently. Germany and Japan, starting from almost a zero base after World War II, recorded fantastic productivity gains in the 1950s and 1960s, benefiting from a brand new plant and equipment complex. In the 1970s, these gains slowed. For the remainder of this century, the greatest productivity gains may come from the Third World nations. Not only are they starting at the bottom, their workers are still hungry for the basic needs and are willing to work to get them.

- Wage increases, whether tied directly or indirectly to the inflation rate, have been rising so fast since 1968 that *increased labor costs cannot be offset by increased labor efficiencies and efficiencies in other production costs...as was the case at lower wage inflation levels.*

Suppose you manufacture wastebaskets. In 1967, your labor costs worked out to be 35 per cent per wastebasket. If your operation was typical of all manufacturing, that 35 per cent labor cost remained almost constant from 1957 through 1968 (see chart on the next page). Wage increases in this period had been more than offset by improved efficiencies, creating productivity gains. But from 1969 through 1977, if your experience was typical of American industry, your labor costs rose from 35 per

For the rest of this century, the greatest productivity gains may come from the Third World nations.

If productivity gains cannot
offset inflationary cost pressures,
prices are usually increased,
fueling inflation even more.

cent per wastebasket to 58 per cent! This would mean that all
your other costs—that is, materials, energy, equipment, interest,
depreciation, etc.—would shrink from 65 per cent of unit price in
1968 to 42 per cent by 1977.

How can this occur when these costs have been rising? You
raise the price of wastebaskets. Thus, inflation and productivity
are closely entwined. If productivity gains cannot offset inflationary cost pressures, prices are usually increased (cost-push in-
down in the U.S., and other major imdustrialized countries. In inflation, the more difficult it becomes to offset the skyrocketing
costs with efficiencies.

Now for the last big reason behind the productivity slowdown
in the U.S. and other major industrialized countries. In the past
the U.S. has been a veritable cornucopia of cheap natural
resources: iron ore, copper, coal and, later, petroleum. With few
exceptions, the U.S. had it, often in abundance.

But in the last few decades our avaricious, lusty industrial
economy has significantly reduced this nation's stores of natural
wealth. We are all aware of the situation. While the U.S. is still,
compared to others, a well endowed nation, we must now drill
deeper. We must mine and refine previously marginal ore bodies.
The cream has been skimmed; now it's taconite. The U.S. must
import more of its raw materials. What our forefathers viewed as
unlimited supplies are not. While advancing technology and
more extensive trade can probably cope, it won't be as easy, and
it won't be as cheap. The U.S. is becoming increasingly depen-
dent on foreign sources for many of its needs.

A Bigger Piece Of The Pie

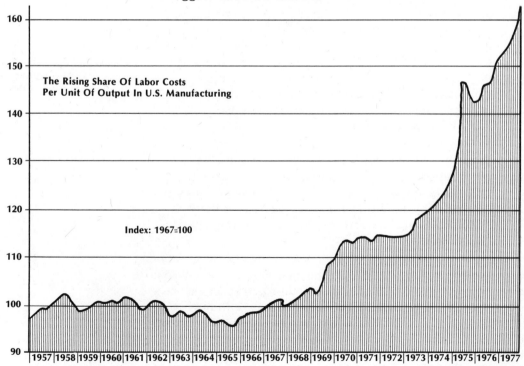

The Rising Share Of Labor Costs
Per Unit Of Output In U.S. Manufacturing

Index: 1967=100

Chart By Boeving

In the past, the U.S. has been on a raw materials binge, including, of course, oil. Finding and extracting reserves was fairly easy and relatively cheap. But no more. And because of the past easy availability, raw material prices have increased slowly compared to the accelerating value Americans have placed on their own labors. To a degree, the productivity gains of the last few decades have been possible because fast-increasing labor costs have been offset by stable raw material and energy costs. Energy costs, of course, were artificially held down. But no more.

In the last few years raw material costs and energy costs have been rising as fast as or faster than labor costs. Better, more efficient production techniques, which for many years were able to offset rapidly rising labor costs, cannot offset the now fast-rising labor, energy and raw material costs. Thus, productivity gains have become increasingly hard to come by in the U.S.

The large increase in energy prices, for example, has increased the operating costs of machinery and equipment to the degree that there is less economic incentive, compared to the old days of cheap energy, to substitute machines for men.

Let's look at another way, using the price of gasoline. Gasoline at the end of 1978 sold for about $1 per gallon. We think this is horribly high compared to the pre-Arab embargo price of about 30¢. But let's go back to 1938. Gasoline then sold for about 26¢ a gallon. In that same year the Fair Labor Standards Act established the minimum wage at 25¢ per hour. Now it's true that at $1 a gallon, gasoline is about 384 per cent above 1938 prices, but the minimum wage at the end of 1978 was at $2.90 per hour, is 1060 per cent higher. So today, a teenager working at the minimum wage can buy almost three gallons of gasoline with an hour's pay. In 1938 (if he/she could find a job), one hour's work would buy one gallon of gasoline for an old Model A. In other words, our society and economy have increased the value placed on worker's time (a commodity than is rarely scarce and always renewable), at a much faster rate than the value placed on gasoline, a product derived from a resource of limited supply and not renewable. The same kind of comparison holds true for most other raw materials.

This has amounted to exploitation of our existing limited, but easily accessible raw material and energy reserves. It has subsidized an over-inflated value of our own worth as workers. It also has been a major reason for past productivity growth. This distortion is the reason why that old TV that still works has no real value when you trade it in. This is why a used refrigerator has little or no value even if it still works. And this is why we have to pay someone to haul away an older model car that doesn't run, even though it has a lot of perfectly good parts. The car is junked because the labor to fix it up, or even strip it for parts, is so expensive. And this is why returnable bottles had virtually disappeared from the scene before the environmentalists got involved. Aluminum, steel and glass have been so cheap, compared with the labor costs involved in collecting, handling and cleaning, that it just didn't "pay" to reuse or recycle.

More efficient production techniques cannot offset the now fast rising labor, energy and raw materials costs in the U.S.

Our society has increased the value placed on a worker's time at a much faster rate than the value placed on raw materials.

With the days of cheap natural resource exploitation now numbered, this distortion will be corrected in future years. Raw materials will, in all probability, increase in value at a more rapid rate than wages, at least in the major industrial nations of the world. The day will come when it will again be worthwhile to maintain and fix things rather than throw them away. Recycling raw materials will be worthwhile from an economic standpoint instead of merely ecologically sensible. This transition can, in many ways, be viewed positively, but with the rich cream already consumed, the economy of the U.S. will have to learn to live a little leaner on what remains. This most likely implies decelerating economic growth and an increasingly hard struggle to keep productivity growing.

Now, Some Other Less Significant Factors:

- Ten years ago Washington subsidized and encouraged a great deal of technological development, emphasizing the defense and space programs. This fostered a lot of positive technological fallout for American industry. Recently the Washington focus is on social programs.

- Many major U.S. corporations seem to be evolving into protective, benevolent, service-providing societies, almost states. Taking care of the citizens' (employees) needs is often more important than bottom line considerations and shareholders' interests. Firings and layoffs, even when clearly warranted, are rare. Payrolls typically grow, even in recessions. Unions also function in a similar way, retarding productivity gains, but their antiproductivity influence is, perhaps, shrinking while corporate benevolence is growing.

The American worker is typically becoming less motivated by work.

- The American worker, in general, is typically becoming less motivated by work, and may not be working as hard. The day's work for a day's pay ethic is, in many instances, becoming a thing of the past. In two-income families and with higher tax brackets, the monetary incentive is not as great.

- While the productivity slide is a very serious problem, the statistical data may be presenting an overly distorted, dismal picture. The broader measures of inflation as well as the narrower measures of industry price increases factored in when calculating overall productivity may be flawed, overstating the actual degree of price increase (see chapter 14 for details). If this is the case, our productivity problem may not be as severe as the productivity data indicate.

Some Questionable Factors:

- The labor force, with the great influx of women and younger workers, is more inexperienced and *maybe* less efficient. (Studies, however, show that women waste less time than men.) At any rate, these negatives, *if,* they ever were negatives, are about over. The absorption is almost completed.

- Younger workers, a growing portion of the labor force, supposedly have different work attitudes and are not content to wait until they are 65 to enjoy themselves. "They want it now." Hmmm! Doesn't everybody? Young and old alike?
- Equal opportunity laws force companies to hire marginally qualified workers, and fears of discrimination charges make corporations reluctant to fire inferior workers. This is probably more "redneck" than real.

Finally, Some Surely Significant Factors Dragging on Productivity: The "Washington Effect"

Perhaps one of the more significant contributors to lagging U.S. productivity is government itself. Consider:

- First we have the federal government's inflationary practices and policies. High levels of inflation make productivity gains, calculated after inflationary impact, very difficult to come by when general inflation levels are 6 per cent and above. Note the earlier discussion of this.
- Then there is the growing local, state and federal bureaucracy that business must spend nonproductive time and money dealing with.
- Finally, there is the government's influence on U.S. worker attitudes: "Why should I work my can off when I can get food stamps, unemployment, etc.?"; "Why should I work my can off when those guys on Civil Service, working for the Highway Department and the Post Office, sit around half the time?"; "The harder I work and the more I make, the more the government takes. It's not worth it."

One of the more significant contributors to lagging U.S. productivity is government itself.

Industrial Productivity Data: The Brighter Side

Let's now look at areas with the best records of productivity gains. The statistics indicate these industries are faring pretty well from a productivity standpoint. Do they tell us anything about how to increase productivity?

Industry	1977 Employees (000)	1972-1977 Annual Productivity Increases
Hosiery	75	10%
Telephone Communications	951	8%
Brewers	51	7%
Synthetic Fibers	101	6%
Soft Drinks	137	6%
Mattresses and Bedspreads	33	5%
Prepared Feed for Animals	74	5%
Copper Mining, Crude Ore	35	4%

Industry	1977 Employees (000)	1972-1977 Annual Productivity Increases
Gas Service Stations	797	4%
Motor Vehicles and Equipment	891	4%
Boxes	106	4%
Metal Cans	61	4%
Pharmaceutical Preparation	140	4%
Air Transportation	309	4%

The outstanding gains in the hosiery industry were the product of recent advances in knitting machine speed, automated drying techniques and new packaging equipment. (Note, that 1977 data, not separated here, indicate a corrective 3.7 per cent productivity decline for the hosiery industry.)

The other gainers also benefited from new technology and heavy investment in new plant and equipment during this period. Almost all are capital intensive industries where the labor component is not a major cost factor. Gasoline service stations, a service industry, are an exception where productivity gains are likely attributable to the trend to self service, decreasing the labor cost factor.

Leaders in productivity gains are almost all capital intensive industries where the labor component is not a major cost factor.

The Productivity Problem Industries

Now a look at the productivity laggers and the productivity problem and disaster areas.

Industry	1977 Employees (000)	1972-1977 Annual Productivity Increases
Bakery Products	240	0%
Footwear	163	0%
Clay and Concrete Products	77	0%
Eating and Drinking Places	4205	0%
Radio & TV Sets	134	0%
Railroads	520	0%
Lighting Fixtures	67	0%
Nonmetalic Minerals	119	0%
Sawmills	184	0%
Printing and Publishing	NA	0%
Steel	544	0%
Cleaning Services	435	0%
Crushed Stone	41	0%
Banks	NA	−1%
Ready Mix Concrete	82	−1%
Hotels and Motels	969	−1%
Motors and Generators	109	−1%
Insurance	NA	−1%
Retail Food Stores	2379	−1%
Furniture	183	−2%
Candy	56	−3%
Construction	NA	−3%
Bituminous Coal	432	−3%
Iron Mining	40	−3%

The industries are, by and large, labor intensive industries. In some of them the problems have resisted solution by innovation. For example, so far automation has not reduced the hotel and motel industry's needs for maids to clean the rooms, etc. In other been too low to encourage management to abandon old plants and invest heavily in new plants with the latest labor-saving technology. In others, unions have resisted improvements (the construction industry), and in others, such as coal, an influx of new, unskilled workers has lowered outper per employe.

Factoring in 1977 data, *coal mining* has now experienced nine consecutive years of annual declines in productivity. While coal output has been increasing, worker hours are increasing even faster. These new workers are inexperienced and not as productive. There are also other factors, such as more stringent safety regulations, the impact of frequent work stoppages and labor provisions requiring extra personnel.

And now a few final comments regarding individual industry productivity data.

Short-term gains in productivity usually are associated with increases in output, and, therefore, tend to move up with general business expansion. In 1976, a strong expansion year, output increases took place in all but four of the industries studied by the Bureau of Labor Statistics, and only six industries had productivity declines in that years.

In 1975, a less vigorous economic environment, half the industries surveyed recorded productivity declines. And, as mentioned earlier, in 1977, 38 per cent of the industries surveyed recorded productivity declines. *This 1977 data is especially disturbing because it was recorded in a pretty fair economic environment.*

All in all, 75 per cent of the individual industries recorded lower productivity gains in 1971 to 1976 than in the preceding period measured. *Thus, the individual industry data confirm the sad state of affairs indicated earlier by the composite data.*

Short-term gains in productivity usually are associated with increases in output and tend to move up with general business expansion.

Chapter 13

How To Profit From Our Productivity Problems

From an investment standpoint, what appears to be the best way to profit from the productivity problems in the U.S.?

A. Invest in the companies and industries with the best histories of productivity increases.

B. Seek out the industries and companies that may be on the verge of a productivity turnaround.

C. Seek out the industries and companies that are best situated to help the industries and companies with serious productivity problems.

D. Sell short the companies and industries with the poorest productivity history.

Problem areas can be the spawning grounds of investment opportunity. And, since many of the readers of this are likely to be involved directly or indirectly with investment management, it is appropriate to discuss some investment management implications of this nation's declining productivity problem. Several strategies are reviewed in the search for investment opportunity.

Problem areas, such as declining productivity, can be spawning grounds of investment opportunities.

- *First (but not best): Go with the best:* Find the industries and companies doing the best job of increasing productivity and buy them. This approach is akin to the classic growth stock approach of the late 1960s and early 1970s. The negative here is that past productivity gains, like earnings growth rates, do not keep marching along. The big productivity winners of the last five years, like say, the hosiery industry, may have about completed their modernization and transition. Future quantum jumps in productivity may not be in the cards. (Recently, productivity for the hosiery industry declined by 3.7 per cent). The same could eventually be true for another recent productivity star, *telecommunications.*
- *Another strategy: Catch the turnarounds:* Find the industries and companies on the verge of a real productivity breakthrough and buy them. If you are right in this analysis, the investment results could be impressive. A dramatic past example of this approach is found with the airlines industry. Remember when piston-driven planes were replaced by jets, increasing speed, capacity, range and operating efficiency? Productivity gains really took off in this period. It may be that the airlines industry is now doing a productivity encore with wide bodies and transportation for the masses.

Catching big productivity turnarounds can be dramatic, but their occurrence is rare. Improving an industry's or company's productivity is a gradual process requiring capital and time. Diluting financing and heavy debt load often accompany a dramatic productivity turnaround. As was the case in the telephone communications industry, the investor who recognizes the productivity upturn early in the game does not necessarily make a bundle. Ma Bell has not really been a big winner, glamor stock.

Improving an industry's or company's productivity is a gradual process requiring capital and time.

- *A third stategy: Buy the problem solvers.* If you are a crack salesman developing a chronic illness, you would most likely undergo intensive and extensive treatment to get better. And, if you survive and are able to regain your old health and vigor, it's all worth it. Your earning power also returns with good health because you can again make the calls, work the long hours, socialize at the country club and close those sales.

But, who really profited from your illness? The internist, the radiologist, the hospital, the drugstore, the folks you (or the insurance company) paid to work on your problem. *And,* even if you don't survive or if you are never quite able to regain that old-time vim and vigor, they still come out ahead. They have profited from your problem, even if they fail to solve it.

Sick companies and sick industries are similar in many ways to people. They will go to great lengths and spend a great deal of money (if they have it or can borrow it) in order to regain their health, or, for that matter, to survive.

In some cases, an industry or company is so sick it should, from a cold, hard business standpoint, fold up the tent and liquidate. But executives who make these corporate life or death decisions don't usually like to be unemployed. They will do almost anything to keep that corporate entity alive as long as possible. After all, they have this responsibility to the employees. (What about the shareholders?) Well, the employee classification usually includes the executives. So, who comes first?

But it's not only the very sick that seek out the problem solvers. The industries and companies with good past records of productivity gains are typically run by alert and effective managements. They know the importance of staying healthy. And they will continue to invest time and money to stay in shape.

All in all, it appears the best investment opportunities will be found among the problem solvers or potential problem solvers. Invest in the doctors, not the patients.

Lagging U.S. productivity is a real and complex problem. It will not go away by itself. It must be treated. It is an illness that is serious in many industries, and it could be terminal in some. Government is probably one of the causes, but the remedy here can only come from the voting booth. So let's examine some of the other causes, factors and problem areas, ones that are now creating and will continue to produce *investment opportunities for investors who can identify the problem solvers and potential problem solvers.*

I. The Broad Sector Approach

A. Improving the Service Industries' Productivity

The service industries, the fastest growing part of the U.S. economy, have been real productivity laggers. As Theodore Levitt of the Harvard Business School said: "Management can achieve the same kinds of productivity breakthroughs in services that it has always done in manufacturing. *There is no reason that in the next 100 years we cannot repeat the successes of the Industrial Revolution,* this time in the service sector."

The supermarket was a pioneering example of a productivity revolution in a service industry. McDonald's is another. Gas stations' move to self-service is a recent example.

What companies have the products and capabilities of improving the productivity of the retail stores? The restaurants and hotels? The attorneys? The dentists and doctors? The mechanics? The banks? The insurance companies?

The Bureau of Labor Statistics' industry productivity data in the previous chapter reveal the recent abysmal productivity

Sometimes an industry or company is so sick it should fold up the tent and liquidate, but the executives who make these corporate life or death decisions don't like to be unemployed.

The service industries, the fastest growing part of the U.S. economy, have been real productivity laggers.

characteristics of such service industries as *Eating and Drinking Places* (zero productivity gain), *Retail Foodstores* (minus 1 per cent), *Banks* (minus 1 per cent) and *Insurance* (minus 1 per cent). No productivity data are available at this time for giant service industries such as *health care, retail, hard and soft goods, repair and maintenance,* and *legal and accounting.*

Estimates are that by 1985, 75 per cent of this nation's labor force will be employed in service-oriented industries compared to 49 per cent 12 years ago. Almost four million workers are employed now in *eating and drinking places,* making it the largest industry tracked by the bureau. Almost two and a half million work in *retail foodstores,* and almost one million in the *hotels and motels* classification. Compare these employment numbers with the two largest manufacturing classifications, *motor vehicles and equipment* (851,000 employees) and *steel* (543,000 employees). *This is a huge market for the productivity problem solvers.*

By 1985, 75 per cent of this
nation's labor force will be
employed in service-oriented
industries.

How do you boost the real output of clerks? Bartenders? TV repairmen? Mechanics? Teachers? Doctors? Lawyers? Cyrus McCormick tripled the output of the wheat farmer and Henry Ford did about the same for the auto worker. But many of the service industries stubbornly refuse to accept efforts to reshape the form of the service. Doctors resist computerized medical diagnostic services. Teachers resist interactive teaching machines. Bankers continue to use personal judgment and intuition rather than a simple computer program to evaluate the merits of even small loans. Chefs abhor the assembly line techniques of McDonald's (even though they recently ranked the McDonald's french fries as the best in the world).

The key to increasing the productivity of the service businesses is the depersonalization of the service businesses. This is difficult for the service providers and the service consumers to initially accept. But the supermarket *did* replace the friendly corner grocer who delivered. The Midas muffler shops almost put the corner filling station out of the muffler business. The fast food business has been the death of many a Ma's Cafe and Joe's Diner. People now are accustomed to pumping their own gas, unheard of five years ago.

The key to increasing the
productivity of the service
business is to depersonalize it.

Truly personal service will undoubtedly survive for those willing to pay for the luxury. After all, a few men still buy their suits and shirts from tailors. Some of us still buy custom-made shotguns and have architects design our houses. But we must pay up for the inefficiencies of the personal touch. To most of us it is "not worth it."

Again, as Harvard Business School Professor Theodore Levitt put it: "The industrialization of service is still in its infancy. There is no reason why in the next 100 years we cannot repeat the success of the Industrial Revolution in the service sector."

Where should one look for the service sector productivity problem solvers?

Here are some specific industries comprised of companies that can be (or already are) instrumental in providing solutions to various aspects of the lagging U.S. productivity problem.

The following are industries that appear to be potentially instrumental in helping improve the productivity of the service industries. The more significant ones, in our opinion, are asterisked.

*Diversified Technology	*EDP Specialized Equipment
*Semiconductors	*EDP Memories
*Impression Technology	*EDP Printers & Displays
*Materials Handling Equipment	*EDP Data Entry Devices
*Small Tools	*Computers, Mini
*Instrumentation	*Medical Equipment
*Vending & Food Service	*Precision Equipment
*Hospital Management	*Office Machinery
*Hospital Supplies	*Data Processing Services
*Computers, Mainframe	Security & Investigation Services
*Telecommunications Equipment	Bank Equipment & Services
Microwave Equipment	Consulting Services
Linen & Work Clothes Rental	Temporary Help & Maintenance
*Solid Waste Disposal	

B. Improving Core Industrial Productivity

Unlike the service industries, the benefits of automation, area. But the poor productivity records of many industries in this area indicate that much more has to be done. The international industry comparisons presented earlier emphasize that our nation's industrial complex is falling far behind the rest of the world.

The availability of capital, combined with the willingness to invest it, are very important factors here. More government encouragement by incentive and subsidy is likely as the long-term ramifications of lagging U.S. productivity are better understood by the politicians and the electorate.

Here are some core industrial productivity problem solvers (the asterisk indicates most significant):

*Mining Machinery
*Machine Tools
 Textile Machinery
 Materials Handling Equipment
*Plant Construction & Machinery
 Instumentation
 Computers, Mainframe
 Computers, Mini
 Precision Equipment
*Process Control
 Switches & Controls
*Technical & Engineering Services
 EDP Memories
 EDP Data Entry Devices
 EDP Specialized Equipment
 EDP Printers & Displays

C. Improving Paperwork Productivity

Many aspects of office procedures, billing, correspondence, reports, collections and inventory control are still in the dark

Although the benefits of automation, organization and controls are accepted in the core industrial area, much more needs to be done.

The handling of office paperwork is still in the dark ages.

ages. Word processing, order processing and, to a lesser degree, data processing are, in most organizations, very underdeveloped.

Techniques and equipment now very productively employed by some large paperwork processors ultimately will be scaled down for broad application in much smaller operations.

This aspect of the productivity problem is found everywhere— the service industries, the core industrial complex, government, charitable organizations, labor unions—literally everywhere. Take the motor vehicle equipment industry as an example. Total employment is about 850,000. But almost 200,000 of those workers are *not* involved in production. Even in the very labor-intensive footwear industry, 13 per cent of the work force is not involved in production. Overall, 30 per cent of the workers employed in manufacturing are not producers.

The potential for productivity improvement through systems and equipment application is huge. Look around your own office. Go to a local retail establishment and watch the clerk still writing up the sale by hand or laboriously special ordering something for you. Better yet, try to make an airline reservation.

The following are some paperwork productivity problem solving industries (asterisks indicate most significant):

- *Impression Technology
- *Computers, Mainframe
- *Computers, Mini
- *Office Machinery
- Office Supplies
- Office Furniture
- *Data Processing Services
- *Bank Equipment & Services
- *EDP Memories
- *EDP Data Entry Devices
- *EDP Specialized Equipment
- *EDP Printers & Displays
- *Telecommunications Equipment

D. Improving Construction Productivity

The construction industry has been slow to adapt many of the efficient manufacturing techniques employed by other industries. With some exceptions, the construction in this country is carried on by many small, thinly capitalized contractors unable to take advantage of the economies of scale. The building trades unions, in the past, have thwarted technological innovation in such areas as automatic nailers, painting equipment and the like. And, typically, the fragmented conglomeration of contractors has been no power match for the organized unions. Incredibly, the manufacturing process of building a house in 1970 was about the same as 100 years earlier.

The construction industry has been slow to adopt many of the efficient techniques employed by other manufacturing industries.

Things finally seem to be changing. Nonunion labor is growing. Technological innovation is no longer being stymied as much as it once was. Major mass producers of housing are emerging, having a stronger capital base. Building codes finally are being modified to allow for new techniques and components.

Construction productivity has been in a long-term decline but this may be changing. However, from an investment standpoint, it is difficult for us to isolate many major beneficiaries of this trend. In stock market terms, we cannot find many pure plays.

Here are some potential construction productivity problem solvers:

> Construction Machinery
> Mobile and Modular Homes
> Plant Construction
> Electrical Components
> Small Tools
> Technical & Engineering

E. Improving Energy Productivity

Productivity is commonly and primarily associated with labor and the application of machinery. However, in recent years the Bureau of Labor Statistics, the American Productivity Center and the Conference Board have take a harder look at the components of the total productivity factor. If a manufacturer or a service industry can make more efficient use of its energy, there is a direct impact on overall productivity. The explosion in energy costs has, of course, greatly increased the potential impact of energy productivity on the total productivity factor.

If a manufacturer or service industry can make more efficient use of its energy, there is a direct impact on overall productivity.

Products and equipment that better control heating and lighting costs, machinery operational costs and transportation costs are in growing demand by American industry. Unless energy prices crack, this demand should continue to grow.

Some energy productivity solvers (asterisks indicate most significant):

> *Trucks & Equipment
> Railroad Equipment
> Plant Construction & Machinery
> Air Conditioners
> *Process Control
> Switches & Controls
> *Container Shipping

F. Productivity Improvement Through Specialized Consulting and Research

With the productivity problem receiving more and more attention, both from Washington and from private enterprise, it is probable that federally financed and certainly privately financed research and consulting contracts will flow to firms specializing in consulting, including engineering and design and management and energy saving techniques.

Specialized consulting and research services may benefit from the quest for productivity gains.

Also, because the employee attitude is commonly thought to be one of the causes of lagging productivity, motivational and incentive specialists may be retained in greater numbers.

Clear-cut investment opportunities in these areas are very limited at this time, although some might be found in the *consulting services* and *technical and engineering* industries.

However, it would not be surprising to see some new firms formed to specialize in these areas...maybe even a few public offerings.

G. Improving Government Productivity By Farming Out Functions

The electorate seems to have had its fill of expensive, wasteful, inefficient state, local and federal government administration and services. *The day may be here when more and more of these services are let out on a contract basis to private companies.* Education, garbage removal, hospitals, food service, mail delivery, administration of government health and welfare programs are some of the possibilities.

To some extent, this has already taken place, and the cost savings and improvement in service has, in almost all cases, been impressive. Some school districts have hired private firms to run schools. Cities have contracted out garbage removal to private firms, saving 50 per cent in some cases. Administration of some state health and welfare programs have been put out for bids. Public hospitals are being turned over to private companies for more efficient cost conscious management.

In response to the electorate's disillusionment with big government in general, this trend could gain momentum. Some of the possible beneficiary areas—industries that can make the delivery of current government services more efficient—are (asterisk indicates most significant):

*Data Processing Services
Security & Investigation Services
Linen & Work Clothes Rental
*Solid Waste Disposal
Vending & Food Services
*Hospital Management
*Telecommunications Equipment
EDP Specialized Equipment

Incidentally, there recently have been some government sponsored efforts made to measure the federal government's productivity in a myriad of areas. The Bureau of Labor Statistics includes such data in one of its publications. Some cynics might, of course, wonder about the objectivity of the data, or at least question the techniques used.

II. The Troubled Industry Approach

In an earlier chapter, using data from the Bureau of Labor Statistics, the specific industries with particularly poor records of productivity gains (losses) were identified. Here is an attempt to identify the doctors, hospitals and perhaps even chiropractors who might be employed to diagnose and treat these sick industries. Individual companies included in these industries are listed at the end of this chapter.

We would like to emphasize this is not a detailed analysis, only a thought-provoker, a strong point for further analysis.

The trend of farming out government services to private contractors could gain momentum.

Who are the doctors who might treat the sick industries?

Poor Productivity	Companies That Can Help
Steel	Plant Construction & Machinery Process Controls
Machinery	Machine Tools Plant Construction & Machinery Switches & Controls
Railroads	Railroad Equipment Computers & Minicomputers
Clay & Concrete	Process Controls
Furniture	Small Tools Minicomputers
Bakery Products	Process Controls
Mineral & Ore Mining	Technical & Engineering Services Machinery, Construction & Mining
Sawmills	Process Controls
Food & Drink Services	Tissue & Disposable Products Office Equipment Minicomputers
Printing	Printing Equipment
Foodstores	Office Equipment Computers & Minicomputers EDP Specialized Equipment EDP Memories EDP Printers & Displays EDP Remote Entry Devices Data Processing Services Business Equipment
Banks	Bank Equipment & Services Consulting Services Data Processing Services Computers and Minicomputers EDP Specialized Equipment EDP Memories EDP Printers & Displays EDP Remote Entry Devices
Insurance	Office Equipment Computers & Minicomputers Data Processing Services Consulting Services
Cement	Process Controls
Construction	Small Tools Construction Materials Mobile Homes Technical & Engineering Services
Coal	Technical & Engineering Services Machinery, Construction & Mining

Some Conclusions

So far in this book, we have shown that inflation is bad for both equity and fixed-income markets in general. Historically the stock market has performed poorly in periods of high inflation, and fixed income investments, in aggregate, have not preserved the value of the invested dollar.

In every investment environment, however, there are investments which go against the general trend. While the inflation

While the inflation environment hurts most investments, some may profit from these conditions.

environment may be hurting most investments, there are some which profit from the very conditions that seem to be so disastrous.

The key is to identify those industries and those stocks within the industries which are likely to prosper. As we noted, one of the causes of inflation (or perhaps to some extent the effect of inflation) is a declining rate of productivity growth in the economy. Increasing productivity is one way of overcoming the effects of inflation on an individual company. If many companies attack the effects of inflation this way, then those that can help will prosper. However, productivity gains by private industry can't do it alone. (For instance, government and consumers must restrain their deficit spending inclinations.)

As companies strive to increase productivity to reduce their costs, industries that provide equipment or services which can help improve productivity will prosper. And, while the stock market overall might be stagnant, companies in these helper industries should do significantly better than the market.

This is one way to profit in the stock market in an inflationary environment, but it is truly difficult. It is not, as the conventional wisdom about the stock market being an inflationary hedge might suggest, merely a matter of buying stocks in investment grade companies and holding on to them, or of buying the Standard & Poor's 500 through an index fund and relaxing. The market will not normally protect you once inflation gets above 4 per cent. And, if you go the fixed income route, you are unlikely to be protected by the fabled "real" rate of interest that economists and historians have tracked all the way back to the prehistory of 1954.

No, the investor who wants to emerge whole from a period of inflation will have to do much homework. He or she will have to use careful analysis, building upon the foundations suggested in this chapter, to identify those companies which are best situated to profit from a lagging productivity inflationary environment.

The investor who wants to emerge whole from a period of inflation will have to do much homework.

Major problems create major investment opportunities, at least for those investors who are able to identify the companies and industries potentially instrumental in the problem-solving process.

In this chapter we have suggested the investment areas standing to reap the greatest rewards because they have the capabilities of contributing to the solution of the nation's productivity problems.

We believe this chapter has focused on what is becoming a major stock market conceptual investment thesis, perhaps similar in scope and magnitude to the smokestack thesis, the energy thesis and the electronics rage of the early 1960s.

An in-vogue Wall Street concept play can be a powerful market force. We believe this one—let's call it the Productivity Play Thesis—has now emerged. However, it is not fully recognized on a broad conceptual basis, and therefore, it could be a profitable investment concept for many years to come.

The Details: Where to Look for Productivity Plays

In this chapter, we have suggested seven ways to profit from an all-out effort to improve the sad state of U.S. productivity.

Herein, using the Piper, Jaffray & Hopwood MicroGroup Project (the most exacting and detailed stock group work available in the investment world), we have isolated a variety of industry groups that could profit in a full-fledged battle against declining productivity. Three points:

1. All the component stocks of each qualifying MicroGroup are presented. Not all are productivity plays. We have, however, asterisked (*) companies which appear to have above average appeal. This is only meant to be a first filter.

2. Many groups have potential in several productivity plays areas. These are coded by applications A through G (see below).

3. The MicroGroups that we now view as especially favorably situated are designated with a **P.** *Note:* Our fundamental research at this point is still underway. Do your own homework.

Key to Productivity Thesis Application

    A = Improving Service Industry Productivity
    B = Improving Core Industrial Productivity
    C = Improving Paperwork Productivity
    D = Improving Construction Productivity
    E = Improving Energy Productivity
    F = Specialized Productivity Consulting and Research
    G = Improving Government Efficiency

MICROGROUPS	PRODUCTIVITY APPLICATION
Mining Machinery:	B
*Bucyrus Erie Co.	
Caterpillar Tractor Co.	
Chicago Pneumatic Tool	
*Joy Mfg. Co.	
*Elgin National Inds.	
American Hoist & Derrick	
Barber Greene Co.	
CMI Corp.	
Harnischfeger Corp.	
Koehring Co.	
National Mine Svc. Co.	
P Machine Tools:	B
*Cincinnati Milacron	
Excell O Corp.	
*Warner & Swasey Co.	
*Kearney & Trecker Corp.	
Acme Cleveland Corp.	
Brown & Sharpe Mfg. Co.	
Cleanso Works	
Mesta Machine Co.	
Monarch Machine Tool Co.	

MICROGROUPS	PRODUCTIVITY APPLICATION

Mechanical Meters: ABE
- Badger Meter, Inc.
- Moore Products Co.
- Tokheim Corp.

P Impression Technology: AC
- Alphatype Corp.
- *Compugraphic Corp.
- *Eltra Corp.
- *Harris Corp.
- Wood Inds., Inc.
- *Xerox
- *Savin

Textile Machinery: B
- *Crompton & Knowles
- Leesona Corp.
- Reece Corp.
- Union Spl. Corp.

P Materials Handling Equipment: ABD
- *Hyster Co.
- Manitowoc, Inc.
- Northwest Engr.
- Pettibone Corp.
- *Raymond Corp.
- *Signode Corp.

Electrical Components: AD
- *Burndy Corp.
- Crouse Hinds
- Grainger W.W., Inc.
- *Hubbell Harvey, Inc.
- *Thomas & Betts Corp.

Trucks & Equipment: AE
- Cummins Engine, Inc.
- Dana Corp.
- Fruehauf Corp.
- Paccar, Inc.
- Signal Cos., Inc.
- White Motor Corp.

Railroad Equipment: E
- *A.C.F. Inds., Inc.
- *Amsted Inds., Inc.
- Brenco, Inc.
- *GATX Corp.
- Pittsburgh Forgings Co.
- Portec, Inc.
- *Pullman, Inc.

Mobile & Modular Homes: D
- Champion Home Bldrs. Co.
- Fleetwood Enterprises
- Golden West Homes
- Philips Inds., Inc.
- Redman Inds., Inc.
- Skyline Corp.

Plant Construction & Machinery: BDE
- *Combustion Engrg., Inc.
- *Fluor Corp.
- *Foster Wheeler Corp.
- *Parsons
- *Pullman

151

MICROGROUPS	PRODUCTIVITY APPLICATION
Automobile Additives:	E
Ethyl Corp.	
Filtrol Corp.	
*Lubrizol Corp.	
Wynns Intl., Inc.	
Air Conditioners:	E
Carrier Corp.	
Copeland Corp.	
Fedders Corp.	
Tecumseh Prods. Co.	
*Trane Co.	
P Small Tools:	AD
Aro Corp.	
Black & Decker Mfg. Co.	
Omark Inds., Inc.	
Snap On Tools Corp.	
Stanley Works	
Starrett, L.S., Co.	
Easco	
P Instrumentation:	AB
Conrac Corp.	
*EG & G, Inc.	
*E Sys, Inc.	
*Sanders Assoc., Inc.	
*Simmonds Precision	
*Watkins Johnson Co.	
Semiconductors	A
*Intel Corp.	
*Intersil	
*National Semiconductor	
*Unit Rode	
Microwave	A
*California Microwave	
*Farinon Corp.	
*Scientific Atlanta	
*M/A Com.	
P Process Control	BE
*Foxboro Co.	
*General Signal Corp.	
Industrial Nucleonics	
*Manufacturing Data Sys.	
*Measurex Corp.	
Switches & Controls	BE
Ametek, Inc.	
Automatic Switch Co.	
*Johnson Controls, Inc.	
Ranco, Inc.	
Riley Co.	
*Robert Shaw Controls Co.	

A = Improving Service Industry Productivity
B = Improving Core Industrial Productivity
C = Improving Paperwork Productivity
D = Improving Construction Productivity
E = Improving Energy Productivity
F = Specialized Productivity Consulting and Research
G = Improving Government Efficiency

MICROGROUPS	PRODUCTIVITY APPLICATION

Container Shipping: E
- Flexi Van Corp.
- Interpool Ltd.
- Interway Corp.
- Sea Containers, Inc.
- Transway Intl. Corp.
- Xtra Corp.

P Office Machinery   AC
- Addressograph Multigraph Corp.
- *C P T Corp.
- *Data Term Sys., Inc.
- Dictaphone Corp.
- *Lanier Business Prod.
- *NCR Corp.
- Pitney Bowes, Inc.

Office Supplies   C
- American Business Prod.
- Avery Intl., Inc.
- Duplex Prods., Inc.
- Moore Limited
- *Reynolds & Reynolds Co.
- *Uarco, Inc.
- Wallace Business Forms

P Computers, Mainframe: ABC
- *Burroughs Corp.
- *Control Data Corp.
- *Honeywell, Inc.
- *International Bus. Mach.
- *Sperry Rand Corp.
- *Cray Research

P Computers, Mini: ABC
- Computer Automation
- *Data Genl. Corp.
- *Digital Equip. Corp.
- General Automation
- *Management Assistance
- Microdata Corp.
- Modular Computer Sys.
- *Prime Computer, Inc.
- *Wang Labs, Inc.

P Computer Peripheral Equipment: ABC
- Applied Magnetics Corp.
- California Computer
- *Electronics Mem. & Mag.
- Memorex Corp.
- Mohawk Data Sciences
- Centronics Data Comput.
- *Data Point Corp.
- Pertec Computer Corp.
- *Storage Technology

P Medical Equipment   A
- *Cobe Labs, Inc.
- Damon Corp.
- *Frigitronics, Inc.
- Hycel, Inc.
- *Medtronic, Inc.
- Narco Scientific Inds.
- *New England Nuclear

	MICROGROUPS	PRODUCTIVITY APPLICATION

Precision Equipment: AB
  *Beckman Instrs., Inc.
  Itek Corp.
  *Perkin Elmer Corp.
  *Tektronix, Inc.
  Sargent Welch Scientific
  Teradyne, Inc.
  Esterline Corp.
  Fisher Scientific Co.
  *Fluke John Mfg., Inc.
  *Nicolet Instr. Corp.
  Systron Donner Corp.
  Veeco Instrs., Inc.

Office Furniture: C
  G.F. Business Equip., Inc.
  Hon Inds., Inc.
  Miller Herman, Inc.
  Supreme Equip. & Sys.
  Tiffany Inds., Inc.

P Data Processing Services: CG
  *Automatic Data Process
  Bradford Natl. Corp.
  Compuserve, Inc.
  *Computer Sciences Corp.
  *Electronic Data Sys.
  *On Line Sys., Inc.
  *Tymeshare

Security Services: AG
  *American Dist. Teleg. Co.
  *Burns Intl. Security Services
  *Pinkertons, Inc.
  Wackenhut Corp.

P Bank Equipment & Services AC
  *Brinks, Inc.
  *Diebold, Inc.
  *De Luxe Check Printers
  *Docutel Corp.
  *Harland, John H., Co.
  *Purolator, Inc.

Consulting Services: ACF
  *Little, Arthur D., Inc.
  Market Facts, Inc.
  *Nielsen, A.C., Co.
  Science Mgmt. Corp.

Technical & Engineering Services: BDEF
  Bolt Beranek & Newman
  CRS Design Assoc., Inc.
  Flow Gen., Inc.
  Genge, Inc.
  Jacobs Engr. Group, Inc.

A = Improving Service Industry Productivity
B = Improving Core Industrial Productivity
C = Improving Paperwork Productivity
D = Improving Construction Productivity
E = Improving Energy Productivity
F = Specialized Productivity Consulting and Research
G = Improving Government Efficiency

MICROGROUPS	PRODUCTIVITY APPLICATION

Temporary Help & Maintenance: ABC
 Allied Maintenance
 *American Bldg. Maintenance
 *Kelly Services, Inc.
 National Kinney Corp.
 Prudential Bldg. Maintenance
 *Servicemaster Inds., Inc.

Linen & Work Clothes Rental: AG
 Angelica Corp.
 Means F.W. & Co.
 National Service Industries, Inc.
 Superior Surgical Mfg.
 *Unitog Co.

P Solid Waste Disposal: AG
 *Browning Ferris Inds.
 SCA Services, Inc.
 *Waste Mgmt., Inc.

Vending & Food Service: AG
 *ARA Services, Inc.
 Cornelius Co.
 Macke Co.
 Saga Corp.
 *Servomation Corp.
 UMC Industries, Inc.
 Vendo Co.
 *Sysco

P General Hospitals: AG
 *American Med. Intl., Inc.
 General Health Services
 *Hospital Corp. Amer.
 *Humana, Inc.
 Medenco, Inc.
 National Med. Enterprise

Hospital Supplies: A
 *American Hospital Supply
 *Baxter Travenol Labs
 *Becton Dickinson
 *Johnson & Johnson
 United Industrial Corp.
 *Bard C.R., Inc.
 General Med. Corp.
 Ipco Hospital Supply Corp.
 Puritan Bennett Corp.

Extended Care Centers: A
 Berkeley Bio Med., Inc.
 Beverly Enterprises
 Charter Med. Corp.
 Hillhaven, Inc.
 National Health Enterprises

Chapter 14

Today's Indices of Inflation Are Seriously Flawed

Which of these statements is most correct?

A. Our major indicators of inflation, the Consumer Price Index, the Producer Price Index and the Gross National Product Deflator, are understating U.S. inflation by 2 per cent or more per year.

B. These major indicators of inflation are very comprehensive and generally quite representative of the U.S. price changes.

C. These major indicators of inflation are overstating U.S. inflation by at least 1 per cent to 2 per cent per year.

D. These major indicators of inflation are reasonably acceptable but do understate U.S. inflation by insignificant amounts.

Tracking and measuring inflation is far more complex than it might appear. Even in the computer age, with all the sophisticated reporting and computation procedures, getting a precise fix on how much prices and the cost of living are rising or falling is a long way from perfect.

Obviously the measures employed today are far superior to those used a century ago, but there is room for many improvements. In recent years we have studied cost of living data purporting to go back as far as the year 950. These ancient data are based on a series of laborious academic reconstructions of typical consumer market baskets, including the basics of food, clothing, fuel and in some cases shelter. Old ledgers and sometimes personal diaries and journals are the sources of prices for items. This work tracks the prices for a particular locality — Stockholm, for example, Valencia, or Oxford, England. Sometimes two or three years of data could not be found for an item, so estimates and extrapolations were necessary. Even though the end product of this tedious research is not all encompassing or precise, it probably is fairly representative of long-term trends of consumer prices for the locality studied. But this is a topic for a later chapter.

Today's most widely used price indices appear to be quite sophisticated compared to the old historical data. But even at today's state of the art, there is need for improvement because so much is now at stake. Tens of millions of dollars, huge volumes of computer time and hundreds of thousands of man hours already are spent annually to provide the primary U.S. indices of prices.

Some may view this as a waste of taxpayers' money. What difference does it make? We don't need some fancy index to tell us prices are going up. Besides, what's the difference if we err by a fraction of a percentage point or even a percentage point or two?

The Most Important Statistics

Before concluding that efforts to increase the accuracy of these statistics is a waste of taxpayers' money, subsidizing a few statistical freaks' compulsion for precision, consider this:

The Consumer Price Index, our chief indicator of inflation, has become *the most important statistic produced by our government*. It influences consumer confidence, capital spending, investment and economic policy. But more importantly, a change of 1 per cent in this one index can trigger billions of dollars of income change, directly affecting more than two-thirds of the U.S. population. This is a conservative estimate. For example:

- About 32,000,000 Social Security recipients have their payments tied to the CPI by a cost of living escalator.
- Almost 3,000,000 military and civil service retirees have retirement benefits tied to the CPI.
- The index also directly affects food stamp allotments for another 20,000,000 or so.

- School lunch subidies for about 25,000,000 children are based on the CPI.
- There are millions of beneficiaries of health and welfare programs where eligibility levels (poverty level) float upward, tied to the CPI.
- A CPI escalator clause is tied to many private rental contracts and even child support payments.
- There are at least 9,000,000 union workers who have CPI measured cost of living clauses as part of their legal employment agreements. It is estimated that 50 per cent of collective bargaining agreements now have "COLAS" (Cost of Living Adjustments) compared with only 36 per cent in 1975.
- Millions of nonunion workers have CPI linked adjustments as part of their compensation packages. Even if this is not done formally, most private employers feel it is only fair to voluntarily provide annual salary increases that at least match the inflation rate established by the CPI.
- The impact of a CPI error on benefit payouts, contributions and actuarial planning can be huge from the pension administrator's point of view. States, municipalities and corporations, those that make the contributions, have billions of dollars at stake here.

The bottom line of the above is simply this:

If the CPI exaggerates inflation by even what appears to be a minuscule amount, millions of people get more than they should, more than they are entitled to. This in itself feeds the inflation that is supposedly being measured. And, conversely, if the CPI understates the actual rate of increase in consumer prices, all these folks would lose. Therefore, efforts to improve the accuracy of the CPI are far more than an ivory tower quest for perfection. *This one statistical series is the most important and influential statistic produced in this country.* Every day, as more things are inflation indexed, it becomes increasingly significant in our lives.

Another important inflation statistic is the implicit Price Deflator of the Gross National Product. While the newspapers and citizens focus on the CPI, economists usually prefer the GNP Deflator because it goes beyond consumer prices as kind of a composite index. Thus, its action plays an important part in public and private economic policy decisions, at least where our nation's 100,000-plus economists play a role. Also, components of the GNP Deflator act as key adjustment factors in arriving at productivity statistics for individual industries and the nation as a whole.

The Wholesale Price Index, recently renamed the Producer Price Index, is also a very important statistic. It serves as an escalator in more than $100 billion of long-term materials purchase contracts. There are many other direct implications, including the SEC's requirement it be used as an accounting stan-

Efforts to improve the accuracy of the CPI are far more than an ivory tower quest for perfection; they affect the outcome of millions of people.

dard in revaluing corporate assets at replacement cost. The
Justice Department uses it in its search for monopolistic practices, and many investment and economic analysts employ this
statistic as a forecaster of consumer prices. Its components also
are used in productivity calculations.

Clearly, these are vital statistics, with the CPI being especially
vital. Errors and flaws can mean billions of dollars in our
economic system. Even in this age of computer precision, there
appear to be very serious flaws in all these prime inflation
measures.

*Errors and flaws in our basic
economic indices can mean
billions of dollars in our
economic system.*

Professors Lorie and Fisher noted in *"A Half Century of Returns
on Stocks and Bonds"* that the reader should "keep in mind that
there is inherent upward bias through time in the CPI," adding
that "the magnitude of the bias in the CPI is unknown but 1 per
cent to 2 per cent per annum is considered reasonable."

Now let's take a closer look at the CPI, the Producer Price Index and GNP Deflator. The snowballing implications of a com-
pounding error of even 0.5 per cent per year are very serious. In
1979, the error appears to have been a 5 per cent overstatement
in the CPI, all things considered.

Our Distorted Consumer Price Index

Each month the Bureau of Labor Statistics sends out 500 data
collectors to visit a sample of computer-selected stores and
sources to price a variety of consumer items. The reports are
analyzed and combined with other price information. In about
the fourth week of the following month out pops the Consumer
Price Index. Occasionally, some of these data collectors get a little lazy and fake it, perhaps going back to bed instead of making
the rounds. But the bureau has taken some steps that appear to
minimize this practice which it refers to as "curbstoning."

Another more serious data gathering flaw is that prices are
checked only at regular outlets, not at discount chains. In reality,
most Americans shop around. Also, no special discounts, such as
the discount fares offered by airlines, are considered.

The Market Basket Problem

A more significant problem, one that experts say gives the index a continuing upward bias, is found in the mix and markup of
the consumer market basket priced each month. Even the new index version, introduced in 1978, is based on a consumer expenditure survey conducted in 1972 to 1973. Times and consumer
spending patterns have changed significantly since then. Oil
prices have more than quadrupled, and food prices shot up
dramatically in the mid-1970s. Because of these changes, the
typical consumer no longer buys as many gallons of gas as he or
she did in 1972 or as much of the most inflated food items, such
as steak, lettuce, etc. Cars now average 20 miles per gallon compared to 13 to 14 miles per gallon in 1972, and drivers don't drive
as much as they did in 1972. Car pooling and increased use of
mass transit also are factors. The grocery shopper substitutes,
switching from higher priced to lower priced items. Still, the 1980

*The CPI basic market basket
ignores changes in life style and
consumer spending patterns.*

CPI continues to be calculated on the assumption that the 1980 consumer is buying as much gas and steak as in 1972 and 1973. In 1972, people in the U.S. ate 120 pounds of beef per year. Currently, they consume less than 90 pounds. Chicken is much cheaper and its consumption has increased by three or four times since 1972. The CPI ignores these changes.

The Bureau of Labor Statistics admits the market basket makeup is obsolete, but unfortunately these consumer expenditure surveys are traditionally done once every 10 years. This is in the the process of being rectified, but it won't be until the mid-1980s that the result of a new continuous expenditure survey will be incorporated into the index. This flaw will eventually be corrected, but one wonders why it will take so long. Maybe the bureacracy should hand the job over to Procter & Gamble or General Foods or a private survey organization; it might not take more than six months for a comprehensive consumer survey...not six years.

Product Improvement Adjustments

Yale University economist Richard Ruggles has studied in detail what he thinks could be a flaw that is overstating inflation, as measured by the CPI, by 2 per cent or more per year. In fact, Ruggles claims that if the CPI measured prices correctly, the index actually would have declined in the 1949 to 1966 period instead of the 36 per cent rise reported.

Here is the problem according to Professor Ruggles: The CPI methodology does not adequately compensate for improvements in the quality of consumer products. If the manufacturer of an appliance improves the product so it lasts 10 years instead of two and as a result he increases his manufacturing costs by 50¢ a unit, the 50¢ price increase should *not* be viewed as inflation; it is quality improvement. The consumer may be paying more, but he or she is getting more. The consumer who does not want this improvement has the option of buying a cheaper model.

The Bureau of Labor Statistics does attempt to adjust its CPI calculations to allow for some of these product improvements. It substracts the costs of a new feature *only if a price increases* and only if the improvement is very obvious and easy to value. If, on the other hand, the product is improved and the manufacturer absorbs the added cost, perhaps for competitive reasons, keeping the consumer price the same, the bureau ignores it and no adjustment is made. If the product is improved and the retail price actually declines because of competition or improved manufacturing technology, the bureau ignores the product improvement factor no matter how obvious or easy to value. Although the bureau acknowledges the principle of the product improvement, it chooses to apply it only if the retail price is increased. This would certainly appear to be an arbitrary one-way street.

Economist F. Lee Moore has compiled some examples that dramatically focus on this major CPI flaw in the product improvement area. In 1934, the standard tire sold for $13. Recently,

The CPI may be overstating inflation by 2 per cent or more a year.

using CPI data, it's $68, up 423 per cent! At least that is the way CPI measures it. But wait a minute! The standard tire in 1934 was a four-ply cotton tire, that would handle a 1.45 ton auto at 40 mph for an average life of 7,000 miles. Today's $68 standard tire can handle a two-ton car at 50 mph for a minimum of 40,000 miles. The net is that even though the price went up 423 per cent the cost per mile driven went *down* 9 per cent. The cost per ton mile has actually fallen 32 per cent. With these improvements in performance, is the cost of tires up or down?

Considering improvements in performance, the cost of many products may be down, not up.

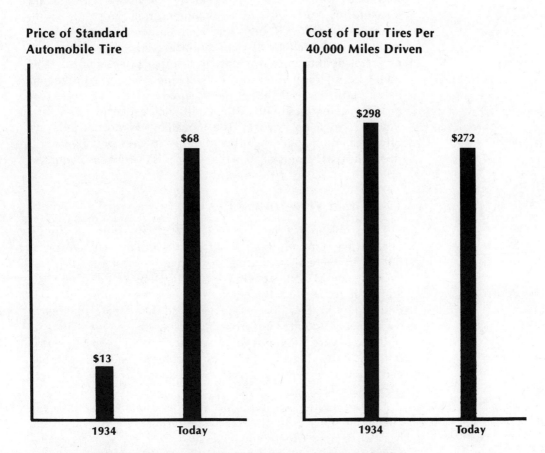

Price of Standard Automobile Tire

- $68
- $13
- 1934
- Today

Cost of Four Tires Per 40,000 Miles Driven

- $298
- $272
- 1934
- Today

Statistically the CPI measurement of personal care items is sharply higher because it ignores product improvements such as fluoride in toothpaste, improvements in razor blades that lengthen their useful life by five or 10 times with less nicks and cuts. We know deodorants work much better, although no one has calculated the cost per hour of protection.

Motor oil prices have increased 234 per cent since 1935, but considering the better performance and longer life, economist Moore calculates that the cost per mile traveled has actually declined by 52 per cent. Light bulbs are another common example. Shouldn't the price be measured in lumen hours provided, not cost per light bulb?

Then there is the major consumer expense item of taxes, a very significant portion of the CPI. Property taxes, sales taxes, license fees and other costs of government are factored in each month.

Government costs have
skyrocketed over the years, but
the services provided have also
expanded greatly.

These have, of course, skyrocketed over the years, but the government services provided also have expanded greatly. Some of us might argue with the degree of real improvement in services provided by state, local and federal governments, but no one would argue that government is not doing more for us today than, say, 15 years ago. A portion of this service expansion is taken into account by the CPI, but not much of it.

This entire issue initially would appear to involve a great deal of subjectivity. What constitutes an improvement in quality amd what does not? If it is an improvement, how do we separate and measure its cost within the manufacturing process? Northwestern University's Robert Gordon and others say that there are mathematical techniques that can effectively isolate the price effect of quality improvements from other price changes. This could be computerized and it is claimed that the Bureau of Labor Statistics could adapt the program to the more important product categories with little additional expense. Economist Moore sums it up, saying, "The prevailing method of indexing price has not changed significantly since it was formalized early this century. The only change that counts is the change in quoted price."

Two Other Flaws in the CPI

The Consumer Price Index is calculated from the price changes each month in a myriad of individual consumer items, but when technology introduces a new, important consumer item, it can take the government a long time to get around to adding it to the list. Prices of new consumer items often fall dramtically in their first several years on the market; the digital watch and calculator illustrate this point. However, the Bureau of Labor Statistics did not get around to including the calculator until 1978. By that time prices of calculators had fallen 90 per cent from initial levels. All of this decline was missed by our price recorders.

A subtle and difficult to measure
flaw in the CPI involves changes
in living patterns.

A more subtle and more difficult flaw to measure involves changes in living patterns. Consider entertainment. Movie tickets have gone up 330 per cent since 1948. Tickets to sports events and other entertainment also have gone up greatly. But today the consumer is getting the same kind of entertainment for a small fraction of the 1948 cost via television. Two hours of television cost about a dime. Home Box Office and cable television cost about $15 to $20 per month.

All in all, if Ruggles, Moore and other critics are correct, and it appears they are, the CPI may be an overstatement, causing a good deal of inflation instead of just measuring it. All the people whose wages and other payments are based on CPI data may be getting as much as 2 per cent per year too much, feeding the wage-price spiral.

The Wholesale Price Index—A Real Horror

If the CPI has faults, the WPI has Grand Canyons. Fortunately not as much is riding on this statistical horror. But, as noted earlier, it is still very important. This index almost surely creates inflation instead of just measuring it. First, WPI never did measure wholesale prices, but finally after decades this error has been corrected. It is now the Producer Price Index, although few call it that yet. It purports to gauge prices of producers in manufacturing, mining and agriculture. Each month the Bureau of Labor Statistics sends forms to 3,000 volunteering firms, asking them to report their prices on about 10,000 items. From these "quotes," price indices are calculated for almost 3,000 commodities. These, in turn, are combined into weighted averages based on the quantities of goods shipped in 1972. Three statistics are now reported monthly: Raw goods, intermediate goods and finished goods.

This sounds pretty comprehensive, but it only covers 27 per cent of the products produced by the 550 major U.S. industries. Then, on examining the 27 per cent that is covered, it is found that many of the individual product price changes are based on reports from only one or two firms, which does not seem very representative. Even worse, many of the companies that voluntarily participate habitually report their list prices. List prices are often fiction. While they may sometimes be the same as transaction prices when demand is strong, they are not when demand softens. When orders slow, or even during good times in highly competitive industries, cash discounts or other price concessions from list price are common. Free delivery, buy 10 and get one free, bonus points, the variety of concessions from list price is unlimited. Then, of course, businessmen are often secretive about their prices. Even a bureau official admits, "We think we are getting good price quotes, but it's hard to tell. Price is a sensitive topic for most businessmen. The accounting department gives us prices but it may not be aware of discounts used by salesmen."

But there is more. The firms that voluntarily report are primarily the larger firms. Nonparticipating smaller firms are more competitive in their pricing.

Then, like the CPI, the Producer Price Index is not, according to many critics, properly adjusted for product quality improvements, especially in durable goods such as appliances which have become increasingly reliable and energy efficient.

It has been noted that the list or product prices included in the PPI cover about 27 per cent of the products produced. This, at first glance, may appear to be a pretty good sampling. But this arbitrary list is sadly out of date in some instances. For example, the office machinery category has shown increasingly higher prices in a period when computers have *dramatically reduced* the price of computation. In 1952 it cost over $1 to do 100,000 multiplications. Today, the cost is less than one cent. This very dramatic effective price decline in a major product was completely missed by the index. Computers, in fact most types of modern office equipment, are not even components of the index, but mimeograph machines still are. At least this was the case in 1978 when our study took place. The net result of all this is that not only is the price collection process out of touch with the

The Wholesale Price Index covers only 27 per cent of the products produced by major U.S. industries.

The universe of products making up the Wholesale Price Index excludes major areas where very significant price declines have taken place.

reality of transaction prices, but the universe of products making up the index is not representative, excluding major areas where very significant price declines have taken place.

These major flaws have not gone unnoticed by the Bureau of Labor Statistics. A program has been outlined to overhaul this index, including broader, more up to date industry coverage, larger samples of individual product prices, more scientific sampling techniques and a better method of determining actual transaction prices instead of the "token" list pricing now used.

This is all great but, again, it is a long, long time away. With current funds available, the bureau thinks it may be able to accomplish some of the easiest revisions by the mid-1980s. The wheels of bureaucracy turn slowly. In the meantime, this statistical horror will continue to overstate inflation, sometimes by absurd amounts, misleading the analysts, the businessmen, the press, the politicians, the Justice Department, the SEC, the economists and the man on the street. Remember more than $100 billion in long-term contracts (government transfer payments, cost of living adjustments, etc.) have delivery prices tied to this data.

Before moving on to the third major indicator of inflation, the GNP Deflator, we will quote an item as it appeared in the May 22, 1978, *Business Week*. Keep this in mind every time you see a reported monthly change in the PPI on the front page of your newspaper.

> "Today the Labor Dept. announced that, in some sense reflective of statistical truth, the annual rate of increase in wholesale prices of finished goods reached 16.8 per cent in April, more than doubling the 7.4 per cent pace set in March. But an unusually large part of the pick-up originated in one sector—jewelry. The department monitors this area with monthly samplings of the prices charged for earrings, necklaces and birthstone rings.
>
> "If there was ever a time when these items threatened to catapult the economy into a meteoric inflationary spiral, it was April. With birthstones accounting for virtually all the movement, the Labor Dept.'s wholesale jewelry price index shot up by 31.3 per cent in the month, which works out to an annual rate of 2,525.3 per cent. 'Sometimes what happens,' says one former Labor Dept. price expert, 'is that an index keeps coming in flat for three years, until someone decides to make an extra phone call. Then you get it all at once.'
>
> "In any event, *Business Week*'s ad hoc wholesale price index for 'finished goods less jewelry' also shows a pickup in April, but only to about an 11 per cent annual rate."

One could conclude this index should be junked now. Perhaps no index at all would be better than the distorted picture presented by this one.

Perhaps no index at all would be better than the distorted picture presented by the Wholesale Price Index.

The Gross National Product Deflator — Garbage In, Garbage Out

This is the last of our three most relied-on indicators of U.S. inflation. This index, the one preferred by most economists, is calculated by the Commerce Department's Bureau of Economic Analysis. Its original purpose was to "deflate" the current GNP calculation to constant dollars, so we can get a fix on underlying economic growth trends, excluding inflation or for that matter, deflation. This measure of inflation is preferable to many because of its breadth, incorporating consumer prices, producer prices, government costs and everything else that goes into calculating GNP. Most productivity calculations are based on this index.

The GNP Deflator is preferable to many because of its breadth.

Unfortunately, the Commerce Department uses the flawed CPI subsets of data to deflate many classes of consumer outlays and even uses the more flawed WPI data for many classifications of capital goods. So, it is that old computer age problem of "garbage in, garbage out." Now, it is true the Commerce Department relies on other special indices, such as a telephone equipment index provided by AT&T, but the CPI and WPI derived information has great impact.

There are other problems too. Almost half of the GNP is made up of services, not goods. No attempt is made to adjust for improvement in the quality of services. All increases in the cost of, say, haircuts are chalked up to inflation. The quality of haircuts may have improved, with styling, conditioning, maybe even a massage, but it is difficult to measure and, therefore, no quality improvement factor is attempted.

Then, from a practical usage standpoint, the GNP Deflator is reported late and is subject to many revisions as additional data trickle in from non-CPI/WPI sources. Early reports of the GNP Deflator are merely estimates and the revisions sometimes are quite significant in terms of magnitude.

In summary, government statisticians are aware of the problems, and a few criticisms, such as some of those related to the quality improvement factors, are arguable. But being aware of a problem and doing something about it are two different things. Collecting, tabulating and analyzing data has become vastly more efficient in the computer era, but it is taking the bureaucracy longer and longer to get anything accomplished.

Government statisticians are aware of the problem, but being aware and doing something about it are two different things.

These indicators are no longer statistics of passing interest, presenting approximations of price trends. They have become vitally important keystones of our entire economic and social matrix. Distortions can mean tens of billions of dollars in unjustified economic transfers in only a few years. The indices themselves certainly appear to be creating a signficant portion of the inflation they purport to only measure.

Further, these distortions can affect government policy decisions. The government might follow more restrictive monetary or fiscal policies than appropriate because it is misled by the apparent upward bias of the indicators.

And finally, businessmen and investors may be misled by the biased data. It is no secret that many U.S. corporations have held off capital investment in the past five years because of the high inflation figures. Might they not have proceeded with those investments, with resultant productivity improvements, if the inflation figures they worked from were lower?

If stock and bond market investors are getting incorrect data on inflation, how can they make correct investment decisions? If inflation is 2 per cent per year, the stock market will most likely have a good year. If it is 5 per cent, the stock market is more likely to have a poor year. But if the real inflation rate is 3 per cent while the indicators are saying it is 5 per cent, what will be the outcome?

Obviously, the investment analysis in this book has been based on the inflation figures *reported* by the CPI, be they flawed or not. The indicated approaches have worked in the past, but this could change if and when the flaws and biases in the inflation indices become more widely understood and are no longer relied upon as the gospel.

Postscript

As a postscript to this chapter, here is the author's early 1980 plea for action, taken from the investment strategy publication, *Perception for the Professional.*

"Stop the Bleeding"

In recent weeks much has been made in the press about a flaw in the Consumer Price Index, a flaw that even the government admits has caused as much as $5 billion in overpayment of benefits and wages tied to cost of living increases. The Congressional Budget Office says that in 1979 the method of measuring changes in home prices and mortgage costs pushed the CPI up by 3.3 per cent more than was justified by the actual increases in these costs.

Janet Norwood, commissioner of labor statistics, said however that no change would be made in the official index at this time, deploring the thought of a "quick fix."

Some of our readers may remember that exactly one year ago *Perception for the Professional* featured a detailed article entitled "The Inflation Indices as a Cause of Inflation," in which we discussed many flaws in the CPI, the GNP deflator, and the Producer Price Index. Yale economist Richard Ruggles and Northwestern's Robert Gordon, among others, have also been severe critics of the methodology employed to arrive at government produced inflation data.

The CPI is the single most important statistic produced by the U.S. government and clearly has continuously overstated inflation, not just in 1979, but for decades. And, as we and others have pointed out, there are numerous flaws and faults in the CPI's construction. *It is not just a matter of home prices and mortgage costs.*

To quote from the February, 1979, issue of Perception:
"In Summary..."

"Government statisticians are aware of the problems. But, being aware of a problem and doing something about it are two different things. Collecting, tabulating and analyzing data have become vastly more efficient in the computer era, *but it is taking the bureaucracy longer and longer to get anything accomplished.* If it is going to take government bureaucracy six years to remedy even the simple acknowledged flaws in these indices, perhaps the task should be farmed out to some private organizations. Time is of the essence.

"These indicators are no longer statistics of passing interest, presenting approximations of price trends. They have become vitally important keystones to our entire economic and social matrix. *Distortions can mean tens of billions of unjustified economic transfer in only a few years.* The indices themselves certainly appear to be creating a significant portion of the inflation they purport to only measure."

The sad part of the entire matter is that government statisticians have been well aware of many of the CPI flaws for years. *Still the massive overpayment hemorrhaging of taxpayer dollars has gone on and on.* A year ago, when researching this subject, we were told it might take six years or more before even the most easily corrected flaws were remedied.

If there ever was a case where "time is money," this is it. Literally hundreds of billions of dollars are at stake, not only in government benefits and salaries but also in the private sector's CPI-linked labor contracts and salary policies.

Yet Commissioner Norwood deplores the thought of a "quick fix." Careful study, review and analysis, with extensive model building, testing and re-review, are essential standard operating procedures in the bureaucracy before any action at all can be taken. That is the Washington way. So what if another $50 billion or even $100 billion of taxpayer money spills away in the meantime.

We suggest Commissioner Norwood and staff at the Bureau of Labor Statistics do all of us a favor and take a remedial crash course in Army Medical emergency procedure. I still clearly remember my instructor, 18 years ago, laying out the priorities for the battlefield.

"*First. Stop the bleeding!* Rags, leaves, stick your damm fist in the hole if you have to, to stop the bleeding! Then protect the wound and treat for shock. Do it quick. Do it now. The experts can take care of the niceties later with all their tests, equipment and consultations and precision. But if *you* don't act and act fast, *they* will be working on a cadaver."

Well, this nation's citizens are being bled white by inflation and by government. The CPI itself is one of the causes of the hemorrhaging. Its overstatement of inflation (perhaps by as much as 5 per cent to 6 per cent in 1979, all flaws considered) results in massive overpayments of government benefits and wages. And, because so much of our total economic system, public and private, is indexed to this one statistic, the CPI itself actually causes a significant portion of what it purports to measure.

If there ever was a need for an emergency "quick fix," the time is now. Stop the bleeding, Commissioner!

Chapter 15

Metamorphic Inflation: The Great Cycles

Which of the following statements are true?

1. During the last 1,000 years, the great cycles of inflation have occurred with a great deal of regularity.

2. Long-term inflationary trends seem to be fairly consistent from nation to nation.

3. Money supply seems to be the root cause of long-term inflation cycles.

4. The inflation surge of the last 70 years is essentially unprecedented.

5. Inflation existed about 60 per cent of the time, in the years from 950 through 1979.

Most economists ignore the
human aspects of the economic
equation, which cannot be easily
quantified.

Economists' Blind Spots: History and Change

What is the major failure of the art and science of economics practiced today? Most economists ignore the human aspects of the economic equation. These factors cannot be easily quantified, nor can the changes they cause be predicted or projected. Thus, economists shelter themselves from reality by viewing economic systems as machines powered by enduring natural laws and formulas, machines that can be adjusted by predictable cause and effect relationships.

Any serious analysis of world economic history would reveal the absurdity of this view of the economic world. Economic systems are created, controlled and manipulated by man with all his erratic, often irrational, behavior. The pseudo-science of economics is not physics. There are few, if any, ever-present, all-powerful natural laws of gravity the economist can rely on to keep order in his universe.

It's true that during a short-term period, even for decades, an economic system can be viewed as a machine of gears, wheels and levers that can be manipulated and adjusted with predictable results. Pump up the money supply and the economy is stimulated. Raise taxes to slow it down. In the 1960s, some of these pseudo-scientists even believed the machine could be fine-tuned to such a degree that cyclical economic contractions could be all but eliminated.

Unfortunately, these clockwork machines don't operate smoothly for long. Other human attitudinal factors, like greed and fear and quest for power, keep getting in the gears. Then major social change or a series of dramatic technological breakthroughs can cause the machine to no longer work at all. In these periods, the old machinery can become totally inadequate, obsolete...a buggywhip economic system in a jet propulsion age.

Man is not yet capable of disrupting the solar system. He can not invalidate the laws of physics. But man can, in the phraseology popular a few years ago, make an economic system "inoperative."

Man cannot invalidate the laws
of physics, but he can make an
economic system inoperative.

Most economists existing in their closed little world, a world constructed out of recent past economic trends, either purposely ignore the potential of major change or don't know any better. A few years ago, after listening to a speech of his, I asked one of today's economic superstars to compare current inflation with post-World War II inflation. "Why?" he said. "That's ancient history. It means nothing." Economists, as a race, prefer today's theory to the lessons of hard economic history. Lord Keynes scoffed at the significance of past economic history saying, "History is for undergraduates." Remember, it was only 10 years ago when most of the U.S. economic establishment insisted gold was no longer significant, calling it a barbaric metal and a relic of the economic past. "What is the possible utility of a metal one digs out of the ground in one place and then reburies in Fort Knox?"

As David Warsh, an economic thinker and writer, noted in an excellent 1977 *Forbes* article on inflation, "Why do economists generally despise history? I think it's because they live in Newton's clockwork universe...a clock doesn't have history; it has mechanisms. An economist's world doesn't need history, for it is like a clock." Unfortunately, a clock is of little use if one has no idea what time zone he is in.

History, Economists and Inflation

Harry Truman supposedly once said (maybe it was really James Whitmore): "The only thing new in the world is the history we don't know." This may have been a borrowed thought from Confucius who said: "To study the past is to divine the future."

But one of the best introductory quotations for a history lesson comes from Willie Nelson, a favorite noneconomic philosopher. Readers may not be familiar with Nelson's work. He is still obscure in academic circles, not yet included in most philosophy survey courses. However, unlike most noneconomic philosophers, Nelson seems to have done quite well monetarily. And, in the world of money and investment, this decidedly increases his credibility. In 1978 both *Time* and *Newsweek* included feature articles on Nelson and his work. Even President Carter listens to him.

At any rate, in 1974, Willie Nelson released a record album called "Phases and Stages." It's the album's bridging theme that serves as an excellent introductory quotation to a history lesson:

"Phases and stages,
"Circles and cycles,
"Scenes that we've all seen before
"...let me tell you some more."

Now, history may or may not be the key to understanding the current inflationary cycle. It is remotely possible we have entered a really new age. But the more one studies the inflationary past, the more it is believed there is much to be learned from it. Basic human interaction, emotion and reaction have changed very little. While mankind appears far more sophisticated than it was 400 years ago, underneath the same driving forces prevail. Greed, fear, self-esteem, survival and competitive drive may be clothed now in a three-piece suit or blue jeans, driving a Buick or a Ford pickup, but, underneath all the dressings of our society, these primeval traits still exist. As they emerge, the outer layer of reason and rationality is often shattered. The political and economic systems of the world are created by man. They also are irrationally manipulated and irrationally destroyed by man, be it by war or inflation.

History rarely repeats itself in the strict sense. Part of the Willie Nelson lyric borrowed to introduce this history lesson may, to some, seem to imply regular repetition: "Phases and stages, circles and cycles, scenes that we've all seen before." This should be viewed in the larger sense. "Phases and stages" mean change is to be expected, sometimes dramatic change. "Circles and cycles" may seem to indicate a clockwork regularity to these changes, but circles can be of varying sizes and cycles, meaning evolution and metamorphosis can be sudden or

The more one studies the inflationary past, the more there is to be learned from it.

drawn out. The "scenes that we've all seen before" are the scenes of disruption and imbalances brought on during the process of change.

To many, cycles seem to imply some unknown supernatural governing force that causes various events to recur on a regular basis. The word "cycle" comes from the Greek word for circle. But there is no implication that a regular period of time is involved. If regular time periods are present, a cycle is labeled a "rhythm." Rhythms are commonly found in biology. Salmon, owl, hawk and rabbit populations peak every 9.6 years, lemmings rush to the sea every 3.9 years (probably led by an economist), and there are regular peaks and valleys of heart disease in New England.

The long-term inflation/stability cycle examined here is not rhythmic in nature nor do we believe it to be governed by some unknown supernatural force.

> The long-term inflation/stability cycle is not rhythmic in nature, nor is it governed by some unknown supernatural force.

Throughout centuries, man has expanded his knowledge, learned new skills and consequently modified his life style. These changes, when combined with human elemental constants, such as greed, fear and competitive drive, can occasionally ignite to blow apart the existing state of social and economic equilibrium. At that point, the economists' tidy, little organized world no longer exists. He pulls the levers, pushes the buttons and shifts the gears, but they no longer work. That is what this history lesson is all about. The lesson to be learned from economic history is that economic systems, no matter how "scientifically" administered and regulated, have, in the past, eventually reached a point where they cannot cope. A state of disequilibrium erupts, usually accompanied by inflation. Eventually, a new system evolves that accommodates the changes. The pressures are relieved, equilibrium returns and inflation subsides.

Social, technological and life style changes, although most difficult to build into an econometric model, are, in the long run, far more important economic considerations than changes in M-1, interest rates, or measures of consumer confidence. But the typical economist pays only token attention to these, preferring to remain isolated in his secure little quantifiable world of formulas and data derived from the last 15 years. In stock market parlance, he is so intent on determining tomorrow's market action that he fails to recognize a major move in the making.

Now, let's examine the major socio-economic moves of the last 1,000 years and the inflation that accompanied them. What then, can the economist learn from history?

The Thesis of Metamorphic Inflation

The chart demonstrates there have been four great periods of sustained inflation during the last 1,000 years, ranging from 70 to 170 years. Each of these explosive inflation surges coincides with a period of extremely significant socio-economic metamorphic change. As man and his society adjust to and digest this change, and as the changing factors stabilize, price equilibrium eventually develops for extended periods of 100 to 250 years. The

> Each explosive inflation surge coincides with a period of extremely significant socio-economic metamorphic change.

The Metamorphic Surges
of Inflation
950-1979

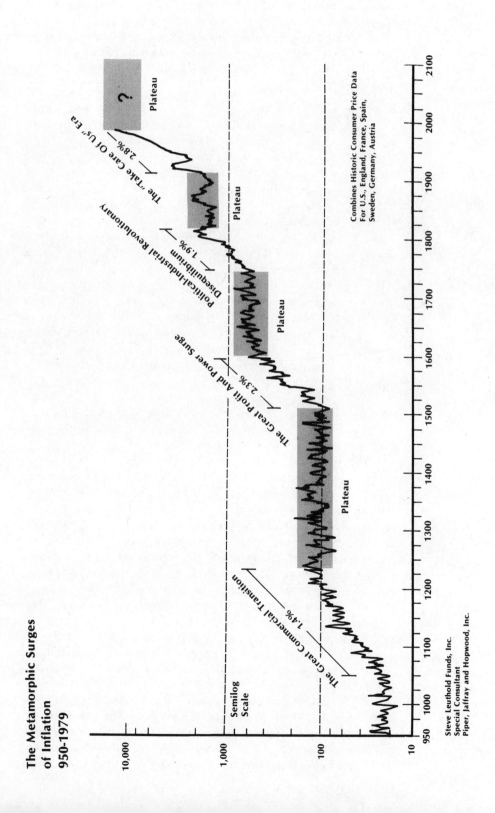

Steve Leuthold Funds, Inc.
Special Consultant
Piper, Jaffray and Hopwood, Inc.

economic system has finally adapted to the changed conditions and inflation, except for cyclical and extraneous inflationary/deflationary swings, disappears. Relative price equilibrium has prevailed for very long periods, sometimes for centuries. In terms of duration, these very long-term phases and stages are irregular. The inflationary periods of great change do not recur on any particular time schedule. These supercycles are not clocklike, not governed by some powerful natural law.

The Data

Before examining the reasons underlying four great inflationary spasms, the techniques used to track and measure 1,000 years of consumer prices should be explained.

In 1975, an article in *Forbes* magazine called attention to a remarkable consumer price index purporting to represent 700 years of consumer price trends in England. Oxford economic history professor E. H. Phelps Brown and his assistant, Sheila Hopkins, laboriously reconstructed a market basket of basic consumer goods an English working man would require and, using old records, they priced its contents back to 1264. The contents of the basket changed from time to time reflecting usage patterns. This index was a starting point for our chart. We sought, blended and weighted other western European consumer price data into this landmark work, including French consumer prices back to 1276, Swedish information back to 1460, as well as German, Spanish and Alsatian data.

When comparing the consumer price trends in eight western European localities with Phelps Brown's index, a remarkable degree of consistency was found. The accompanying chart demonstrates this. It's true that comparative year by year data were, at times, inconsistent, but the big picture trends were amazingly similar for all series examined.

The price information prior to Phelps Brown's 1264 starting point is the product of *Forbes'* David Warsh. Warsh combined reliable price data from other scholars, developing an estimated measure back to 950. Obviously this work, and Professor Brown's for that matter, is hardly precise and is subject to error, but it certainly is valuable in portraying long-term trends.

Turning to more recent times, U.S. consumer price data were introduced into our long-term index in 1800. From 1914 to date, only U.S. consumer price data are used in our index.

All in all, it is believed this index is probably a fair approximation of long-term consumer price trends experienced by the relatively advanced surviving Western economic societies of Europe and North America. As noted, the trend variance from nation to nation based on reseach done so far is much less than expected.

The index is not meant to be a world inflation index. It incorporates no data from South America or China. The index also excludes that 1,000 per cent-plus smashing hyperinflation of, say, post World War I Germany, inflation that literally destroys a nation's economy. However, there are years of 60 per cent to 100

We believe our index is probably a fair approximation of long-term consumer price trends experienced by the relatively advanced surviving Western economic societies.

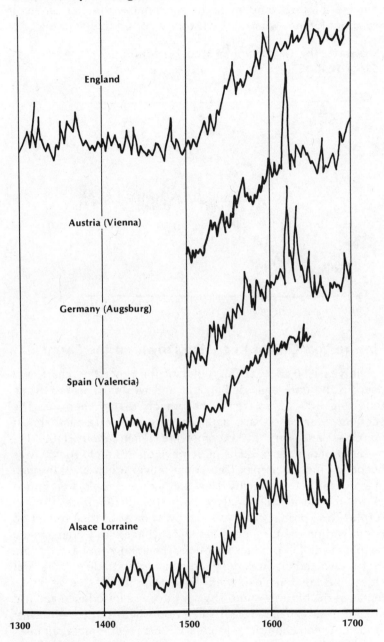

England

Austria (Vienna)

Germany (Augsburg)

Spain (Valencia)

Alsace Lorraine

1300   1400   1500   1600   1700

per cent annual individual national inflation incorporated in the
composite index. Our usage test was: Does some form of
workable economic system survive?

Hopefully, scholars in the future will do more work on expanding our knowledge of historic inflation trends. The Confucius
quotation, "To study the past is to divine the future," does not
imply history will repeat, only that it will help you better concep-
tualize future developments.

A few years ago, a widely respected economic figure said flat-
ly, "This new wage-price explosion is altogether unprecedented."

That level of ignorance is a poor base on which to build a rational analysis of future economic trends. Unfortunately, this man has a lot of company in the economic world. Remember, it was Lord Keynes who said, "History is for undergraduates."

**Spasm I - The Great Commercial Transition
(Circa 1050-1220)**

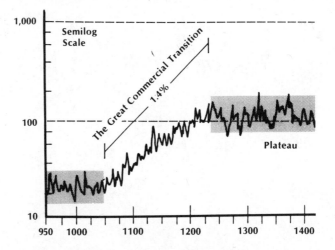

How're You Gonna Keep 'Em Down on the Farm?

The year 950, the starting point of the preceding chart, was deep in the dark ages of England and western Europe. In the following 100 or so years, not much really changed. The economy was simple and agrarian, very few craftsmen, almost no cities and very little commerce. Then about 1100, the metamorphosis started. The underdeveloped simple society was becoming more complex. The prime mover was a breakthrough in agricultural productivity. New methods and tools, iron tipped plows and horse collars, along with specialization, resulted in surplus food production. No longer was most of the production consumed on the farm or in the local village, nor were so many people needed to produce the food. The immigration from country to town and city was on. People moved to trade centers, and cities like London developed. Trade was facilitated as coins replaced the barter system. The contract was introduced and use of credit was expanded. Craftsmen flourished, as did merchants. Trade between countries was greatly expanded. A more complex form of government, feudal monarchy, emerged and the kings went on crusades. Continental and English population started to grow again in this period, a response to agricultural productivity increases.

A pure monetarist might say the money supply increase, Arab gold, coins, credit and contracts brought this dramatic economic expansion, but that's putting the cart before the horse. What impact would increased money supply have had if the increase in agricultural productivity had not freed people from toiling in the fields? Money supply growth was the *response* to the major changes taking place, not the cause. Population growth and

About 1100, the underdeveloped simple society began becoming more complex, due largely to a breakthrough in agricultural productivity.

other factors sometimes cited as a cause of this inflation period were, in reality, fallout from the agrarian productivity increases.

This great metamorphic change—the move from farm to city—was too much for the old economic ways to handle. Until a system was developed to facilitate the quantum jump in economic activity, metamorphic inflation existed. A new equilibrium level apparently was established in the early 1200s. The long metamorphic inflation thrust was over, replaced by shorter term cyclical inflation/deflation cycles, an erratic course that prevailed for at least 250 years. Assuredly there were dramatic bouts of both inflation and deflation in this span caused by events such as the Black Death and the 100 Years War. But the net for the entire period, after all the roller coaster ups and downs, was little or no net increase in consumer prices in a period of 250-plus years. Why this long net stability? No new major societal metamorphosis really emerged until the early 1500s.

The great metamorphic change from farm to city was too much for the old economic ways to handle.

Spasm II - The Great Profit And Power Surge
(Circa 1500-1600)

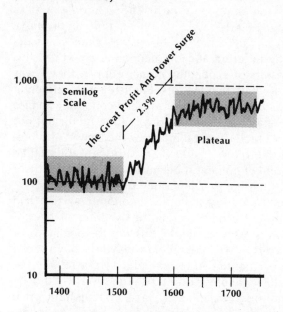

Around 1500 another dynamic age of metamorphic change emerged, one sometimes referred to as the "dynamic century." In this period, the church stopped viewing charging interest and making profits as wicked. Actually, the pursuit of monetary reward came to be encouraged by the priests, and this was very significant in the church-dominated society that existed then. Large accumulations of private capital took place. Also in this period, government's role was expanded, even bureaucratized to some degree, as the dynamic monarchies of England, France and Spain centralized power. In this period, taxes were broadly applied for the first time.

Commercial colonialism expanded greatly, bringing world markets and active trade. With this trade and discovery came the gold and more importantly the silver from the New World, which

The period beginning around 1500 marked the real emergence of the modern western world we know today as the complexities of society increased socially, politically and economically.

By the early 1600s, a more complex economic system had evolved, adapting and digesting the dynamic changes of the previous 100 years.

expanded the money supply. All in all, during this period, the mix of jobs and occupational specialties grew incredibly. Population in Europe also renewed its growth. The complexities of society increased, socially, politically and economically. This period marked the real emergence of the modern western world we know today. Foreign affairs and diplomacy, both with guns and words, came into sharp focus in this century. Powerful nations vied to expand their horizons and control. In this 100-year period, there were only 25 years when no large-scale warlike operation was going on in Europe.

This was a century when profits and accumulation of capital grew tremendously for selected members of society. Materialism and mercantilism were encouraged by church and government. Government power and involvement expanded, both domestically and abroad. Economic and political power became much stronger, more concentrated and centralized.

The old decentralized commercial economic system that had endured for several centuries could no longer cope with these surging powerful changes.

Some historians would point to renewed population growth as a major factor underlying this dynamic 100-year metamorphosis, but it appears this was more of an effect than a cause. Monetarists say the inflation and the economic growth in this period were the results of expanding money supply, that it was all those precious metals flowing into English and Continental economies that was the root cause of all the economic changes and inflation. This may have been a contributing factor but not the root cause. The precious metal mines of the New World produced far more in the following 100 years of price stability than in this 100-year period of metamorphic inflation. Obviously there was far more to it than the simple money supply theory.

By the early 1600s, a more complex economic system had evolved after adapting to and digesting the dynamic changes of the previous 100 years. As an example, this was the beginning of modern credit markets as we know them today. Although social and economic change continued to take place from 1600 to the mid-1700s, it was slower and less dramatic. The system could apparently handle it fairly well, and a stage of long-term price equilibrium again prevailed, interrupted at times by some zigzags from nasty wars and political upheavals. Spain, even with its massive inflows of gold and silver continuing, was a financial disaster. In this period, the Dutch, then the English developed very sophisticated and effective financial systems.

The mid-1700s marked the beginnings of the third period of great metamorphic change in England and Europe. The prevailing estalished economic-political systems, ones that had fairly well accommodated the socio-economic changes of the last 150 years, broke down. And, as in the past, a dramatic surge of inflation erupted. But finally about 70 years later, in the early 1800s, another period of equilibrium was achieved. This was to prevail for 100 years, until the early 1900s.

A wave of political change swept across Europe and other parts of the world in this dramatic period of industrial and

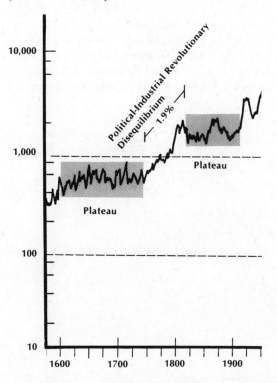

political revolutions. The old concepts of absolute monarchies, "divine rights" of kings and church rule were swept away. The French Revolution and the American Revolution were the most dramatic products of the new political philosophy: Government was for the people and by the people. England became a limited monarchy, and the modern parliamentary system was born.

Prior to this sweeping change, guilds had controlled much of the industry in Europe, restricting membership and output, and opposing new methods. The guilds, already on the decline, fell with the monarchies. So did many of the restricting tolls and taxes that previously had restricted trade and economic development. The wars and turmoil in this period brought intense pressures to bear on the financing resources. Fortunes were lost and interest rates soared. The power of the church declined and people were no longer preoccupied with religion.

Accompanying all this massive political and philosophical change was the Industrial Revolution, with the steam engine and the growing use of coal. There was widespread introduction of machines to do the work of humans. Canals and turnpikes were built. Manufacturing became a big business, and industrial capitalists and powerful commercial bankers emerged. Bloody-clawed capitalism came into being, and the doctrine of *laissez-faire* came on the scene. Industrial freedom marched hand in hand with the new democratic forms of government. The attitude toward business and capitalists was essentially "hands off."

Inflation peaked in the early 1800s, and prices came down sharply after the last decade of the Napoleonic Wars. With the

Accompanying a massive political and philosophical change was the Industrial Revolution, with the steam engine and the growing use of coal.

advent of peace, the economies of western Europe and England got down to business. Total output and productivity leaped ahead with the new technology of the Industrial Revolution. The 19th century became the industrial age, and the metamorphic inflation of the previous 70 years disappeared. Consumer prices in 1910 were no higher than they were 100 years earlier. There were, of course, cyclical bouts of inflation and deflation, but clearly a new equilibrium had been achieved, and it prevailed for more than a century.

**Spasm IV - The "Take Care Of Us" Era
(1910-?)**

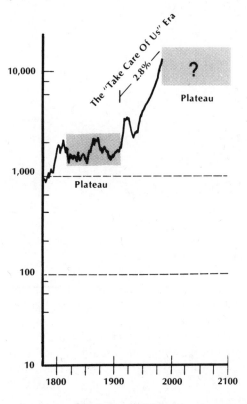

So it was that the 1800s were prosperous and fairly stable in the advanced countries of western civilization. It was a century of little armed conflict. The new forms of democratic government took a *laissez-faire*, more or less hands-off, approach in economic and social affairs. It was a new form of government but generally an era of minimal, almost innocuous, government. Government responsibilities were seen as keeping domestic order, providing an appropriate degree of pomp, providing protection against foreign enemies and providing a court system. The economic benefits of the industrial revolution extended far down the economic order as increased productivity and fairly free international trade raised the standard of living in even the lower economic classes. Hard gold-backed currency prevailed in this period and inflation, except for a few fits and starts, was nonexistent. Consumer prices ended the century below what they had been at the century's beginning.

The 1800s were prosperous and fairly stable as new forms of democratic government took a hands-off approach in economic and social affairs.

The Social Winds of Change

But around 1900, a new pervasive metamorphic change began emerging in England, then the most advanced industrial, political and economic power in the western world. The "take care of us" era appears to have started in that first decade of the 20th century. Parliament, now a government by the people and for the people, responding to the desires and power of the newly mobilized laboring classes and partially under the banner of the Fabian socialist philosophy, enacted a new kind of legislation — social legislation.

By 1910 the first broad pension, health and unemployment insurance and income tax legislation had been enacted. Other advanced European nations followed England's lead. To the east, there was the Russian revolution, at least incorporating some of the same concepts of government's changing role. The U.S., being a younger, less advanced country than her European brethren, lagged. The "take care of us" metamorphosis did not begin in U.S. until the early 1930s, in the depths of the Depression. The "New Deal" programs were, in many ways, adaptations of that original English social legislation of the early 1900s.

By 1910 the English government was beginning to take the place of the church and charity by caring for the old, the hungry and the disadvantaged. Government, responding to the electorate, in effect got religion and developed a social conscience. This new government role in society was a radical departure from the previous century, and it greatly increased the breadth and the expense of government. In the coming years, this change dramatically affected the economic and social fabric of society. And, as was the case in the preceding three periods of dramatic change, the metamorphic changing process also brought inflation.

Government, in the early 1900s, got religion and developed a social conscience.

The System Breaks Down

In the early 1900s, the English economic system was able to cope fairly well with this new government role and its associated costs; at least this was the case up to World War I. Between 1914 and 1918, English taxes tripled but still only 28 per cent of the war expenditures came from these taxes. The national debt of England was increased 11-fold in this period. Historically, wars have always strained financial systems, but a guns-and-butter combination was really taxing. Financing and administering the social and military efforts further expanded government's role in the war years, and, unlike the past, when peace came, the government's war-expanded role did not significantly contract.

A short 12 years after World War I, the western world found itself in a depression. In these hard times, the social and economic role of government surged ahead. The economic doldrums and lower revenues coupled with this increased role of government and its associated costs were more than most existing economic systems could cope with. The large and efficient world credit markets, which had previously served the western

After World War I, world credit markets could no longer provide the huge amounts of capital required by increasingly socially oriented governments.

world's economies so well in the 1800s and early 1900s, could no longer provide the huge amounts of capital required by increasingly socially oriented governments. Politicians would not and could not (if they wanted to stay in office) hold down the pressures for greater social expenditures. Government deficit spending suddenly seemed a necessity, not a sin.

In 1931, these combined pressures blew the lid off. England abandoned the gold standard. By the end of 1932, 34 other countries followed. Only a handful of hard currencies remained. The wraps were off the printing presses and for the most part the days of hard currencies were over. National priorities had shifted in the most powerful countries. Hard currencies and fiscal responsibility took a distant backseat to full employment, social security and health and welfare.

The "take care of us" era had dramatically emerged. Responsibility for the old, the unemployed, the sick and the hungry was now clearly perceived as primarily government's responsibility, and no longer, as was the case in the 1800s, mainly the responsibility of church, charity or relatives. As this social and political metamorphosis proceeded, monetary discipline went out the back door. The fourth great sustained inflation surge was well underway.

The Die Had Been Cast

The Great Depression was a terribly important event in this period. Throughout history, economic contractions and depressions have brought deflation, and the 1930s also brought deflation but only temporarily. In a larger sense, this depression actually intensified and accelerated the metamorphic inflation of this "take care of us" era.

The 1930s were hard times for a great many people. Fifty or a 100 years earlier, it would not have been perceived as government's prime responsibility to take care of the citizens, nor for government to actively participate in solving the economic problem. But, as pointed out, by the 1930s, this hands-off attitude was long gone. Governments in the U.S., England and western Europe mobilized, often with untried potential solutions. Many programs involved spending money the governments did not have, borrowing heavily and in the process, degrading the currencies.

As in past depressions, a rebound eventually came. In many nations, this rebound was stimulated by the pre-World War II buildup. Then the war itself provided additional stimulus for many economies. But even as the economies rebounded, the momentum for more government services and programs continued. A temporary stabilization developed during WWII with its full employment and priority military spending. But this pause was only for the duration. The die had been cast, and when the war was over, the social and economic roles of government began growing again. The U.S. government also took on a new financial responsibility, rebuilding western Europe. This was in some ways an extension of the "take care of us" perception of government, a social conscience, so to speak.

The momentum for more government services and programs continued during the pre-World War II buildup and during the war itself.

The government role grew even more in the 1950s and 1960s. Government spending—federal, state and local—marched onward and upward, financed directly or indirectly by higher taxes, more borrowing and deficit spending. By the time the Vietnam war came along, the U.S. leaders had come to believe that government could handle a massive social war and a military war at the same time. Guns and butter. We can do it all! This period could well go down in history as the apex of big government.

Prime Considerations

But is government's expanded role really the underlying cause of the great 20th century inflation surge?

Certainly part of the inflation during this period was war related. World Wars I and II brought bursts of inflation as did some lesser conflicts. Historically, wars have created short-term inflationary pressures because their costs abnormally stretch the economic resources of the involved nations. But this wartime inflation also quickly subsided when the conflicts were over. The pervasive inflation since 1910 can not be explained away by wars.

As in the earlier three periods of massive metamorphic change and the accompanying metamorphic inflation, the monetarist will attempt to rationalize and explain the inflation as merely a matter of money supply expansion. Again this ignores the big forest and, to mix a metaphor, it puts the cart before the horse. The very long-term expansion of the money supply in this period was necessary to accommodate and facilitate the dynamic expansion of government's sphere and more recently to accommodate government deficits.

Inflation usually begets money supply growth, not the other way around. If a dollar is worth less because of inflation, more dollars must be provided to keep an economic system on an even level. In the short-term, if money supply growth exceeds inflation, it may be stimulative and perhaps accelerate inflation. If money supply growth is less than inflation, it may act as a drag on the economic system, thus slowing inflation. But in a broad brush sense, the supply of money expands to accommodate a nation's economic growth, be it private or government growth. If long-term endemic inflation exists, it also must be accommodated by a corresponding growth in money supply just to maintain an even level.

Inflation usually begets money supply growth, not the other way around.

On the surface, the population/inflation theory seems to work in this phase of history. Population growth in the U.S. and Europe has accelerated fom 1910 to date, but has the inflation merely been the result of too many people chasing too few goods? Before accepting this thesis, consider that population also increased as dramatically in the 1800 to 1910 period, a period that had no net increases in consumer prices.

In summary, although the major wars and the Great Depression were extremely important events in the 1910 to date period, the root cause of our great metamorphic inflation seems to be the massive expansion of government's role within the social and

Inflation is not a relatively
simple matter, but rather a very
complex affair with social
causes.

economic segments of society. As was the case in the earlier eruptions of massive societal change, the previously existing economic system proved to be inadequate. And again, a major inflation spasm resulted. Inflation is not, as most economists (including Keynes and Friedman) seem to believe, a relatively simple matter with social *consequences*. Rather, long-term inflation trends are very complex affairs with social *causes*.

The western world is still in the throes of this most recent massive spasm. The economic systems have not yet adjusted to the metamorphic change. However, there are some encouraging indications and some evidence that the adjustment process has begun. This is the topic of the final chapter.

Some Numbers to Chew On

The long-term inflation study charted earlier in this chapter yields some interesting statistics, data that are helpful in maintaining perspective. The working base is somewhat crude, but over longer spasms it probably represents the inflationary and deflationary trends experienced by the western world's established economies.

Over the entire millennium, the annual compound rate of inflation for this index is 0.6 per cent per year, and the median rate is 1.3 per cent. Approximately 47 per cent of the years have been inflationary (more than 1 per cent) and 41 per cent deflationary (prices down more than 1 per cent). The remaining 12 per cent of the years are classified as stable, (1 per cent inflation to 1 per cent deflation).

The Great Inflation Spasms

Now let's examine the four great metamorphic inflation spasms. Starting and ending dates may not be as precise as they appear because of the crudeness of the data. The same holds true for rates of change.

	Approx. Duration	Years	Starting Index	Ending Index	Increase	Annual Compound Rate
The Great Commercial Transition	1050-1230	180	20	150	650%	1.35
The Great Profit and Power Surge	1509-1597	88	92	685	645%	2.30
Political - Industrial Revolutionary Disequilibrium	1744-1813	67	518	1,881	263%	1.94
The "Take Care Of Us" Era	1910-79	69	1826	13,268	627%	2.92

There are also four periods when metamorphic inflation was absent and relative long-term price stability prevailed. Cyclical inflationary and deflationary moves are found in these periods, but no metamorphic inflation appears to exist. The first such period, 950 to 1050, may have existed longer than the 100 years indicated. No data prior to 950 are available in workable form.

Examination of these tables and the 1,000-year chart on page 173 demonstrates that inflation has not been a permanent,

	Approx. Duration	Years	Starting Index	Ending Index	Change	Annual Compound Rate
Plateau I	950-1050	100	20	20	0.0	0.0
Plateau II	1231-1508	277	128	121	− 5.5	0.0
Plateau III	1598-1743	145	670	712	+ 6.3	0.0
Plateau IV	1814-1909	95	2297	2268	− 1.3	0.0

always-present part of economic history. Also, it appears great inflation surges and subsequent periods of relative stability do not operate on any regular clock. These are superinflation cycles but they have no real rhythmic characteristics. Uniformity in terms of elapsed time between occurrence magnitude and duration is not to be found. All we can say is that they last a long time. As man's knowledge continues to expand, great metamorphic societal change may occur somewhat more frequently and future economic systems may succeed in adapting somewhat more quickly than in the past. We will leave that for Herman Kahn to speculate upon.

As man's knowledge continues to expand, great metamorphic societal change may occur somewhat more frequently and future economic systems may adapt more quickly than in the past.

Intermediate-Term Inflation History

A summary of intermediate-term inflation periods may be helpful. Most of today's observers might classify our intermediate-term periods as permanent conditions because they include only inflation bursts of 25 years or longer. These periods represent major cyclical inflation moves of varying intensity as well as isolated events of inflation resulting from wars and other extraneous factors. These intermediate bursts are sometimes found within the entended plateau periods as well as within the metamorphic inflation surges.

The primary purpose of this exercise is to place the current inflation burst, starting in 1933, in proper historic perspective. The short-term accelerations, such as 1966 to date, and the flares of three or four years in duration are not examined. Again, the data employed in the following table are quite crude prior to 1900. But nevertheless, the data are valuable for comparison.

Intermediate-Term Inflation History

Duration	Years	% Change	Annual Compound Rate
1000-1020	20	+106.3%	+ 3.7%
1050-1075	25	150.0	+ 3.7
1080-1140	60	166.7	+ 1.6
1190-1230	40	114.3	+ 1.9
1283-1316	33	200.0	+ 3.4
1343-1370	27	119.0	+ 2.9
1464-1483	19	88.4	+ 3.4
1504-1531	27	90.2	+ 2.4
1537-1557	20	217.1	+ 5.9
1558-1597	39	197.8	+ 2.8
1604-1649	45	103.2	+ 1.6
1691-1711	20	80.3	+ 3.0
1744-1774	30	98.3	+ 2.3
1779-1813	34	169.3	+ 3.0
1834-1867	33	67.1	+ 1.6
1895-1926	31	173.9	+ 3.3
1933-1979	46	613.5	+ 4.0

Chapter 16

Economists or Shamans?

Today you are 25. If inflation continues at a rate of 7 per cent, how much would today's $7,000 compact car cost you when you retire at age 65?

A. $10,500

B. $26,000

C. $47,000

D. $105,000

The final chapters of this book deal with the future. Most of what has preceded has been history; some, very ancient history.

As discussed earlier, most of today's economists have very little sense of long-term economic history. Lord Keynes set the tone when he said, "History is for undergraduates."

Confucius, on the other hand, said, "To study the past is to divine the future." Because most practicing economists are, to a large degree, in the business of making future short- and long-term predictions, there seems to be a contradiction here. Who do we believe? The modern economic contingent that scoffs at the musty old stuff or those voices from the past like Confucius or, as quoted earlier, Harry Truman?

Well, it's certainly true that trained economists are becoming more numerous and more important in our world. Their professional ranks are expanding faster than a South American nation's money supply. But, we must remember the great economic contributors of an earlier time were often not even trained as economists. Adam Smith was a moral philosopher. David Ricardo was a stockbroker. Economics as a specialized profession is a relatively new development. The American Economic Association was not founded until 1885 and by 1925 membership numbered only 3,000. MIT's economics department, now viewed as one of the best, did not even exist in the 1930s.

The great economic contributors of earlier times were often not even trained as economists.

Today membership in the American Economic Association is 20,000, but this is only the tip of the iceberg. The U.S. Department of Labor figures there are more than 115,000 working economists in the U.S., one economist for every four lawyers, one for every two CPAs. Economics may be our society's newest profession and, although it doesn't have as many practitioners as the "oldest profession," there are now just as many economists as dentists and, according to Paul Samuelson, as many as chiropractors.

The old definition of an economist as one who knows all about money but doesn't have any no longer fits. The professions' superstars make $400,000 per year and more; and the typical business economist is on a par with the typical lawyer in terms of earning power. Adding up all the salaries, book sales and economic services, you find the industry is a $2 billion per year proposition. Not so long ago, an economic consultant firm was sold for over $100 million.

In days of yore, the idea of economic forecasting and manipulating the economy never occurred to people. A century ago, the world economic system was becoming very complex, but it was not the government's function to do anything about it. Predicting the future was the territory of the astrologers and sorcerers; today it's the economists'. We are now inundated by economic forecasts. To quote from a January, 1979, issue of *Pensions & Investments* magazine:

In days of yore, the idea of economic forecasting and manipulating the economy never occurred to people.

> "Late December/early January is the traditonal thermal pollution time in the investment business. The atmosphere is temporarily clouded by the hot air of forecasts, prognostications and predictions for the

New Year. Unfortunately though, in 1978 some brokers and investment managers came on hard times and can no longer afford those inhouse economists who traditionally disgorge this material. (Rumor has it that Jimmy the Greek and Jeanne Dixon have ghostwritten several of the more troubled firms' 1979 outlooks and forecasts.)"

Economics has become a big business populated with Ph.D.s running computer models and massaging detailed data bases. The reams of computer printouts and miles of charts put forth a very scientific image, building confidence in the output. But in recent years, as detailed earlier in this book, the forecasts emanating from all this don't seem to be much more reliable than what the astrologers and sorcerers whispered in some king's ear centuries ago. In view of the dismal recent record, why do so many pay so much for these forecasts and pay so much attention to them?

Art Versus Science

In the last two decades, economists have become taken with the quantifiability of their art. The input is so orderly and the numbers appear so precise. And the computer can do a great job extrapolating all those past numbers, even the revisions to the revisions. Unfortunately, effective economics still remains an art, not a mathematical science. New and different factors, factors not experienced in the past (at least not in that part of the past covered by the modern data base), can blow the best model apart. The first OPEC price increase is a good example. Because it was something new, more than a few economists seemed to pretend it had not happened. First, they were not sure how to deal with it, and, second, because it occurred late in 1973, it was difficult revising 1974 forecasts. Also if a revised conclusion differed radically from what the economic herd was saying, the revisionist ran the risk of looking pretty silly. In the world of economics, looking silly, even if it is temporary, can often be far worse than being wrong. At any rate, in late 1973, few economists anticipated the high inflation in 1974 or the depth of the subsequent recession.

Unfortunately, many economists are essentially highly paid numbers crunchers. How does a statistician assess, say, the Johnson administration's decision to fight the Vietnam war and the war on poverty concurrently? A meaningful assessment required imagination and creative thinking because it was something new, it was not in the data base and it was not a function of projecting the last 10 years of data. This, then, is the *art* of economics.

The extensive supply of economic statistics only creates the illusion of quantifiable science. Economists for the most part appear to have no real sense of longer term economic history. Perhaps it's because the completeness and the easy accessibility of economic statistics of the last couple of decades provide a tempting trap. When an economist says the only important data

> Although the computer can do a great job extrapolating all those numbers, effective economics still remains an art, not a mathematical science.

are those which have been gathered since WWII, he may be limiting his total comprehension. Some economists seem to believe economic history begins where the computer data base begins. Thus, future projections often become projections based on immediate past experience. Longer term trends and cycles, be they rhythmic or not, are lost or not recognized.

The Search for Universal Natural Laws

There are some economic theorists who are dedicated to discovering the universal natural laws that govern economic systems, forces and relationships that are immortal. Mercantilists, Keynesians and now monetarists all think they had the keys to universal economic truth. Today Phillips and Laffer explain a complicated world with simple diagrams. Somehow these economic theorists attract large crowds of sophisticated devoted followers, including politicians, academicians and intellectuals, all looking for the new economic messiah, with the universal truth.

Economic theorists attract large crowds of sophisticated devoted followers, all looking for the new messiah.

These followers must be true believers. They do not ask for proof, extensive quantitative testing or detailed historical/practical application. If the shoe looks good, is momentarily comfortable and seems to fit, they buy it. Invariably they find that one pair of shoes is not practical for changing environments. Soon the shoes develop holes or hurt like hell. Then, it's back to the theoretician for patching and stretching, but alas ultimately the shoe is eventually discarded. What then? Well, it's right back to a new economic theorist's store to select another model that promises to wear forever, that is practical in all environments and that always feels great.

Well, it is one thing to pay $60 and put your feet in a magic pair of shiny, new, untested shoes, but it's quite another to put a multibillion dollar economic system in the same kind of pollyanna merchandise.

Why is it that business and government continue to pay so much attention to today's economists? Why does a major corporation spend millions of dollars on economic projections? It certainly isn't the track record. Why does government initiate costly programs on these same projections? Why do politicians and even academicians so readily leap for an economic magic pair of shoes? Perhaps it's that economists provide politicians and businessmen with a supportive and encouraging crutch. It's true that sometimes economic forecasts improve the chances of being right, but even if they prove wrong, they provide the implementers with a socially acceptable excuse. Even an unproven and untried economic theory can serve to provide the foundation for otherwise unjustifiable government fiscal policy, programs and tax reform.

In some parts of the world, businessmen and government officials still consult astrologers before making a major move, gaining assurance and building confidence that the proposed actions are in tune with the great vibrations of the universe. And some, if they don't like what they hear, get a new astrologer. However, an

In some parts of the world, businessmen and government officials still consult astrologers before making a major move.

astrologer, even if he had a better batting average than an economist, would probably not sell very well in a corporation board room or in Washington. Now maybe, just maybe, if that astrologer had access to an IBM 370 and a big enough pile of printout...

It is of course unfair to tar all economists with the same brush. Some of this writer's best friends are (or were) economists. In fact there are some exceptional original thinkers. There are economists with a strong sense of economic history. There are economists who perceive economic and social change as it is occurring, factoring this change into their thinking. There are economists who view their profession as an art, economists who are not merely slaves to the quantitative data base of the last two decades. But, 20 years of reading and listening to economists have led to the conclusion that these are the exceptions.

"We Can Live With That"

Not long ago in *Business Week,* one of the nation's leading economists projected 7 per cent inflation built in indefinitely, adding, "We can live with that." Actually many economists are now projecting future long-term inflation of at least 6 per cent or 7 per cent. Perhaps these seers have never bothered to take a long look at economic history or at a compound interest table.

Just what would 7 per cent inflation do to a 25-year-old person retiring at 65, 40 years from now?

- Today's $7,000 compact car would be $105,000, 40 years from now!
- Today's $75,000 house would be $1,125,000, 40 years from now!
- A 15¢ stamp would be $2.25, 40 years from now!
- A $6 bottle of cheap whiskey would be $90, 40 years from now!!!

Six per cent inflation compounded over 40 years equals a 10-fold gain in the cost of everything. Seven per cent is a 15-fold gain in the price of everything. Still we hear economists today say, "Yes...we can live with 6 per cent to 7 per cent inflation."

> Six per cent inflation compounded over 40 years equals a 10-fold gain in the cost of everything.

But 6 per cent to 7 per cent inflation over an extended period, in almost all probability, would blow this economic system apart. At no time in 1,000 years has an economic system survived 6 per cent inflation for an extended period, with the possible exception of some South American nations. But, the jury is still out down there. History does reveal that some nations did have long-term 6 per cent-plus inflation experiences. But their economic systems *were literally destroyed.* It is unfortunate so many economists are not aware of this or choose to ignore economic data more than a decade or two old.

In Chapter 1, we reviewed U.S. inflation history from 1790 to date. The analysis of that data demonstrates the following:

- Recent high levels of U.S. inflation are *not* a new phenomenon, having been exceeded on a moving average basis, in the 1790s, the 1860s and the 1910s. Several other periods also came very close to ap-

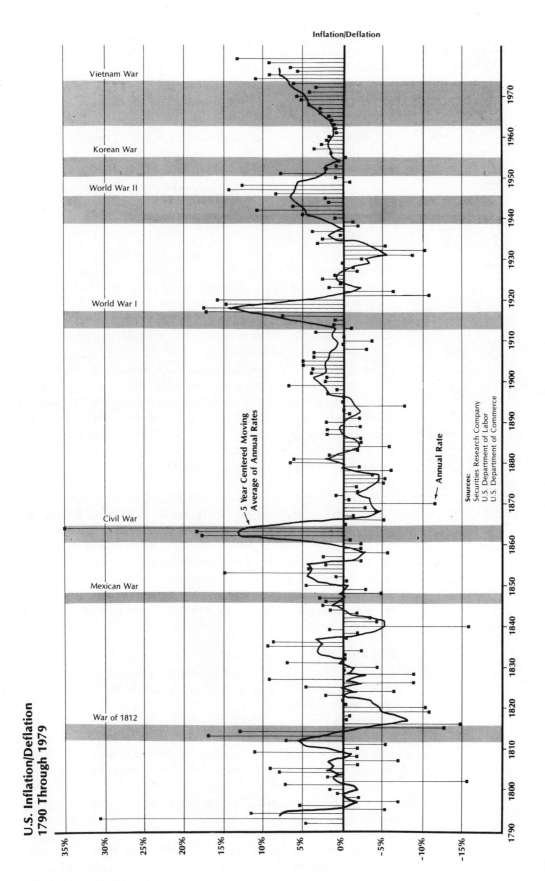

U.S. Inflation/Deflation
1790 Through 1979

Inflation/Deflation

Vietnam War

Korean War

World War II

World War I

Civil War

5 Year Centered Moving
Average of Annual Rates

Mexican War

Annual Rate

Sources:
Securities Research Company
U.S. Department of Labor
U.S. Department of Commerce

War of 1812

proximating recent experience. Numerous individual years exceeded recent peak levels of 11 per cent to 13 per cent.

- Inflation runs in cycles and in the past clearly has not been a permanent fixture in the U.S. economy.
- Prior inflationary peaks have, in all but one case, been followed by a significant correction period of deflation.
- *It is obvious that major wars and high inflation go hand in hand.* The Revolutionary War, the War of 1812, World War I, World War II, the Vietnam War, and the Korean War were accompanied by a build-up of inflation.
- As a superheated war economy cools off, inflation typically has subsided. However, with the exception of the Civil War, relatively high rates of inflation have prevailed for several years *after* each war's conclusion, probably a function of pent-up consumer demand. As this is satiated, the deflationary correction begins developing.
- The shift from an inflationary environment to that of deflation has often been sudden and dramatic.

In summary, the inflation/deflation data from 1791 through 1979 reveal that very long-term inflation in the U.S. is much lower than generally believed. *The annual compound growth rate in consumer prices is 1.2 per cent for the period.* The arithmetical average of annual data is 1.5 per cent and the median is 1.7 per cent.

The inflation/deflation data from 1791 through 1979 reveal that very long-term inflation in the U.S. is much lower than generally believed.

Also, running counter to the belief that inflation has usually been a characteristic of the U.S. economy, the study found that inflation, *on an annual basis, exceeded 1 per cent only 48 per cent of the time,* while deflation of 1 per cent or more was present 32 per cent of the time. Price stability (less than 1 per cent inflation or deflation) existed in 20 per cent of the years.

In total, 56 per cent of the years experienced some upward movement in consumer prices, while in 44 per cent of the years, consumer prices were unchanged or down.

A Look at the Long Term

But is this U.S. history significant in terms of future experience? Before dealing with this, a fast review of the very long-term study is in order.

Interestingly, in our 1,000-plus-year study, we also found that prices rose about 60 per cent of the time and fell 40 per cent of the time. The 1,000-year annual compound rate of growth for consumer prices worked out to less than 1 per cent per year.

In this data, we see four distinct bursts of metamorphic inflation, each taking place during a period of a great social-economic change. When the economic system adjusted to the change, inflation plateaued.

Now, look at those percentages on the chart. In the "commercial transition" period, we see that inflation compounded at 1.4

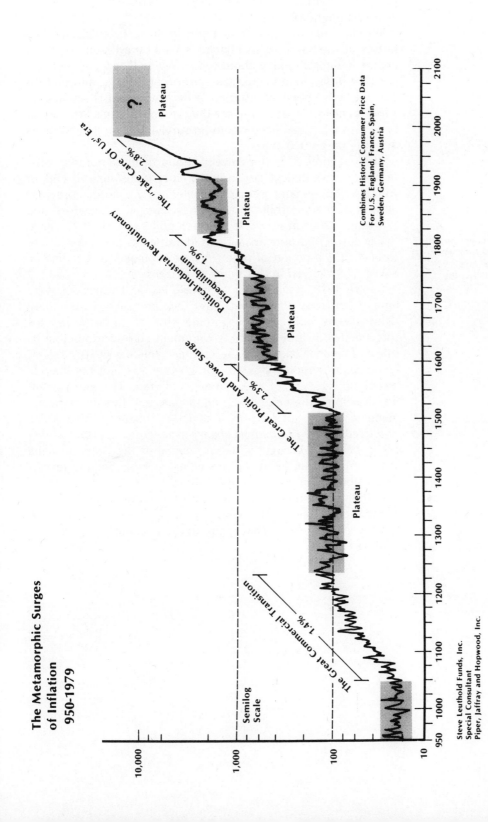

The Metamorphic Surges of Inflation
950-1979

Plateau

?

The "Take Care Of Us" Era
2.8%

Political/Industrial Revolutionary
Disequilibrium 1.9%

Plateau

The Great Profit And Power Surge
2.3%

Plateau

Plateau

The Great Commercial Transition
1.4%

Semilog Scale

Plateau

10,000

1,000

100

10

950   1000   1100   1200   1300   1400   1500   1600   1700   1800   1900   2000   2100

Combines Historic Consumer Price Data
For U.S., England, France, Spain,
Sweden, Germany, Austria

Steve Leuthold Funds, Inc.
Special Consultant
Piper, Jaffray and Hopwood, Inc.

193

per cent per year. In the "profit and power surge" period, it was 2.3 per cent annually over the 100 years. In the "political-industrial revolution disequilibrium" period, the rate was about 2 per cent. Finally, in the current surge, it has been 2.9 per cent per year compounded.

We did not slip a decimal point in these calculations. The historically extraordinarily high rates are a far cry from what you hear economists talking about today, saying that 6 per cent to 7 per cent inflation is the permanent order of things, and that we can live with 6 per cent inflation. If these economists would take a look at history, they would see they are more than a little out of sync with what has been reality in surviving economic systems over the past 1,000 years.

The question is: Is the current period of metamorphic inflation, which we believe began in the early 1900s, near its end, or will it continue and perhaps accelerate? As noted, previous periods of metamorphic inflation have ranged between 70 and 170 years. The current burst has been going for about 70 years.

The current inflationary surge is identified as the "take care of us era." *It is a period of time when government has become increasingly involved in the affairs of citizens.*

The current inflationary surge reflects a period of time when government has become increasingly involved in the affairs of citizens.

Before 1910, government responsibility and functions were limited to providing pomp and circumstance ceremonies, fighting wars and maintaining some form of domestic law enforcement. But around 1910, government started expanding its role in England, taking on the care and feeding of its citizens. Other nations soon followed. The government, not the church, began taking care of the starving children. The government began helping the citizens during plagues and famines. Government, in effect, got religion, a social conscience. *This new attitude represented a dramatic change in government responsibility and expense.* It brought a major change in the economic and social order. And, as in the preceding social-economic revolutions, along came metamorphic inflation.

Is the sun setting on this period of evolutionary social and economic change? Is the metamorphic inflation of the last 70 years on its last legs? That is the topic of Chapter 18, the concluding chapter.

Chapter 17

The Energy Dilemma and Inflation

Which of the following statements are true?

1. The world oil tank is approaching empty.

2. The OPEC oil cartel must be viewed as permanent.

3. Supply/demand considerations dictate that oil prices can only go one way...up.

4. The only solution to the energy problem is U.S. energy independence at any cost as quick as possible.

5. Seventy-five per cent of all the oil wells on this planet have been drilled in the U.S.

6. There are many potentially oil-rich areas where very little exploration activity is going on.

While we are in the midst of a painful energy transition, this provides strong economic impetus to develop energy alternatives.

We expect at this point that at least some of our readers are thinking to themselves, "Sure, all this that I have read so far is interesting, and it certainly is detailed, but what about today's energy crisis and its dramatic effect on inflation? Might we not be in a whole new ball game where history and past statistical studies mean little or nothing?"

We think it's best to deal with these questions before the concluding chapter. First, we will review two previous energy crises, one in England and one in the United States. The parallels with today's petroleum crisis are most interesting and revealing. Then the current oil situation will be examined, in terms of OPEC and probable world oil resources.

Without denigrating the significance of the world's current energy problems, the situation is not unprecedented. We are in the midst of an energy transition, a transition accelerated by high oil prices. While this is a painful period, it provides strong economic stimulus to develop new energy sources before the petroleum tank registers "empty."

The current oil situation is obviously inflationary, but it is in reality a very large dose of that species of inflation described in Chapter 1 as "Isolated Factor" Inflation.

Before directly dealing with the current energy crisis, let's go back some 500 years to the beginnings of an earlier energy crisis. During the Renaissance, wood was the critical energy component in European economies, just as petroleum is today. Wood, of course, was employed in almost all construction and was the provider of heat, light and food preparation. England ultimately became a large wood importer, having chopped down its domestic wood supply.

Prices rose as wood became more and more scarce. Some industries could not afford these rising energy costs and breweries and bakeries went out of business. The citizenry rebelled at having to pay such exorbitant rates for firewood to heat their homes, provide light and cook food.

In 1593 and in 1615, energy conservation acts were enacted, limiting the use of wood, especially in construction. The use of brick was mandated, but unfortunately it took more firewood to bake the bricks than it took to build an equivalent wood structure. From 1600 to about 1650, the price of firewood increased 800 per cent as demand exceeded the shrinking supply. Better grades of wood advanced even more.

As can be seen in our earlier chart of consumer prices, this was not a period of metamorphic inflation, but wood led the inflation parade in moving consumer prices erratically upward. The cheap, easily accessible wood was a thing of the past. Not only had wood become prohibitively expensive, the supply was restricted severely. Some families were forced to burn furniture and even parts of their houses to survive the winters. In one year alone, the price of firewood, if one could get it, advanced 300 per cent! This was an energy crisis that in social magnitude was at least as severe as today and, in those days, the government was not around to provide subsidies to the freezing families.

The high price and scarcity of wood ultimately brought an energy revolution, the coal revolution. In the early 1600s, people were aware that coal was an alternative energy source, one that could be substituted for wood. But, prior to the period of skyrocketing wood prices, coal was too expensive. Chopping down trees was easier and cheaper than digging coal out of the ground.

However, the wood energy crisis caused coal to become price competitive with the now high-priced wood. As the coal industry grew, mining sophistication and technology advanced, reducing the extraction costs. Coal was soon found to be a superior industrial fuel and, with mining efficiencies, it became relatively low in cost. Iron production became cheaper with a better quality metal produced. Industrial technology, as a result, took a great leap forward with the invention of steel, steam and then the steam engine. The Industrial Revolution was underway. The root cause of this great period of technological advance may well have been the wood energy crisis. If there had been plenty of forests in England back around 1600, society would have had little incentive to develop and discover the real potential of coal.

The wood energy crisis caused coal to become competitive with the high-priced wood.

An Energy Crisis in the U.S.

But there has been a more recent historic energy crisis. Let's go back to the early 1800s here in the U.S. Since colonial times, the primary source of light had been whale oil. But, by 1850 the whales in the Atlantic had become few and far between. The price of whale oil and sperm oil doubled, then doubled again. New whaling technologies had to be developed to maximize oil recovery from the whales that were taken. The high prices of whale oil also made it economical to take smaller and smaller, lesser yield whales.

America was growing fast and the supply of whale oil was obviously being depleted. There were no adequate substitutes available and the price of oil skyrocketed, up 600 per cent in 30 years. Then, in 1848 the shortage was alleviated, but only temporarily by the discovery of the South Pacific whale herds. Soon, however, by the advent of the Civil War, this new field was played out.

By 1866, sperm oil sold at $2.55 per gallon in New York, up from 43¢ in 1823. And ordinary whale oil was $1.45 in 1865, compared with 23¢ a few decades earlier. For comparison purposes, in 1868, 19¢ bought a complete dinner in a New York restaurant. The consumer could buy seven dinners, eating out every night, for the price of one gallon of lighting oil. The restaurants themselves were paying more to light the place at night than they were paying for the food purchases.

Clearly an alternative energy source was a necessity. High prices, population growth and decreasing supplies of whale oil combined into a crisis. In 1858, Edwin Drake set out to find an alternative. At Titusville, Pa., he found it. The U.S. entered the Petroleum Age. By 1867, kerosene, refined from Pennsylvania crude, broke the whale oil market. By 1900, whale oil prices had

By 1866, high prices, population growth and decreasing supplies of whale oil combined into another crisis.

fallen some 70 per cent from their high, but whale oil lamps had still become became collectors' items. Kerosene had, with production efficiencies, become even cheaper. More importantly, just as with the development of the coal industry some 200 years earlier, a chain reaction of technological and economic development was initiated. Oil became the new foundation of the economy, not merely a source of night light.

Now and Then

The parallels drawn between today's petroleum crisis and those earlier energy crises in wood and whale oil are obvious. The solutions to those earlier periods of discomfort and uncertainty resulted in quantum leaps forward, economically, technologically and socially.

These earlier solutions did not come about overnight and the period of transition was a difficult one. Back then, as today, the stimulus that brought the advance was economic. Wood and then whale oil became so expensive that it became economically worthwhile to develop alternatives. Great fortunes were made by the developers of the coal mines in Europe and by the industrialists who learned how to make use of this superior energy source. The same, of course, was true for the oil barons of America and subsequent developers of the automobile industry, the chemical industry and a host of others.

History demonstrates that most societies oppose change; doing it the old way is easiest. Without the wood crisis and the accompanying economic incentives, the development of the coal industry and even the Industrial Revolution may have been delayed for centuries. If there had been ample wood supplies, society, in general, would have remained content with sawing down trees the way the earlier generations had done. Without the whale oil crisis, the petroleum seeping into those ponds and creeks in Pennsylvania would have continued to be viewed as a nuisance for who knows how many years.

In those earlier days, what if the government had the power and inclination to ration supplies and artificially hold down prices, destroying the incentive to innovate and find solutions? Perhaps one day the 17th century Englishman would have awakened to find not a stick of wood available anywhere at any price and alternative sources of energy still only wild eyed dreams. Perhaps the American of the 19th century would have awakened one morning to find the last whale had been taken. Suddenly most social and commercial activity would have had to take place before the sun went down.

History demonstrates that most societies oppose change — doing it the old way is easiest.

Today's Solutions

We will not attempt to survey today's energy alternatives to petroleum. There may be new ones before this book is published. We will, however, note that the progress toward solutions is accelerating at a much faster rate than most thought possible five years ago or even two years ago. And, as in those earlier energy crises, the primary stimulus is economic.

Finding and developing economic alternatives to oil at $30 or $40 per barrel is far more feasible than when oil was selling at $3 or even $20 per barrel. Syncrude from coal, photovoltaic cells and sophisticated energy conservation techniques are no longer wild pie-in-the-sky dreams. They are quickly becoming economically viable solutions. And, if past experience is a guide, the solutions to the current energy crisis may be the springboard to yet another dramatic chain reaction of technological, industrial and societal change. And, as in the past, many of the individuals and corporations developing the best solutions will profit handsomely.

> Solutions to the current energy crisis may be the springboard to yet another dramatic chain reaction of technological, industrial and societal change.

But, the $64 billion dollar question is, can and will these solutions become practical reality soon enough? Will we all wake up some morning and find the gas tank empty, with industry and society as we know it grinding to a painful halt? This, then, is the subject of the last section of this chapter. How much petroleum remains in the world's tank? What about OPEC? Does the current energy crisis make all the inflation trends and relationships examined so meticulously in this book not applicable? Let us look at today's energy myths and realities.

Myths Among Today's Perceived Energy Realities

> "It may almost be taken as an axiom that the most popular concerns of the day will not be the ones that result in future trouble."
>
> — CHARLES O'HAY

The two most popular concerns of the day are oil and inflation. And, obviously there is some relationship between the two. Will oil shortages and high prices, be they brought about by real short supply or artificially controlled short supply, continue to be a major trouble area in coming decades? Or will the late Charlie O'Hay's "almost axiom" prevail?

OPEC: The Artificial Factor

First, let us examine an artificial factor, the oil cartel. Historically, cartels have not held together very long because the divergent interests of the participants eventually break the alliance. The diamond cartel as administered by DeBeers has had a remarkably long life compared to short-lived tin, copper and steel cartels, but diamonds may be a unique situation.

> Historically, cartels have not held together very long because the divergent interests of the participants eventually break the alliance.

If artificially high prices and short supplies do not encourage development of alternative materials or new production methods, the divergent interests of the aligned parties in the cartel eventually cause a few participants to break away. Once the united front is broken, the remaining cartel participants are hard pressed to keep it together. Once erosion sets in, it quickly accelerates, especially if those "break aways" seem to be prospering relative to the still aligned parties.

OPEC is fully aware of the importance of maintaining some form of unit, allowing increasingly wide nation by nation internal pricing variations. But nations such as Libya and Nigeria have stretched this pricing band to the breaking point and Saudi

Arabia's steadying influence within the cartel is all but gone. *Internal OPEC frictions appear to be increasing rapidly as individual nations seek more autonomy.*

Unity is strength, but *as people or nations become more prosperous, they also tend to become more independent.* This is the major reason that militant all for one, one for all unionism is almost a relic of the past in the U.S. And, it's probably the reason that even the much softer, more accommodating unionism of today is losing ground.

OPEC also has distressing external problems. Mexico, an emerging oil production power, is not a member of the club. Other non-OPEC nations also appear to have very significant future oil production potential. If these outsiders price their oil higher than OPEC, the more greedy and needy OPEC members may join the outsiders, regardless of the existing OPEC pricing band. *Cartels can be broken apart on the upside as well as on the downside.* As this is written, this appears to be happening.

Production quotas also are falling by the wayside. How long can or will the rich establishment members of OPEC control world oil supplies by cutting back their own individual production? *The emergence of non-OPEC oil producers will make this supply control increasingly difficult.* More on this later.

Within OPEC, economically troubled members such as Iran, Venezuela and most African producers need to sell as much oil as they can (maybe for as high a price as they can) right now. Would the Saudis voluntarily cut their own production back by, say 80 per cent to keep world supplies in control? Or would *they finally say to hell with all this and sign a long-term supply treaty with the U.S. for all their production in return for a U.S. NATO-type defense commitment?* For the already rich Saudis, the Russian bear becomes more ominous day by day. Are a few dollars more per barrel worth the risk? Or is it now more important to protect what they have?

The Energy Alternative Factor

The higher the price of oil, the more practical the alternatives become. Supposedly, syncrude can be produced for $35 to $40 a barrel without subsidy. Solar, tidal, hydro, wind, etc., all start to make economic sense at some point. Remember the earlier energy crises in wood and whale oil. The transitions to coal and petroleum were the products of scarcity and high prices. *Keep in mind that higher oil prices accelerate alternative technological research and development at almost a French curve rate.* This research thrust could someday produce a miracle solution to the current energy dilemma such as an oil alternative from water, or electricity so cheap it would not be necessary to meter it (have you heard that line before?).

Of course we cannot base our future on the hope of some water-into-wine technological miracle, but it *could* happen. Oil could eventually be transformed from its current position of black gold to a messy, dirty, unattractive ecological nuisance, best kept deep in the ground. Yes, the mighty oil-based corporate giants of today, if this should occur, might well become the

OPEC production quotas are already falling by the wayside.

The current research thrust could someday produce a miracle solution to the present energy dilemma.

buggy whip corporate dregs of the year 2,000 — at least those oil and oil service companies (unlike Exxon and Mobil) that aren't diversified.

The Oil Supply Factor

Forgetting about energy alternatives and future miracles, higher oil prices have more immediate implications for today's situation. They greatly stimulate exploration. Higher crude prices make it worthwhile to employ more sophisticated exploration techniques and to look for oil in what had previously been viewed as unlikely or unavailable places. Some of you may be saying, "Sure, sure, but where else is there to look? For heaven's sake, we have even explored the Arctic wastes!"

Jude Wanniski, in an article appearing in the October, 1979, issue of *Harper's* titled "Oil in Abundance," addressed this common misconception. On this planet, 3,200,000 oil wells have been drilled and 2,400,000 of those have been drilled in the U.S., most of these being in the oil producing southern states.

Of *all* the exploratory wells ever drilled on earth, 95 per cent were drilled in the industrial countries with 75 per cent in the U.S. alone. *Africa, Latin America, South and Southeast Asia and China have hardly been touched.*

Of all the exploratory wells ever drilled, 95 per cent were drilled in the industrial countries.

Wanniski partially explains this concentration of past exploration by the very favorable political, legal and economic environment that has existed in the U.S. compared to other nations around the world. A combination of stable government, private ownership of land with accompanying mineral rights, available capital and technology have until recently focused the search for oil on the U.S.

An examination of Dr. Bernardo Grossling's tables and statistics as presented in *New Perspectives on the International Oil Supply* (1979) demonstrates the point. The petroleum-prospective area, onshore and offshore to a depth of 200 meters, is estimated for 11 regions of the world. Three of the regions, Latin America, Africa-Madagascar and the U.S.S.R., are thought to individually have more potential and developed petroleum acreage than the U.S. Yet, these three regions *combined* have drilled but one-fourth of the wells drilled in the U.S.

Here are some summary statistics we have extrapolated from one of the charts in this study. Our calculations may not be precise, but then their estimates may not be either. Still the reader should get the idea.

	Oil Production & Prospect Area (U.S. equals 100)	Wells Drilled To Date (Exploratory & Development)
Latin America	120	110,000
Africa-Madagascar	120	20,000 (or less)
U.S.S.R.	107	525,000
U.S.	100	2,425,000
South & Southeast Asia	78	25,000 (or less)
Australia & New Zealand	70	5,000 (or less)
Canada	57	150,000
Middle East	40	10,000 (or less)

	Oil Production & Prospect Area (U.S. equals 100)	Wells Drilled To Date (Exploratory & Development)
Western Europe	40	75,000 (or less)
China	26	20,000 (or less)
Japan	14	10,000 (or less)

Keep in mind, when examining the table, that the number of wells drilled dates back to when the oil industry started over 100 years ago. While this writer is hardly an oil expert, we know that many of those 2,400,000 wells drilled in the U.S. do not compare in terms of productivity to the kind of wells drilled today. The first U.S. well in Titusville, Pa., was a far different affair than the first well drilled in the Persian Gulf. Thus, this well-to-acreage comparison may be somewhat misleading.

Nevertheless, the table certainly does support the conclusion that *there is a lot of untapped potential around the world.* In total, the U.S., with only a small fraction of the world's oil acreage potential, has produced 35 per cent of the approximate 330 billion barrels of oil taken out of the earth so far.

Exploring for and developing oil fields in foreign lands has become a high risk proposition for capitalists.

Exploring for and developing oil fields in foreign lands has become a high risk proposition for capitalists. You spend a lot to find and develop it, and they take it away. Thus, international oil companies now will get involved only if prospects look so good for a major find that they can turn a profit damn quick before nationalization or confiscatory taxation. Go for the cream because you probably won't have the time to make anything on the milk. There is little economic incentive for expensive long shots or slow payoffs.

Here are some specific examples of the current low level of exploration going on in potentially oil rich areas.

- Australia and New Zealand have an oil production and prospect area 70 per cent as large as the U.S. and a minuscule number of wells. *Still in 1978, only 53 exploratory wells were sunk.* Half of that number were drilled the year before. Why? Most of the land is owned by the government and the drillers have real problems negotiating with the bureacracy.

- *The Middle East has far more production potential than is found in the developed fields.* Still, since 1974, the number of exploratory wells drilled in the entire Middle East has averaged 95 per year, in Saudi Arabia but 10 per year and in Iraq a lowly one per year. Why? Sheikhs in their current catbird seat have no reason to flood the market.

- Only 83 wells have *ever* been drilled in Madagascar, a country almost the size of Texas and one of the world's most promising oil areas. This huge island, located off the southeast corner of Africa, lies in one of the world's largest sedimentary basins where oil is most likely to be found. The problem here appears to be political. Prior to 1975, the French controlled this country, allowing almost no exploration. If oil was found, they were afraid they would be thrown out under the new government. Since 1975, little more has been done because the new government does not trust the international oil companies and they, in turn, don't trust the new government.

As we see them, the *myths* among today's perceived energy realities are:

Myth: *OPEC is here to stay.* We think not. Almost all cartels have broken up. Either alternative materials or diverging interests of cartel members have broken past efforts to severely regulate supply and price of a commodity. The oil cartel price fixing now seems to be breaking apart on the upside and controlling supplies as new and cash-needy oil producing nations emerge will become increasingly difficult.

Myth: *The world oil tank is approaching empty.* We think not. There is still a vast number of potential oil producing areas on this planet that are relatively unexplored. In some cases, the problem is political. In others, it's been a matter of lack of incentive. And, in many areas, it's a combination of the two. Today's high prices are starting to resolve both of these impediments.

There is still a vast number of potential oil producing areas in this planet that are relatively unexplored.

Myth: *Nationalization and confiscatory taxation will block significant new oil exploration.* We think not. The oil reserve plum has become juicy, and underdeveloped nations are going to be increasingly willing to "give enough" to the internationals to warrant their participation. They need each other, no matter what the politics may be. As one oil executive told me, "We can now work with any government, Communist or not, as long as it is relatively stable."

Myth: *Oil prices can only go one way: Up.* We think not. No matter what it may look like, the laws of supply and demand have not been repealed when it comes to oil. The demand for oil is not currently inelastic; consumption does drop off some when prices go up. Technology is stimulated to find ways to get more miles out of a gallon of gas or more effectively employ the BTUs in heating oil. Recessions, of course, also curtail industrial usage. So far OPEC, by regulating supply, has been able to manage the situation, thanks to Iran and the strong secular increase in demand from the newly emerging industrial nations.

The demand for oil is not inelastic — consumption does drop off when prices go up.

But as more nations develop their untapped oil resources and as the effectiveness of the cartel erodes, these artificial supply constraints will become increasingly difficult to maintain. Many of the emerging-nation oil exporters are otherwise poor. The total cash flow is more important to them than the price per barrel. *Long-term considerations are top priority for only the rich.* Those that don't have it, want it now. Selling a million barrels of oil today at $30 per barrel is better than selling 500,000 barrels of oil at $40, at least for those nations with hungry mouths to feed.

Then, as a postscript of sorts, what would the oil rich nations of the world do with their horded reserves of black gold if it really appeared that a cheap oil alternative fuel source was actually a prospect? The world could see the biggest liquidation sale in history.

Myth: *U.S. energy independence, at any cost as soon as possible, is our only current alternative.* We think not. This idealistic energy independence goal, while politically appealing, is not our immediate salvation. There are many raw materials in which the U.S. is not self-sufficient. It, of course, is appealing to be self-sufficient in all vital raw materials, including oil, but those days are gone for the U.S. We have already taken out too much. *Nations have survived and prospered for centuries without a rich store of natural resources.* As long as international trade is relatively open, with alternative sources of supply, even a large oil importing nation *can* prosper. This condition may develop much sooner than many think.

In the next few decades at least, the U.S., must rely on other nations for some oil. Our once great reservoir has been fairly well worked compared to other areas of the world where the surface has barely been scratched. While it appears technology, with proper stimulus, can be expected eventually to come up with new energy sources, oil must be relied upon in the interim.

With significant new world supplies in prospect and the united power of OPEC being destroyed, our nation will not exist at the mercy of the Arabs, if in fact this ever has been the case. Freer trade, not isolation, should be our intermediate course.

> Nations have survived and prospered for centuries without being self-sufficient in natural resources.

Today's world energy problem is not a myth. There is no doubt that on a long-term basis the world's economies *must* find energy alternatives to oil. While world oil resources are obviously far greater than most believe, energy consumption will, on an overall basis, be increasing as more and more Third World nations progress up the economic ladder.

Even though there are still huge untapped and undiscovered oil reserves hiding under the earth's crust, in all likelihood they will eventually be depleted. Conservation and new discoveries merely postpone this potential day of judgment.

However, we have more time to solve this dilemma than is commonly believed. *The situation is not as critical as the surge in oil prices in the last five years would indicate.* Gas lines and high oil prices do not mean the world is running out of oil right now. There is, by most estimates, an adequate supply of oil to see the world through the transitional phase to other energy sources, whether it takes 50 years, 100 years or even longer. And, as pointed out earlier, the current energy crisis is not unprecedented. We have been through this before.

There is an adequate supply of oil to see the world through to other energy sources, whether it takes 50 years, 100 years, or longer.

While it is hard to realize when waiting in a gas line or taking out a second mortgage on the homestead to buy fuel oil, the oil problems of the last five years have been a long-term blessing. Call it an alert, an early warning. The world's oil energy tank is not yet on reserve, much less running on empty. *But, it is no longer at a comfortable level.* We must seriously start planning where and how we are going to get a refill and start doing something about it now. The really good news is some have finally started doing something about it.

Looking through the musty pages of history we find that crises such as the current energy crisis are the catalysts of dramatic progressive change, great technological leaps forward, new eras. Thus oil, the "isolated factor" component in today's inflation, is transitory. We have travelled this road before. High oil prices make the development of energy alternatives economically feasible. As the new methodologies are developed and perfected, the cost of energy should decrease. That's the way it has worked in the past and that's the way it will be in the future. The lessons are there if one bothers to look.

Chapter 18

The Future:
How Big Is Big?

Since 1930, the advent of the "take care of us era" in the U.S., government spending at all levels has risen from 10 per cent of total national income to over 40 per cent. The federal government is now the biggest single employer, the biggest consumer and, of course, the biggest borrower. This is hardly a revelation, but the following examples vividly demonstrate the quantum growth of government's role in employment, spending, regulating and controlling the citizens, corporate and private.

Item: In 1949, total federal spending was $40 billion. In 1980, our deficit *could* well equal that, 100 per cent of 1949's total spending!

Item: In 1978, Americans paid $16.7 billion *more* in taxes than they spent on food, clothing and shelter *combined*! (From *Harper's* magazine, March, 1978.)

Item: The Department of Health, Education and Welfare now has 1,100,000 people directly and indirectly in its work force, more than the U.S. Army. This department has an annual budget of $180 billion, an amount greater than any national budget in the world except Russia and the U.S. This new budget is 3.3 times the world-wide annual sales of the largest industrial company in the world, General Motors.

Item: Currently 87 government agencies have been created to regulate some aspect of business and Congress has authorized 25 bureaus in 14 different departments to handle water pollution alone. And, no one is obliged to investigate whether these agencies with multi-million dollar budgets are tripping over each other's feet in duplication.

Item: Let's examine one of the most spectacular growth areas of government, transfer payments. Transfer payments is government language for money transferred from income of people working to people not working. (In the United Kingdom, this is referred to as "the dole.") It includes unemployment compensation, Social Security retirement money, welfare money, and so on. In 1966, these payments in the U.S. totaled $44.7 billion. By 1978, they were over $250 billion, up 450 per cent in a little over a decade.

How much is $250 billion? $250 billion is over five times *all* the dividends paid to U.S. stockholders in a year. $250 billion is over 22 per cent of *all* the money paid in annual wages and salaries to every man, woman and child in the U.S.

Item: By some estimates, 80,000,000 people in the U.S. currently depend on government—national, state and city—for their primary source of income. This includes public employees, such as police officers and the like. It also includes people on unemployment, welfare and Social Security, the recipients of the transfer payments. Currently only 71,000,000 are employed by private enterprise and nongovernment employers in this country. So, in effect, each citizen working outside government is also supporting and providing the primary income for another. (Sometimes I think the person I am supporting must have 10 children, vacation in Hawaii and eat steak every night.)

In effect, each citizen working outside government is also supporting and providing the primary income for another.

Certainly this massive expansion of government's role did not take place without the endorsement of the majority of citizens. Polls indicated less than eight years ago that 70 per cent of Americans had a favorable attitude toward government. Big government was perceived as being good, providing wanted services and looking after those who were unable to care for themselves. In the last few years, however, a dramatic change has taken place in American attitudes toward government. A similar poll in 1979 found that 70 per cent or more of Americans have a negative attitude toward government. For the most part, big government is now disliked, distrusted, almost viewed as the enemy of the people it was originally designed to serve.

For the most part, big government is now disliked, distrusted, almost viewed as the enemy of the people it was originally designed to serve.

Vietnam and Watergate have been factors, but items such as those that follow have (when totaled) played a more significant role in destroying the previously held American belief that government was good.

Item: It is estimated that there are now over 900,000 totally ineligible welfare recipients receiving billions of dollars annually.

Item: A Washington, D.C., contractor was paid to paint 2,400,000 square feet of the General Services Administration headquarters, even though the entire building has an area of only 1,900,000 square feet! During a Senate hearing, a congressional committee was told that theft among GSA employes amounted to $66,000,000 a year. The fraud, theft and waste in the GSA continue at a rampant rate, costing taxpayers as much as $25 billion annually!

Item: Some $3 billion is stolen annually from government health programs and yet the federal government has fewer people investigating than it has manicuring the White House lawn.

Item: It costs the taxpayers well over $1,000,000 a year to pay the salaries, staff and fringes of *each* and *every* Congressman in Washington.

Item: The U.S. Secretary of Labor has two chauffeurs available for private and business use, with combined salaries of $70,000 per year. That's the *chauffeurs.*

Item: Senator Proxmire's Golden Fleece Awards call taxpayers' attention to these kinds of government studies: $375,000 for a Pentagon study of the frisbee, $159,000 to teach mothers how to play with their babies, $80,000 to develop a zero-gravity toilet, $121,000 to find out why some people say 'ain't,' and $29,324 for a study of the mating calls of the Central American toad. Some of these are justified, although they do sound absurd, but clearly not all.

The Golden Fleece Awards call attention to wasteful government studies.

Item: A few years ago, Dow Chemical made a comprehensive study of its regulatory costs. Compliance with federal regulations cost Dow $286,000,000 in 1976, up 27 per cent from 1975. The 1976 figure was equal to 50 per cent of Dow's after-tax profits and 6 per cent of sales. And none of these dollars produced one product or any service. Worse, Dow found that $69,000,000 — or better than one-third of their 1976 compliance costs — actually overlapped or conflicted with other regulations. Former President Ford stated that $130 billion in taxpayers' money is wasted each year on what he termed "useless" regulation. Democratic leaders have said the same thing. That $130 billion equals about 24 per cent of the entire federal budget, about $560 for every man, woman and child in the country. It was estimated in 1977 that current regulations increase the price of a new house anywhere from $1,500 to $2,500 and the price for an average new car by $666. Undoubtedly the figure is higher now.

Item: The Interstate Commerce Commission is a good example of ridiculous and costly overregulation. Suppose a trucking firm has an ICC license to haul from Richmond, Virginia, to Albany, New York, and wants to haul goods from Richmond direct to Boston. The ICC dictates that he must pass through Albany, even though it adds hundreds of miles to the route. If that trucker is carrying tobacco, for example, he would have to return empty to Richmond because he lacks an ICC license to carry

The Interstate Commerce Commission is a good example of ridiculous and costly overregulation.

another commodity. A survey conducted a few years ago showed that approximately 38 per cent of all ICC-regulated vehicles must return empty to their point of origin because of ICC restrictions. The cost of this sheer waste forces transportation rates higher and higher and dissipates needed energy resources. Therefore, every time you make a purchase of just about any product—including almost all groceries—you are paying 20 per cent more for the cost of getting those products to market than you should, thanks to a bureaucratic dinosaur called the ICC.

Item: In the past few years, the Department of Energy has come into being. Already it has 20,000 employees and a budget in excess of $10 billion. The primary function of DOE is to regulate exploration, production and pricing of energy. Already the federal government is spending more money per year regulating energy than the entire net profit of the petroleum industry. Maybe prices are being regulated, but the industry is not.

The leading U.S. public opinion polls now show that only 14 per cent of the citizens have a high regard for those who govern and 50 per cent believe government is "run by people who don't know what they are doing." Citizens now feel very strongly that government has become oversized, overly powerful and horribly wasteful. About 81 per cent are in favor of a constitutional limitation on federal spending, probably because another poll shows that 82 per cent feel federal government spending is "too much," while only 17 per cent feel it is too little or about right. In addition, 72 per cent feel the federal government is too strong.

Citizens feel very strongly that government has become oversized, overly powerful and horribly wasteful.

While the public does not have an especially high regard for business, 77 per cent feel it is run more efficiently than government. This attitude is coming to prevail in other parts of the world, especially in the highly socialized countries. Here are the results of a poll conducted in May, 1976, in the United Kingdom by Market and Opinion Research International. At that time, there was proposed legislation in Parliament to nationalize the British banks. The poll showed that the public opposed this nationalization 76 per cent to 14 per cent with 10 per cent saying they didn't know. Amazingly, as a class, the Labour Party voters, the ones that are supposed to be antibusiness and antibanking establishment, opposed banking nationalization 63 per cent to 25 per cent and opposed a companion piece of legislation that would nationalize the insurance industry by a margin of 64 per cent to 23 per cent.

Even in the industries that had already been nationalized, taken over lock, stock and barrel by the government, public ownership was opposed. For example, in the case of the gas and electric utilities, 40 per cent were in favor of government owner-

ship and 51 per cent opposed nationalization and public ownership.

This public attitudinal change in the United Kingdom was
somewhat surprising, but it seems to be part of a growing trend in
many industrial nations—Sweden, Germany and Japan. The
public attitude toward government is becoming increasingly
skeptical. In most recent elections, the Socialists and other
strong central government advocates are losing ground for the
first time in 30 years.

The public attitude toward
government is becoming
increasingly skeptical in many
industrial nations.

The Soviet Union now permits collective farmers to cultivate
small, private plots in their own spare time and sell the produce
for their own profit. Two years ago, these plots accounted for a
mere 4 per cent of the land under cultivation in Russia. Yet by
value they produced one-fourth of the country's food. When this
system of private plots was instituted under Nikita Khrushchev,
his critics said the Soviet Union was going capitalist. Khrushchev
replied, "Call it what you will. Incentives are the only way to
make people work harder."

Is the "Take Care of Us Era" in Its Closing Stages?

In 1978, Vermont Royster speculated on this in his *Wall Street
Journal* column. Royster, an admitted skeptic and cynic, said:

> "Clearly something is going on here. Politicians are
> slow to change, but when the political winds shift,
> they can tell a hawk from a handsaw. You almost
> begin to wonder if we haven't—after all these many
> years—reached a turning point in the public attitude
> toward government spending.

> "Turning points are rarely recognized when they oc-
> cur, and things don't always move swiftly in the op-
> posite direction after they have passed. Only in
> retrospect, and after much fighting, was Midway
> seen as the turning point in the Pacific War. In 1932,
> few realized that the election that year was pivotal
> in American politics. So it could be here.

> "But in the affairs of men, the important thing is not
> always where we are but where we are headed. Dare
> we hope that someday we can look back on 1979 as
> a turning point in the affairs of the nation?"

It may be that the "turning point," as Royster calls it, was in
actuality a few years ago. I happened to be in London when then
Prime Minister Jim Callahan addressed the Labour party's national conference in Blackpool. Americans typically view the
British Labour party as a strongly socialistic, left-wing political
unit which, left to its own devices, would socialize and have
government control as much of British industry and society as
possible. Lord Keynes' economic theories, although warped and
reshaped to fit, make up the economic doctrine of the Labour
party. But in this speech, Callahan sounded like a combination of
perhaps Barry Goldwater, Taft, even Reagan. These are quotes
from his speech:

The American view of the British
Labour party as a strongly
socialistic, left-wing political unit
is not altogether accurate.

"The cozy world which we were told would go on forever, where full employment could be guaranteed by a stroke of the pen by deficit spending, is gone. Britain has lived too long on borrowed time, borrowed money and borrowed ideas."

Another quote:

"Unemployment is caused by paying ourselves more than the value of what we produce."

With this, the delegates to the conference began booing and shouting, but Callahan added, "Firms must be able to earn a surplus," and that is a euphemism for saying they must make a profit.

Before he left the stage, he added, "We used to think that you could just spend your way out of a recession and increase employment by cutting taxes and boosting government spending. I tell you in all candor that that option no longer exists and it only ever worked by injecting inflation into the economy."

I ask you, who does that sound like? Does it sound like some rock-ribbed conservative out of Kansas? Does it sound like Milton Friedman, or some other representative of the business establishment? No, it's Jim Callahan, the leader of the Labour party in the United Kingdom and former Prime Minister.

Some people would say that Callahan didn't really mean a word of it, that he was just mouthing the phrases to make it easier for the United Kingdom to get the financing it needed to get it out of a financial crisis. But *The Economist,* a leading London business publication distributed all over the world, and a publication that is not exactly naive, referred to Callahan a few years ago as the best conservative Prime Minister Britain could get.

So, at that point a strange new element of political leadership in the Labour party was emerging. It would appear that it reflects the changing view of the man in the street, a dissatisfaction with big government and inflation. I didn't do a Gallup poll, but here are some of the comments made by taxi drivers, pub frequenters, barmen, clerks and the like.

A strange new element of politicial leadership in the Labour party was emerging.

"We've had our run since the war with our government running it all, and it's a bloody mess. It's time to get them out of business and out of our lives."

"So many regulations now, you can't turn around. One thing politicians don't have is common sense be they Labour or Tory."

"I'm a working man all my life. I fought in the war and I'd fight again for this country, but I am sick and tired of paying taxes so all those bastards can sit around on the Dole."

"Jim Callahan is the first one of them that's made any sense. We can't keep spending more than we take in."

"I'm Labour, but I'm for Callahan. He's the first one that's had the courage to tell them damn politicians what they ought to hear instead of what they want to hear."

The same mood prevails in the U.S. where in 1978 Governor Dreyfus pulled off an upset victory in Wisconsin with a campaign slogan that declared government has three functions: 1. Defend our shores. 2. Deliver our mail. 3. Stay the hell out of our lives!

But it is not only the conservative and new era politicians that recognize the new mood of the people. Tom Hayden, student radical leader of the 1960s, said this about Proposition 13, "It is in many respects a legitimate grass roots populist revolt against the stupidity of government."

Not only conservative and new era politicians recognize the new mood of the people.

Trends in humor often reflect changes in public attitudes and in the last year or two the following lines always seem to bring the house down.

"What are the three most common lies heard in the U.S.?
1. The check is in the mail.
2. ...of course I will respect you tomorrow.
3. I am from the government and I am here to help you."

Peter Bernstein, in a beautifully written article titled "The Tide in the Affairs of Men," put it this way in the summer of 1978:

"A man standing on the beach when the tide turns will never know for certain precisely when that event occurs. For some time afterward, waves will continue to lap up to almost the same point as the last wave of high tide. Only after a period of time, when successive waves fail to reach the former levels, can he then say that the tide has turned.

"The turning point of great historical forces is just as difficult to identify and for just the same reasons. Forces in motion tend to stay in motion, and the stronger they are, the greater the inertial characteristics they acquire. The change in the tide in such cases is a complex, even attenuated, process, in which the old force still seems to be very much in control even while the new forces are only beginning to gather strength.

"The events of the past few months are giving fragmentary, if dramatic, evidence of a vast sea change whose turning point is hidden in the violent turbulence of the past 10 years: A mass decision to curtail the role of government in our lives. *We stress that we do not believe this is the moment when the tide is turning; rather, this moment is a confirmation that the tide has turned."*

What Peter is saying so eloquently is that the "take care of us era," the long period of expanding the role of government, is over, and so may be the long metamorphic supercycle inflation that accompanied it.

The long period of expanding the role of government may be over, though reversals of the tide are difficult to recognize.

This is difficult for most of us to accept because reversals of the tide are difficult to recognize and because we are so conditioned by immediate past experience.

Keep in mind that one of our major shortcomings in economics and investments is that our thinking is too often warped by very recent history, immediate past experience.

- Many bought classic growth stocks at the end of the line in 1971 and 1972 because of their great 10-year record.
- Many are avoiding stocks now because, since 1968, total return has been minimal.

Twenty years ago, when I started in this business, it was almost universally believed, among other things, that:

- The dollar would absolutely never be devalued...JFK said so.
- 6 per cent was the most bonds would ever yield.
- You couldn't lose buying utilities.
- Stocks were a great inflation hedge.
- The U.S. would absolutely rule the financial and industrial world for 100 years.

These truisms of the 1960s look silly today, just as many of today's truisms (such as, 6 per cent inflation is built into the system) will look silly 10 years from now.

The Winds of Change—The End of an Era

What will get us out of today's inflation fire? Red Adair isn't going to put it out. Think back to the 1,000-year inflation history chart. This last great surge of inflation accompanies the "take care of us era," that major socio-economic change discussed. The sun is setting on that change—perhaps it has already set. The growth of government spending, government services and government involvement in our lives is slowing down, stabilizing. This is true not only in the U.S., but also in most industrial nations.

In the U.S., the change is not coming from Washington or from economic experts—it is coming from the people.

Here in the U.S., the change is not, at this point, coming from Washington. It is not coming from old, out-of-touch representatives in the House or Senate. It is not coming from Keynesian economic experts. *It is coming from the people.*

The people of this country are fed up with big government getting bigger. They are sick of inflation. They are sick of bureaucratic waste and federal deficits. This is not, as some people still think, just a few nuts in California (I remember when Proposition 13 was what happened to me on my second night in San Francisco).

This is a major historic turning point. Tax limitation and spending limitation proposals are now found in almost every state. A proposal to require a balanced federal budget has worked its way through 30 state legislatures. We may not see a constitutional convention called, but Congress will be forced to pass such a law to prevent the constitutional convention. Either way, it's a victory for the people against the Washington establishment. The public is learning how to change things by direct action.

This is not just a taxpayers' revolt. Sure people are sick of paying out more in taxes than they do for food, clothing and shelter combined. But most Americans don't want to do away with good schools, most don't want to let the needy starve and freeze, most don't want to see old people begging in the streets.

There will be no backtrack to the good old days of bloody clawed capitalism, survival of the fittest and minimal government interference and regulation of our lives. History demonstrates that such backward moves are rare. The good old days won't return...nor were they always so good.

However, now it appears as though government growth in the U.S. has slowed, maybe stopped. The economic system can now catch up, learn to live with and adjust to the "take care of us era" of the past 50 years, just as happened in the "profit and power surge," the "political-industrial revolution" and the "commercial transition." This adjustment could mean we are entering a long period, 100 years plus, of relative price stability, interrupted, of course, by temporary bursts of war-induced inflation, cyclical business inflation or special factor inflation like OPEC. These other factors are important, but history demonstrates they do run their course in relatively short periods of time.

> We may be entering a long period, 100 years plus, of relative price stability.

And, when all the smoke is blown away, it appears the major immediate cause of the last decade of abnormally high inflation levels in the U.S. is the U.S. government's continuing policy of spending more money than it takes in, covering the difference by degrading the currency. OPEC is also a factor, but not merely as important.

In the more advanced stages of "the take care of us era," government's role expanded so dramatically the revenues could not keep pace with spending. Business and labor could not really be faulted for raising prices and wages; they are only trying to keep up. The root cause has been big government getting bigger, big spending getting bigger.

But the winds of change are starting to blow. Government spending, combining all levels, has *already* stabilized when measured as a percentage of national income. To assume that the government growth of the last 10 and 20 years is the die cast for the next 10, 20, or 30 years is almost certainly myopic and naive.

> To assume that the government growth of the last 10 and 20 years is the die cast for the next 10 and 20 years is almost certainly myopic and naive.

In summary, this book has demonstrated:

- High inflation is *not* new.
- Inflation has *not* been a permanent fixture in the U.S. or other world economies.
- Shifts from high inflation to minimal inflation or deflation can be *swift*.
- Inflation in the U.S. may have peaked in 1974 and now is moving jaggedly downward, perhaps momentarily interrupted by the energy factor.

Still economists and politicians project future long-term inflation at 6 per cent or 7 per cent, saying we can live with that. They would be wise to take a look at history and at a compound interest table.

Remember, 6 per cent inflation compounded over 40 years equals a *10-fold gain in the cost of anything.* Seven per cent is a 15-fold gain in the price of anything. Still we hear, *"Yes, we can live with 6 per cent to 7 per cent inflation."*

At no time in 1,000 years has an economic system survived these levels of inflation for such an extended period.

Herein we identified the root causes of today's inflation. First we had the 50 years of metamorphic inflation accompanying the massive socio-economic change, when government's role was redefined as taking care of the people. Then, in the last decade, this has been accentuated by huge inefficient bureaucratic spending and chronic federal deficits.

But "the times, they are a-changin'," led not by old establishment political leaders or economists, but coming from the people. Such a reversal is in the works now. This is difficult for most of us to actually accept because reversals of the tide *are* difficult to recognize, and because we are so *conditioned by immediate past experience.*

From a personal standpoint, five or even three years ago, it would have been difficult for me to believe such a meaningful change could take place, that the pendulum could be swinging the other way, but it is happening. The attitude toward government is indeed changing. And ultimately our government is still for the people and *by* the people.

Not many years ago, I thought hyperinflation and destruction of our economic system as we know it was really in the cards. I was close to agreeing with the James Dines and Harry Browns of the world who firmly believe it's always darkest before the lights go out completely. I no longer believe this. As Peter Bernstein says, "The tide has turned." The nation has come upon the right path.

The tide has turned. With a few interrupting cyclical peaks and valleys, the basic inflation rate is expected to be below 3 per cent 10 years from now. Within the next decade, expect at least one or two years of no inflation or actual deflation. This indeed may be accompanied by some economic hardship, but, to most of us, that would certainly be more tolerable than the inflation ravages of the last decade.

"The times, they are a-changin'." One need only look, listen and then take a long look at history.

Though difficult to believe that the pendulum is swinging the other way, it is happening.

"The times, they are a-changin'."